# THE UNDERWORLD CAPTAIN

Captain Alexander Shannon has been a member of HM Armed Forces since 1983. He took part in the Falklands conflict, completed six tours of Northern Ireland and also served in Bosnia. He has risen through the ranks to become a captain and currently works as a Permanent Staff Administration Officer.

David Leslie has worked for the *News of the World* since 1970 and has focused on the Glasgow crime scene since 1990. He is also the author of the bestselling *Crimelord*, about Tam McGraw, as well as *The Happy Dust Gang; Mummy, Take Me Home; The Hate Factory* and *The Gangster's Wife*.

# THE UNDERWORLD CAPTAIN

## FROM GANGLAND GOODFELLA TO ARMY OFFICER

### CAPTAIN ALEXANDER SHANNON
### WITH DAVID LESLIE

MAINSTREAM
PUBLISHING
EDINBURGH AND LONDON

First published in Great Britain in 2011 by
MAINSTREAM PUBLISHING COMPANY
(EDINBURGH) LTD
7 Albany Street
Edinburgh EH1 3UG

ISBN 9781845967673

A catalogue record for this book is available
from the British Library

Printed in Great Britain by
Clays Ltd St Ives plc

1 3 5 7 9 10 8 6 4 2

# CONTENTS

# PROLOGUE

Peering into the night through a late autumn drizzle flecked with the first scattering of snow, the soldier watched and listened.

In the distance, he could see the dull orange glow of street lamps reflecting on damp roofs. Now and then a harsher light would show as a door was opened, perhaps for a cat to go about its stealthy business. It was the task of the soldier to track details such as that.

The night-sight glasses that let his eyes wander through windows and into homes were constantly misting over and he was irritated by the necessity to clear them. Even his slightest movement, like drying the glass, could betray him, putting not just his life at risk but also those of his colleagues.

He focused on a single dwelling huddled among the drab rows. Days ago, he had pointed out to those with him how the angle of its television aerial set it apart from others and had shown how a link in its drainpipe differed from those of neighbouring buildings. What his superiors had ordered him to keep to himself was that the house was the base of a man suspected of being a terrorist killer. The fewer who knew that, the better and safer for all.

Now and again, he was tempted to steer his sights to the home of a young and buxom brunette who lived three doors to the left and whose bedroom blinds seemed rarely closed. He wondered if his fellow soldiers had at times succumbed to a similar curiosity. Thinking about her drew his mind to his own troubles. A marriage in danger of falling apart. Family members seemingly forever at odds with the police and others who were intent on bringing them violent harm. Friends who had died. And then there was he himself.

To his credit, he had achieved so much, despite growing up amidst poverty, an unsettled education and long spells in children's homes. Those from such backgrounds often spent most of their lives in conflict with the better off in society, who wanted to restrict men like the soldier to their own class. Those from humble origins were traditionally allowed a step on the bottom rung of the promotion ladder, but not encouraged to climb. The soldier had taken all this in his stride and had been determined. And he had succeeded.

Now, the very society that so often despised his kind was depending on him for protection – even the mere ability to walk streets in safety.

Many just like the soldier had died at the hands of self-styled patriots who shot from darkness, blew up innocent families and funded their evil by milking the fruits of the very trades they purported to despise.

He realised his mind was beginning to wander.

Suddenly, he was jerked into awareness. A light shone, a door banged, a dog barked and through the increasingly thick dusting of snowflakes he saw the glow of a cigarette. He was sure his quarry had no inkling of where those who were watching him lay, but at the same time the soldier was careful to mask his movements. After glancing at his watch to check what time the man had appeared, he was almost disappointed to see the cigarette being extinguished and the smoker returning indoors.

He was certain, though, he had seen his man. Now, he would carry on watching, waiting for his target to disappear on one of his occasional sorties or to welcome late-night visitors. If he moved out, then the soldier would need to get word to others further afield but equally alert.

For now, he went back to waiting. He could feel the snow brush his blackened face. Somewhere only a foot or two away a rat scurried across a sleeping colleague. The soldier had faced bombs and bullets with near disdain, but a childhood often spent watching rats creep over his own bedding and that of his brothers and sisters had left him with a violent disgust for these rodents that seemed to stalk humans.

He could hear the gentle breathing of his friends as they contorted their bodies in the tiny, damp space open to the sky and its snowflakes, desperately trying to find the sleep for which they so longed. At least the air would dilute the appalling smell of men encased in an outdoor nest for days.

Inches to his right, a man whispered a request for the time, but it was hours before the next watch began. Until then, the soldier was alone with his thoughts. He knew he was too disciplined to sleep when it was not his turn to do so, but concentration was often a problem, overcoming the boredom of staring for hours into the unknown.

His safety and that of the men around him was his responsibility alone and going over and over a checklist in his mind helped keep him on his mental toes, but what all too often caused his thoughts to drift off was the knowledge that the streets he watched, and the men, women and children, animals even, living in them, were a mirror of his own past.

There were times as he was watching during the day when he felt he knew even the content of conversations held hundreds of metres away. He had never been in any of these homes but was sure he could see the cheap furniture, worn carpets and marked walls. Within those walls, there would be drunken rows, blows, tears, the cries of children, despair.

He had fought his way out of hopelessness, but as the hours passed he wondered if he was being sucked back. The soldier's thoughts took him to a place that had been his home and which was forever calling him back, somewhere that held many secrets, his own among them.

*  *  *

Glasgow, the Dear Green Place, sitting astride the River Clyde. A home to heroes and villains: heroes who had shown bravery in arenas the world over, and villains whose deeds had made them heroes in the eyes of some. Sadly, the city's reputation was too often based on the exploits of those concerned with crime rather than courage.

Much of the violence so prevalent in Glasgow was blamed on religious differences. The reality was that religion was but a secondary cause – money lay at the heart of most of the trouble, with alcohol a frequent trigger.

Yet the city had also produced its share of those whose selflessness was beyond challenge. The Highland Light Infantry was the city's regiment, leaving tales of courage and honour wherever its colours flew. Then the story of the 16th (Service) Battalion (2nd Glasgow), better known as the Boys' Brigade, Glasgow Battalion, was the stuff of real-life adventure yarns, inspiring many young men to take the King's shilling. At the Battle of the Ancre during the Somme offensive in November 1916 about 60 soldiers from 'D' Company were cut off behind enemy lines and surrounded by hordes of well-armed German troops. All efforts to relieve them failed, but despite suffering a horrific bombardment they refused to surrender. Finally, when enemy troops stormed their trench, they found just fifteen alive, all of them wounded, three of whom would die soon after.

Countless other acts of bravery had received public recognition. The very first Victoria Cross to be awarded to a soldier went to a Glaswegian, Major John Simpson Knox, who had run away from humble origins and lied about his age to join the Scots Fusilier Guards at the age of only 14. Throughout Glasgow lie the graves of others who have received this highest of honours. Private George Rodgers, of the Highland Light Infantry, won the VC during the Indian Mutiny in 1858. A year earlier Gunner Hugh McInnes had joined the illustrious ranks of its recipients at the Relief of Lucknow. His remains are in St Peter's RC Cemetery on London Road. Private John McDermond was another VC winner during the Crimea. Like so many others, he came from humble beginnings and when he died his grave remained unmarked in Paisley. The soldier had often wandered into St Kentigerns unaware he was passing within feet of the grave of Sergeant Robert Downie, formally recognised for his courage at the Somme in 1916 with a VC.

# THE UNDERWORLD CAPTAIN

Such men had been willing to give their lives to preserve their friends, but while heroism abounded, it was Glasgow's vicious gangland that gave rise to the real headlines. These same cemeteries also marked the end of life's journey for some from the underworld whose deeds attracted much greater publicity but less acclaim.

So many young men were faced with the choice, even before leaving school, of whether to pursue a legitimate career or to take the path into crime. The soldier had opted for the former by joining the army, but his service career was inextricably entangled with the criminal world. He would face courts, risk imprisonment, be suspected of involvement in terrifying gangland murders and set out to kill and maim outside of the army Rules of Engagement, which gave service personnel protection from prosecution. His skills as a soldier would attract assassination offers, which, had he accepted, would have made him wealthy. The fact that he refused put his own life at risk, but at the end of the day a love that so many had doubted would last had set him on an honourable course.

Yet so many of his peers, members of his own family even, had become criminals. Most entered the underworld not through a deliberate choice but because they simply grew into it – relatives were gangsters and so offspring naturally drifted into gangland, largely because they knew no different and believed it was their destiny from birth.

Glasgow had seen its share of men placed on pedestals because they killed, robbed and hurt. The book *No Mean City* describes in frightening detail the cruelty of an individual known as the Razor King, who slashed rivals almost for fun. It was based on a real-life individual and while the story could not be blamed for the prevalence of knife and razor carrying, it did nothing to discourage those who did. The Razor King ended up lonely and poor, but few remembered that.

Patrick Carraher then swaggered his way through the streets of the city, slashing and gouging all who stood in his path. Cronies fawned to his every whim. He escaped the gallows when skilful defence by a lawyer saw one murder charge fall by the wayside, but years later a second left him dangling from the end of a rope in Barlinnie prison.

At the time the soldier had enlisted in the army, Glasgow was effectively under the control of a handful of powerful men who made their own laws and dictated how the lives of thousands of others would run. Many of these men were faceless, known only to a few. They had slipped out of Glasgow and headed to the great cities of England from where they ran highly lucrative criminal empires. One who remained on his home territory was Arthur Thompson, known as the Godfather, a revered, almost idolised, figure who posed as a legitimate businessman while running a series of rackets from a sprawling home known locally as the Ponderosa.

An arm's length from Thompson was Thomas 'the Licensee' McGraw, an at times shadowy man who ran a successful safe-cracking gang known as the Barlanark Team before graduating into the hugely profitable world of the drug smuggler. McGraw was seen as the logical successor to the Godfather.

Known to both, at one time as an associate, if not friend, was Paul Ferris, born less than three years before the soldier. Ferris would never claim to want to usurp Thompson or McGraw, but his involvement with Thompson in particular, and the aftermath of the association, would have a near devastating effect on the soldier and on the lives of many others. Ferris was likeable, intelligent and forward-thinking. He was also loyal, an attribute that was to deprive him of years of liberty.

* * *

As the soldier was watching his terrorist quarry, Ferris was the subject of an intensive police surveillance operation. Yet while one could be said to be the gamekeeper and the other the poacher, both were targets. Each knew there were those who had vowed to have them killed and each took precautions to stay alive. Both would experience the dangers and disloyalties of Glasgow gangland. They would suffer in their differing ways from the treachery of a Judas whose love of gold led to betrayal and murder. That Judas would flit in and out of the life of the soldier with devastating effect.

## THE UNDERWORLD CAPTAIN

This, then, was the Glasgow the soldier knew so well. But as the years rolled by he would often wonder whether its very reputation was a blight on a career in which he mingled with the lowest to the highest, often doubting if either could be trusted.

# CHAPTER ONE

My name is Alexander Shannon. Friends call me Alex, while to most of my family and closest friends I am Ally. I was born in Rottenrow Hospital, Glasgow, on 16 February 1966. It's the same hospital where the Moors murderer Ian Brady was born in 1938. Like me, he came from a poor family.

All of us have at some stage in our lives tried recalling our very earliest memories. Mine are of growing up in old tenement buildings in Cowcaddens before we moved to the relative comfort of newer houses in Wellfield Street, Springburn, in the northern part of Glasgow. I say 'newer' because here we had inside toilets, a real luxury for many families even at this time. Our home faced the Edgefauld Flats, at the bottom of a hill, where a Benefits Agency building now stands.

It's of my time in Springburn that I have my clearest memories because it was here that I started school at what was St Aloysius. The school stands to this day, a Grade-A listed building, and there must be thousands of former pupils who pass it and cast their minds back to those first days at the beginning of the 1970s. Many of my fondest and happiest times came during this period of youthful innocence, free of the cares that overshadow the lives of parents, especially as there was so much poverty around and it was often a real struggle for survival. I was determined to keep the memories of these happy times stored so I could bring them out occasionally when things seemed black. They are all the more special for spanning just a few short years. Little did I know, it would not be long before the course of my life changed dramatically.

For a short time, I went to Garscube nursery school. I had no way of knowing it at the time, but it would play an unusual role in later years when my brothers and I were stockpiling weapons for an ongoing feud with some of the rival Springburn Mob, as we called them. We had been offered a double-barrelled shotgun but before buying it wanted to test it out. We did this by firing it on the side door of the school. It wasn't the brightest thing to do because it was ten o'clock one Saturday night. The row was horrendous. In seconds, everybody was at their windows, peering out, wondering what was going on. We just carried on walking, as if the loud bang was nothing to do with us.

I remember turning up for one of my early days at school wearing my Sunday best, which for me, in those days when money was short, was Wellington boots, a duffle coat and shorts. Some of my new mates mocked me, just to make me feel at home. Among them were the McGovern brothers: Steven, Tony and Tommy. They would remain friends for life, albeit at times from a distance, and then during some difficult periods in the early 1990s that would test our resolve and friendship.

From time to time, my parents would talk about Jimmy Boyle. A small-time crook with a vicious streak, Boyle was relatively unknown even after he was jailed for life in 1967 for the murder of 'Babs' Rooney. Murder was a crime so frequent in Glasgow that it usually rated merely a few paragraphs in the local media. It was only after he took umbrage at the violent behaviour of prison officers that he achieved near cult status. Boyle's so-called 'dirty' protests at the beatings, cruel treatment and hard conditions inside regularly led to rioting, which brought on headlines and stories about the things he was supposed to have done on the outside before he was sent to prison. Some of these were incredible and made Mum and Dad laugh. Boyle never encouraged anyone to follow his example of violent lawlessness, but the fact was many did.

I never knew Boyle, but he had stayed with Mum and Dad for a spell when they lived in London. My sister Roseanne, six years older than me, was born while he lodged with my parents and not long after that they all returned to Glasgow.

# THE UNDERWORLD CAPTAIN

I think most people in Springburn knew somebody who was in jail, but then we were so young the word 'gangster' meant nothing to us. It was really only when I became a teenager that I came to understand the meaning of the word. Mum and Dad used to tell us a funny story about William 'Tank' McGuinness, whose killing in 1976 led to Patrick 'Paddy' Meehan being cleared of a murder in Ayr for which he had been jailed. He was given a Royal Pardon and compensation.

McGuinness used to run about with my uncle Sonny, who was only about five feet tall. The story goes that they would start at one end of Cumberland Street, each on one side of the road, and run to the other end having a competition to see how many people they could slash on the way. I don't know if there was much truth in this, but that's what I heard, and it was known that the pair did a lot of bad things together.

During this early period, our summer holidays were spent in Blairgowrie, in Perthshire, where we stayed for up to seven weeks, picking berries for local market gardens. It was the only time we got to meet our relations, who came from all over Glasgow. Every fortnight Dad or Mum would disappear back to Glasgow. We didn't know why then, but would later work out they had gone back to sign on, so they could continue picking up the social security handouts on which the whole family had to survive.

It was a great time, but I remember there seemed to be more drinking and fighting than berry picking. Everyone stayed in camps, with a camp for those from Glasgow, another for the Dundee pickers, a separate one for the Edinburgh crowd, and so on. The camps were very territorial and you were not really meant to stray, but we often found ourselves kicked out of one camp because of the trouble and looking for another that would allow us in. Often we would not be welcome anywhere and on a couple of occasions fortunately managed to find an empty building in the town centre where we would cuddle up next to Mum and Dad until morning and the warmth it brought with it. Even though it was summer, the memory of how cold those nights were remains vivid. We'd wake up shivering and damp, and then head round the pubs to look for other friendly pickers to see if we could get into any of the other camps. Normally we did, but then the whole cycle of drinking and fighting would start again.

Dad was an alcoholic, and my mum Ellen was a very young and attractive woman who had five kids early in life. A year after Roseanne came James (Jamie), followed by Thomas (Tam), me and then the youngest, John, who, from the day he was born, was known as Pawny. Even he doesn't know the reason why he got that tag. Looking back, Mum was probably stupid and naive, and I don't mean that in any cruel sense. Her own dad had been in the forces and she was brought up in an army camp at Carmunnock, on the outskirts of Glasgow. Until her early 20s, she neither smoked nor drank. So often she was on the receiving end of the violence dished out by Dad. He died in December 2009 from cancer and other related illnesses and it was only in later years that I came to realise the reason he lifted his hands to Mum was jealousy. She was attractive to other men, who often looked admiringly at her, although she did nothing to encourage this. It was inevitable that they would split up and lead their separate lives, but after he and Mum parted Dad never remarried. I know he loved Mum more than she could ever understand, but you don't show someone how fond of them you are by taking your hands to them. That's what your head and heart are for. Long before he died, Dad knew where he had gone wrong, but of course by then it was too late.

I was aged five when we went berry picking for the last time. Soon after we returned home, Dad left Mum. As a result of the stress of everything, she had a nervous breakdown and ended up receiving treatment in Woodilee Hospital in the north-east of Glasgow. It meant we children were taken into care. It was our first experience of being split up.

Pawny went into a nursery, while the rest of us trooped off to Dunoon, on the Cowal Peninsula in Argyll. It had developed as a holiday resort for wealthy Glasgow merchants and many of the beautiful and imposing homes are now hotels and guesthouses. Jamie, Tam and I found ourselves in Dunclutha Children's Unit, while Roseanne was sent to another school in the town. I actually enjoyed my time here – for the first time, I was warm at night and was being fed three times a day. I had numerous friends and it was a welcome relief to discover there was no bullying or fighting. Even from an early age in Springburn I had constantly had to fight to prove myself. The majority of the time the battles were against the McGoverns. It was the way of life then.

When social services realised that they had split us up, they saw to it that we were reunited, and so Roseanne and Pawny both came to Dunclutha. They had to move Pawny next to me in my dormitory, as often when staff came in to get us up in the morning I was not in my bed. They soon worked out where I would be: in the nursery, in bed with Pawny. However, the nursery wasn't next door – reaching it meant leaving my building and crossing the grounds, about 100 metres. I was only five at the time. I still remember that feeling of being so sad and lonely without my sister and brothers right next to me at the beginning of my time in Dunclutha.

I was enrolled at St Munn's primary school in Dunoon and fitted in really well. The school had a policy of zero tolerance to bullying, so I did not have to prove myself as much as I had done in Glasgow. And I made a lot of friends, some of whom were the children of serving American sailors based at nearby Holy Loch, where, following the start of the Cold War, the United States Navy based submarines carrying Polaris nuclear weapons. The American kids introduced me to peanut butter and jam pieces, so I would often swap these for my packed lunches. I was delighted at this – especially because they were only too happy to take my spam sandwiches from me.

At Dunclutha, we all wore the same uniform, which made us all equal; however, it was here that I became aware of a difference existing between Roman Catholics and Protestants. I had wondered why some of my friends went to a different school to me, and someone explained it was because they were Protestant. My mum and dad were Catholic and that's how we were raised, but there was never any bitterness between us children.

I don't know how it came about, but Tam, Pawny and I all became supporters of Glasgow Rangers, while Roseanne and

Jamie were Celtic fans. Looking back all these years later, I believe it must have been a case of us going against the grain, or maybe it was because when we went into Dunclutha, we had come from a tough background where confrontation was almost a way of life and so we simply decided to try rubbing the others up the wrong way. If that was the reason, it didn't work. I recall watching an Old Firm game on television in Dunclutha in the early 1970s and shouting with the Rangers supporters even though I went to the same school as the Celtic fans. Maybe it was that game that sparked my interest in football, but I soon discovered I was pretty good at it.

Of course there were the odd times when I felt sad, especially when, every now and again, we would have to go to the gymnasium and sit in a big square while prospective foster parents came in and walked around us, more or less pointing to the kids they wanted. The Shannons were never chosen – I honestly thought the reason was because I had bright ginger hair! It was only much later that I realised others were being picked because they didn't have parents, whereas we were only there because our mum had suffered a breakdown and we would eventually be reunited with her. Despite enjoying Dunclutha and the kindness we were shown there, we longed for the day we would be back with Mum.

In the meantime, of course, there were consolations. It was during this time that I first came across the game Doctors and Nurses. We all played it, every day and at every opportunity. It was a case of no-holds-barred, and I came to believe it was normal for a boy of six or seven to be behind a shed or under a bed with a girl, even two girls, of the same age playing the game. The occasion I had doubts and wondered if something was wrong was when I went down to the water with a couple of older girls and they disappeared into a hut with an elderly man. I knew they were going inside to play the game with him, and in any case they used to tell me about it. Maybe the reason the girls were at Dunclutha was because they had been the victims of sexual abuse at home. I would never know. I stayed friends with one of them for the next five or six years until we lost contact. I sometimes think about them and hope they ended up happy and settled with someone who took good care of them.

One of the nurses who worked at Dunclutha took a real shine to me and on odd weekends she would take me to stay with her in Glasgow. She was engaged to be married, probably to an American sailor because she was planning to move there after the wedding. They wanted to take me along, but it never came off, presumably because my mum wouldn't agree. In any case, there was no way I would have been parted from my sister and brother.

We stayed at the children's unit for about two years and during that time Mum only came to visit us once. Dad turned up twice. I put the lack of visits down to Glasgow being a million miles away, as it seemed to us, never realising it took only a ferry and a bus ride to reach Dunoon. Mum's second visit, however, would change our lives.

Early in 1974, Mum came to see us, this time to take us away. She had a new partner, James Lafferty, and told us we were all going to live together in a new home she had found. It was new only in the sense that it was different from where we had been previously. Leaving the warmth and cleanliness of Dunclutha, we discovered our new life would centre on a flat at the very top of an old tenement in Kelvinhaugh Street, Anderston. It still had an old communal toilet in the stairs and the place was infested by rats.

Instead of enjoying three meals a day, a warm bed and people around us who showed their feelings, we were thrown into a world of wooden floorboards and generally all of us sharing one bed with our jackets for blankets. Usually, we would get one meal a day and sometimes that consisted of just a tin of soup among five children and two adults. For a long time, we were drinking our tea from jam jars because we hardly ever seemed to have cups. It was as if I had stepped back in time. Mum may have honestly believed she was doing the best for us, but from the beginning she was struggling with life and found it hard to cope with having all five of us back in the house. For much of the time, it was left to Roseanne to look after us, while we experienced a return to the miserable old days of adults drinking and fighting and us children enduring hunger and cold. We were sometimes going for days with a constant pain brought on by hunger, but there was nothing we could do.

Eventually, by the age of eight, as a lot of children do when they have problems at home, I decided the time had come for me to move on. Luckily, something happened that made me put the plan on hold.

Even at that age I knew I had to do things for myself, and that included finding food. One day, when she had some money, Mum bought potatoes, peas and a steak pie for the seven of us for our dinner. I'd seen all this food and the pie made my mouth water. I was hungry, remember, and thought to myself, 'I'll just have a wee taste of that.' Before I knew it, I'd eaten the whole of the inside of the steak pie. Then I ran away from the house. Needless to say, after a process of elimination as to my whereabouts, I was caught out by Mum. By God, what a hiding I took that night. I've remembered it ever since because it taught me a harsh lesson; never steal from family and friends, especially food. What hurt most was not the beating, but seeing my sister and brothers go another day without a meal because of my selfishness and greed.

It is amazing how your mind can come up with ideas for putting money in your pockets to buy food, even when you are young. Just below our home was a very popular pub called Barney's and the guy who owned it – Barney – was great with all the kids. I think he felt sorry for us and was always giving us crisps and drinks. Soon we started to notice there were a lot of trucks that would park on the street overnight, as there were a few bed and breakfasts around. We were quick to realise the potential here. Along with children from another big neighbouring family, we would ask every driver if they would like their vehicle watched for a few hours or during the night. If they said yes, and gave us a couple of pounds, all was well. If they turned down the offer, then the goods inside became fair game and usually disappeared. It was a protection racket and a profitable one.

Just down the road was a busy ferry to Ibrox and at times there must have been almost a mile-long queue of lorries parked nose-to-tail. Inside these giant vehicles were cargoes of almost everything imaginable, but we'd pick and choose which loads were likely to be useful. Electrical goods were a real favourite.

Sometimes a driver who had lost his load would ask around to see if he could find likely culprits and then come to us and buy his equipment back. This was a real starting point for my brothers and me because we soon learned a valuable lesson: if you want something, then go and get it – even if it does not belong to you. At that young age, we had learned that everything had a value. If you could not use it, then sell it and use the proceeds to buy food.

The reason for all of this was simply hunger. We stole to eat.

One evening a Mr Kipling van drove up and parked, the driver making off in the direction of a lodging house. We knew he wouldn't return until the next morning. Cakes were a real luxury for us and we were sure the vehicle was packed full of them. In those days, padlocks on wagons or vans were not as sophisticated or secure as today, and for experienced robbers like us it was only a matter of minutes before we had the doors open.

It is hard for someone who hasn't known hunger to understand just how desperate it feels. When you are starving, you eat whatever appears in front of you, and in this case it was cakes. Big, fancy wedding cakes. I hate marzipan and under the icing these cakes were coated with it, but I threw it down my throat as quickly as possible. They were *exceedingly good* wedding cakes.

We ate with such desperation it was as though we feared someone was going to come along and take the food from us. Within minutes, we were full of dry cake, coughing and choking, but with bloated stomachs. We then had to think what to do with the uneaten cakes. There was no way we'd throw them away. We decided to save them for later, so we stored them in the stairwell of our tenement. When we went back to check on them, just a few minutes later, the cakes were literally teeming with rats. They were everywhere. Soon, not a crumb was left.

Sometimes our money-making schemes would go wrong. One night, we broke into a new factory at the bottom of our street, thinking it was a clothing unit. Imagine our horror when we found that all it contained were nuts and bolts! The sensible thing would have been to leave. Instead, in our anger and frustration, we foolishly set about wrecking the place. In the course of throwing boxes of nuts and bolts around, we obviously made too much noise and as a result the police came and caught us.

I learned a lot of lessons that day. One in particular was that if ever something happened in our area, the police automatically assumed the Shannon family was to blame. I tried to keep out of trouble and away from the police, yet we were constantly being picked up for one thing or another. This added to the strain on Mum, who was already struggling to cope with us. These difficulties at home affected our schooling; teachers found us difficult to control and were unsure as to how we should be dealt with.

My teacher at Anderston primary used to make me use a desk in the corner away from everyone. She didn't realise I was happy with this arrangement; most of the other pupils were Indian, Pakistani or Chinese and, as I hadn't come across anyone from these countries before, I felt apprehensive about mixing with them and was convinced it was better to be stand-offish than to get to know some of them.

Still, life wasn't bad. Some of my fondest memories of Kelvinhaugh Street are of getting the ferry across the Clyde to Ibrox so I could watch my beloved Rangers. When I had been at Dunclutha, one of the nurses, a staunch Catholic, was horrified that I was a Rangers fan and would tell me: 'Alexander, you'll never get to heaven if you carry on supporting that team.' But every time I walked into Ibrox I thought I was already in heaven.

Then there were school dinners. Once we were on the register, it meant we were at least guaranteed one good meal a day, while during the summer holidays we would all march down to another school for our free meal. It was a lovely, warm feeling having a full stomach.

Things picked up even more when I got myself a part-time job cleaning in the Lorne Hotel on Sauchiehall Street.

# THE UNDERWORLD CAPTAIN

Admittedly, it was a bit of a joke because there wasn't a lot I could do, but the other workers took pity on me and used to give me money at the end of each week for the work I had done for them. Gripping my pay tightly in my pocket, I would run home and split it with my mum, so she could go down to the pub for a few drinks. Sadly, my prized job did not last long.

The hotel had organised a sale of jewellery and clothes, and one day a huge van packed with these items pulled up outside. I walked over to the driver and told him my brothers and I would help him unload for a small fee. He agreed, but when we were caught helping ourselves to some watches, I was promptly barred from entering the Lorne again.

About this time I spent Christmas with one of my friend's families. I was the odd one out because I received no presents, but then that was nothing new to me. I had never known what it was like to be given a gift on a birthday or at Christmas. What you have never had, you cannot miss.

In 1975, the Shannons were on the move once more when the tenements in which we lived were demolished. We were to be housed temporarily, until alternative and permanent accommodation could be found for us, in a ward set aside for the homeless at Forresthall Hospital in Springburn. I can still recall the long wards with high walls and no roof. All we kids were sent to bed early, so the adults could watch television. There were about ten families waiting in our ward to be re-housed and frankly we couldn't get out of there quickly enough. It was a cold, unhealthy, miserable place.

I was delighted when I discovered we were moving back to my old stomping ground: Springburn. And it was while I was living there that I met someone who would change my life.

# CHAPTER TWO

I was over the moon about our move from the hospital ward. Anywhere would have done, but the council sent us to Galloway Street in Springburn and it almost felt like going back home. Not quite, though. The majority of Galloway Street consisted of new maisonettes and the prospect of us ever having a new house was a pipe dream. I suppose, in a way, we looked upon the occupants as snobs, though I can honestly say we didn't begrudge them their luck.

For us, it was what was known as the 'old end' of Galloway Street. It was great being there, but all my mates were down at the old part of Springburn itself, near Memel Street. Since I now stayed in Galloway Street, it meant that they and I lived in different parts of Springburn, which may not sound important, but it was. Just about everybody joined the gang that ran your home territory, so I was recruited into the Springburn Peg, while most of my pals were members of Memel Toi.

There were literally hundreds of gangs in Glasgow at this time. Over the years, some have faded away, as boys and teenagers have become more interested in watching television or joining sports clubs and the like, but many still survive. There were some brilliant names, like the Baby Tongs in Calton, the Antique Mob from Shettleston, the Derry Boys in Bridgeton, the Shamrock Young Team at Garngad and the Blackhill Coby. There were even a few girl gangs around, such as Lady Sham in Garngad and the Queen Bees, who ran about the Gorbals. Some of the gangs took their status and territorial rights very seriously, but while the younger kids might have got themselves involved in the odd skirmish, it was relatively harmless stuff. As you grew older, however, things became more serious.

I have often wondered whether it was being a gang member that first piqued my interest in the army. In a way, gangs and army regiments have certain similarities, in that members tend to stick together and look after each other. Discipline is, of course, an entirely different matter, but at the age of eight it's something you tend not to worry too much about. You join a gang because your pals are members and you want to have fun with them. As time went on, a couple of things would happen which definitely planted in my young mind a desire to become a soldier.

Our house move resulted in my mates and me going to different schools. Despite the fact that I was a Roman Catholic, I was sent to Albert primary, a Protestant school, while the McGoverns were still at St Aloysius, a newer school next to the Carron Scheme flats. Sometimes kids from St Aloysius would sing through our gates, 'Proddy dogs eat the frogs.'

Just as gangs fought with one another, so did our schools, and the result of that was years of petty conflicts, squabbles and fights with people I'd always looked on as friends.

The house itself was great. There were three bedrooms, so no longer was there a need for all of the children to share a single bed; however, more rooms and more beds were to cause more problems than you can imagine.

In those days, the mid-1970s, there was no such thing as a duvet, and even if there had been it wasn't something we were likely to have heard of. So, for bed coverings, we simply threw our jackets over us while we slept. Sometimes going to bed could be miserable, especially when the nights were cold. To make things worse, we could not afford to buy coal the majority of the time and, as a result, the living-room fire was rarely on. That, in turn, meant the house was frequently freezing; the fact there were no carpets on the floors for insulation made it worse. The fire had a back burner, so if it wasn't on, there was no hot water.

Nor could we afford a new television. On the rare occasion when Mum had a few pounds to spare, we'd get an old second-

or third-hand black-and-white set from the Glasgow Saltmarket, the Briggate, keeping it until it packed in completely then getting another old replacement. We'd watch programmes like *Basil Brush, Dastardly and Muttley* and *Captain Pugwash*. Times were hard, right enough. Pawny once spotted a TV set on offer for £1 in a jumble sale at his school and beat the teachers down to 50p. I remember him proudly bringing it home.

As children, we saw our move to Galloway Street as an adventure. The second-hand stalls at the Briggate became a regular hunting ground for us. As soon as we began settling in, we went about trying to furnish our new house to make it more comfortable and give it the appearance of being a home. First we got odds and ends of furniture, then Mum took us to buy us clothes. She wanted us to go to school looking smart and tidy, but next day we turned up for lessons in a selection of mismatched and ill-fitting gear. We didn't complain because we knew she was doing her best for us. Mum would say, 'It doesn't matter what the clothes look like, so long as they are clean. You can wear them every day, as long as you wash and dry them each night.'

This didn't go down too well with us. We wore our clothes to bed to try and keep out the cold, but some of us had a habit of wetting the bed, so the stench of urine at school was bad. Needless to say, it didn't go unnoticed by the nurse.

All the pupils could smell it too, but none of them said a word. They knew better. The Shannons may not have been in Galloway Street long, but already we had a reputation as trouble-making thieves. No matter the size of another family, they knew we were always ready for a fight. We would take on anybody who offended us.

I have a particular hatred of bullies, so at that time I tended to look out for those who picked on the weak, then I would target them for a bit of payback. I was small and had a terrible temper, which often got me into trouble with the teachers. Despite all this, I loved school.

As time went on, I became conscious of people laughing behind my back. Maybe it was just because we were poor and wore clothes that had belonged to others. Maybe it was because we never had money. Whatever the reason, here I was thinking myself an adult and deciding I needed to do something about the situation. It was time for me to start back along that old road I knew best: making money so I could dress and feed myself.

* * *

Then something happened that was to have a profound effect on me. I was only eight when I first saw Angela Scullion, but even at that young age I felt there was something special about her. I was too young, of course, to think about love and romance – you don't when there's a football to be kicked around or a pal who wants you to head off somewhere with him – but before we even spoke I liked Angie. And it turned out we had much in common. We were both from similar backgrounds. Angie's mum, like mine, had drink problems. We came from big families – I had three brothers and a sister, Angie had two sisters and four brothers. And each of us knew what it was like to go without. From the day I first took notice of her, I took every chance there was to see her and be near her. The only obstacle was that she was 18 months older than me and had friends her own age, but there was no way I was going to give up on her.

While she kept me at arm's length, soon I had the feeling she might be warming towards me, despite trying to give the impression it wasn't me she was interested in. She knew I was a rascal, but she had had her own forays into crime. She used to go to Bishopbriggs with her pals to steal milk and things like that from doorsteps. Then they'd bring it all back and go knocking on doors selling the milk. With what was left, they would set up a jumble sale in somebody's garden and sell that. They asked me to be their security guard and make sure that nobody else would steal anything that they had stolen. When they had sold everything, they'd go to the chip shop and use the money to buy food, because they didn't get much to eat at home. I was about ten then. I suppose you could say it was the first time I did guard duty.

The army, too, kept coming back to occupy my thoughts. At the beginning of 1975, the dustcart drivers went on strike in

Glasgow and elsewhere and soon bags of rubbish began piling up in the streets, encouraging vermin – rats and mice especially – to forage openly amongst the rotting food and decomposing clothing. As the strike dragged on, the situation became intolerable. There were serious health concerns, especially for children used to playing in these same streets and curious about the mountains of foul-smelling refuse. As a result the army was brought in to start clearing up. The soldiers attracted a good deal of criticism, with accusations of strike-breaking and so on, but I was almost transfixed by the sight of men from the Royal Highland Fusiliers driving into the streets and clearing the rubbish. They might only have been acting as bin men, but they looked smart and disciplined – real men.

The memory of them would often come back to me, especially the white hackle attached to their headdresses. I'd often imagine myself marching about, the hackle proudly standing out.

At home, despite our efforts to make things more comfortable and welcoming, we found ourselves drifting back to the bad old days, witnessing Mum and her partner fighting and drinking. Of course the cause of the trouble was always money, or rather the lack of it.

A close friend of my mum's tried to help us out – or maybe help himself – by robbing a Glasgow branch of the newsagent RS McColl. Actually, it wasn't so much a robbery as a comedy caper. It has to be one of the most ludicrous crimes ever seen on the streets of Glasgow.

His head and face encased in a stocking for a mask, he demanded the money, and the frightened staff handed over a bag filled with about £600 in coins. So far so good. Then just as he was about to set off on his getaway, as he began opening his jacket to stuff the booty inside, the zip unfortunately caught the stocking and as he pulled it, it ripped his mask, exposing his face for everyone to see.

There was worse to come. Panicking, he fled out of the shop and started running towards Balgrayhill, but in his haste he had left the bag open and the coins started spilling out, rolling onto the pavement and road, attracting scores of passers-by, who started picking the money up, most of them getting a good look at the thief. It was inevitable that his name would be passed to the police and he was arrested. However, by the time he went to court, he had discovered God, with the help of Pastor Jack Glass, the well-known Protestant preacher, evangelist and political activist. Pastor Jack, who died in 2004, came from a working-class background in Glasgow and could sympathise with those who got themselves into trouble as a consequence of poverty. He went along to court with the culprit, put in a few good words for him and as a result the decision was a suspended sentence. Everyone felt he was very lucky – it was the intervention of Pastor Jack that saved him from a stretch in prison.

A side effect of all this was that sadly my mum and her partner split up. The worry had caused her to have another nervous breakdown and she was once again taken to Woodilee Hospital. Now, Roseanne became mother to us all, but the absence of our real mum meant we felt free to pursue activities on which she had frowned when she was at home.

Tam and me, and a guy called Mairdo, along with a couple of other friends, set up a small team and started breaking into shops and business premises. Within only weeks, we were wearing made-to-measure clothes and had hundreds of pounds in our pockets.

Mum, meanwhile, had met someone else in Woodilee. His name was Jim Corrigan and when she was discharged, she brought him home to stay with us. To be honest, his presence and her relationship with him didn't really bother us. We were so absorbed in pulling off some of the best turns in the north of Glasgow – and I had not yet even reached the age of 11.

Mum had always known her sons were free spirits who wanted to go about their lives in the way they chose. She realised it was no use her ordering us not to steal because at the end of the day if we wanted to do it, then we would go ahead regardless of what she said. There had been times when she had tried keeping us in the house at night, but we simply waited until she was asleep then climbed down the drainpipe and off we went. Mum at least persuaded us to agree that we would never break into people's houses, arguing that they might be poor like us. We went along with her on this and it became a golden rule for us to avoid residential properties. Usually, we would target premises in Bishopbriggs, in the north of the city.

Tam used to rip me off for my cut of the money all the time by always making sure our mum's electricity and household bills were being paid. I didn't really mind and in hindsight I'm glad he did it because it meant that for the first time we had electricity and hot water. At last the good times seemed to be heading our way.

While we knew problems were always likely to appear just around the corner, for now we carried on regardless. Two really good turns stick in my mind.

# CHAPTER THREE

Everyone involved in crime knows success depends on quality information. One day a guy who lived close to us, and knew we were making big money, stopped Tam and me in the street and asked if he could have a word. We told him to go ahead and what he said made us perk up. He began by telling us that what he had in mind would net us in the region of £20,000. It was 1976, so that was a lot of money then. It sounded too good to be true, so before committing ourselves we wanted to know more.

Our informant agreed to tell us everything so that we could make up our minds about whether to go ahead. Before doing so, however, he wanted a promise from us that if we took the job on, then he would receive a generous cut and, no matter what happened, his name would never be revealed. We had no problem in giving our word on both these reasonable conditions.

His detailed information interested us immediately. He told us that the monthly wages for staff working in a particular business premises close to where we lived were kept in a safe from the Friday until the Monday so that wage packets could be made up and distributed at the start of the week. This might sound like an unusual arrangement, but it was not unknown for some companies to pay monthly. Within hours we had set about getting organised.

Our first task was to put together a team we could trust. The job would entail burning our way into the safe, and our informant told us he knew how we could get hold of the necessary equipment. When we asked where, we were astonished to be told, 'Right there. It's already in the place you'll be doing.' It seemed almost too good to be true.

We assembled a five-strong team and on the Friday night watched as the workers gradually left, the last pair locking up and checking the building was secure. After waiting an hour, just to make sure nobody had forgotten anything and returned to collect it, we broke in through the roof. The plan was straightforward. Since we didn't have the combination to open the door of the safe, we would just use a blowtorch to burn the lock out. We knew it was not going to be easy – the safe would be made from toughened steel – but we had the whole weekend to work at it.

Within minutes we had sparked up the burner and set about making ourselves a fortune. We worked with military precision in shift formation around the clock. While one was burning, another would be assisting, while yet another was keeping a lookout and someone else was going off to buy food. The fifth member would be sleeping. Sometimes we would sleep on the floor, at others sneak back home and go to bed for a few hours, knowing we could get in and out without Mum noticing.

And so it went on, hour after hour. We were working in the pitch dark and so didn't realise the dust from all the burning had blackened our faces until we had the appearance of coal miners.

We carried on from the Friday night until the early hours of Monday morning, by which time we had burned to a depth of around five inches. Try as we might, though, the lock would not budge. You can imagine our despair when we realised we had to call it a day and clear out before the staff came to open up. With an hour to spare, we packed up our tools, wiped everything down to make sure we had left no fingerprints and left to go home, where we caught up on some well-deserved sleep.

In later years, I found out it hadn't been the safe that had foiled us, it was our own lack of knowledge. I took a course aimed at giving me a qualification to become a gas engineer and realised the settings on the gas cylinder and torch had been wrong: we had been burning for the entire weekend with a yellow flame. A simple change in the settings would have given us a much more effective blue flame and we'd have been through the safe in no time! Mind you, the strength of the burner might have incinerated all the money.

Nevertheless, we woke later that day to stories about a professional gang who were only centimetres away from getting their hands on £20,000. The police stated that if the crooks had stayed just half an hour longer they would have been off with the wages. At the time, the news devastated us – the more we thought about the money, the more we kicked ourselves for giving up when we did. We were really down for a couple of days and the problem was everybody had a good idea we were responsible. Doubtless the informant, who had also lost out big style, was putting it about it was the young mob who were behind the robbery attempt. We were constantly wondering whether the police would come looking for us. Shocked and frankly pissed off, there was the consolation of knowing we were still free. Had we got away with it, what would I have done with the money? The usual. I know for a fact I would have gone off and bought myself all the smartly fitting clothes I could afford. I'd obviously have bought food for home and given my mum a good bung. But at the end of the day, if it had been successful, I'd have been locked up within days. Someone was bound to have told the police about the ten year old going around with pockets packed with money. And in those days, as soon as the police stopped you and found you had more than a pound in your pocket, it was taken from you and never heard of again.

While that one didn't work out, another did. Whenever we were short of cash, we would simply go out and steal to fill our empty pockets. But we had to be careful. Not only did we have the police to contend with, but doing turns in someone else's territory could spark off a lot of trouble.

On this occasion, it was one of the wettest days I can ever remember. Rain was just pouring down and kept on coming. My jacket was far from waterproof, but the inconvenience of getting literally soaked to the skin was not going to stop us.

Our target was a carpet shop. Climbing to the top of the premises, we carefully removed some of the slates and, discovering a layer of wood underneath, simply broke through it. It was a Sunday and we had made our entry in broad daylight, yet so far nobody appeared to have seen us because there were no shouts or warnings or the noise of police sirens. However, as we climbed into the shop itself, to our horror we saw customers peering in through the big glass shopfront windows. It was an eerie sensation, like our privacy had been invaded by strangers without the right to do so. Thankfully, they were only window shopping, looking at an array of brightly coloured rugs, doubtless wondering whether to come back the next day to check on prices. I recall thinking to myself, 'They'd better take a good look, because they won't be there in the morning.' There wasn't much we could do until the onset of darkness and so, cold and soaking, we wrapped ourselves in some rugs we found at the back of the shop and settled down to sleep. By the time we awoke, something like six hours later, it was dark. We felt refreshed and dry. Now it was just a case of finishing the job. Stuffing as many rugs as possible into black bags, we climbed out through the roof and started walking, taking care to keep an eye out for police patrols.

Over the next few hours we walked through Bishopbriggs, up onto a railway line, confident no trains would be running, and headed in the direction of our Springburn home. Most gangs have a hiding place where they stash loot safely until it is needed and we were no exception. We used to leave our booty next to the Briggs Bar. Having done so, we headed for our beds. By this stage, it was around three in the morning, so after another sleep we returned next day on bicycles and ferried all the goods back to Galloway Street. For the next few days, we did a roaring trade in tenner-a-time rugs that sold like hot cakes. As word spread, we even offered a delivery service. Now and then we'd pass a police patrol and be given a look that said, 'I wonder what that lot are up to now.' Thankfully, nobody thought to stop us.

With the money we were making, I was able to afford the best clothes and dress smartly. I had always been conscious of my appearance. I was brought up in a city of the haves and have-nots and looked on myself as one of the latter. There was a sense of feeling deprived and it acted as a spur that drove me not only to make a success of anything I did but also to make sure I was seen to be successful. Wearing smart clothes was one way of showing I was doing well. I may not have been from the most affluent areas of Glasgow, such as Bishopbriggs, but I could look as though I came from the same background as many of the well-off who lived there.

I loved the fact that people knew my name. I had it stitched in white thread into my back pockets for everybody to see and insisted on having vivid white buttons, known as 'cat's eyes' because they shone brightly in the dark, on my clothes. I was able to buy trousers specially made for me. You could steal off-the-peg clothes, but not made-to-measure.

I was always able to wear smart shoes, because I stole those from Goldbergs, a famous chain of stores started in Glasgow at the beginning of the century. Goldbergs sold really first-rate gear. I know it sounds crazy, but even though I had enough money in my pocket to buy the shoes, something about the thrill of stealing them and getting away with it really appealed to me. I just got a buzz from doing it. And I wanted to look better than those who could actually afford to buy their clothes legally.

I felt so good and proud that strangers seeing me in my designer gear and with money in my pockets would be under the impression I was from a rich family. In a sense, though, it was a false front, a way of countering what was a basic insecurity resulting from feeling unloved, of not being good-looking and being conscious of my red hair. I could hide my worries under smart clothes and seeming affluence, and appear to be someone who would put a bullet in you if you gave me a wrong look, but that hair would just not go away. Sometimes I felt I was a ginger-haired outcast from whom others wanted to shy away.

My worst memory was when I was aged ten. My mum had saved up for a haircut for me at one of the best hairdressers in Glasgow, but I was turned away because my head was full of lice. I promised myself then that I would never again let anybody pay for anything for me. I determined to sort things out for myself, to be who I wanted to be and wear what I wanted. I believed then, and still do, that what you wear is a statement of your ego and, with the exception of the red hair, mine was massive.

There is a saying that a Glaswegian will spend a pound to stop someone else making fifty pence. It's all about jealousy. Being smartly dressed and having money in your pocket got you noticed, especially in a fairly run-down area like Springburn, which was, at that time, largely McGovern land, or so they liked to think – and few would challenge their right to run the area, or have the temerity to dispute their superiority.

Initially, there hadn't been any difficulty between us. In fact, they seemed quite happy with us coming into their territory and doing a bit of shoplifting or screwing shops, and even on odd occasions we'd do turns together. My mum would go to their ma's house and have a drink because Mum frequented the same pubs as their parents. Sometimes we'd go to their home with Mum. Then obviously jealousy crept in. The fact is the more money you are earning, or the bigger reputation you are getting, the more somebody wants the money and the name for themselves.

In the wonderful gangster movie *Once Upon a Time in America* there is a scene in which a gang of young tearaways are ordered by an older crew to hand over their profits from stealing, or at least a share of them. I found myself in that exact same scenario when, sporting my smart clothes and shiny new shoes, my pockets ringing with coins, I ventured down to the bottom part of Springburn and headed for the local fish and chip shop. There I came across Tommy McGovern and his team.

Tommy congratulated me on our recent exploits in the earning game, but I had the feeling this was leading up to something and I was about to be proved correct. Calmly, Tommy went on to suggest I hand over some of my well-earned money to him and his mates. Now, I had a couple of pals with me, but I was well aware that they were not into the sort of dodgy dealings that were making me money. And they were scared of the McGoverns. I told Tommy where to go in language that was both colourful and anatomically imaginative, and he clearly didn't appreciate my response. A brief scuffle ensued. I knew I was outnumbered and decided that the time had come for me to go, but there was no way I could run fast enough in my new shoes. So, pulling them off and clutching them tightly under my arms, I sprinted for safety. For the next few minutes, I was chased from one end of Springburn to the other in bare feet. Thankfully, my pursuers were no match for me.

I knew Tommy had been trying to make a point – I was in his territory and nothing went down without either his say-so or compensation being paid to him. And while that might have been how it was in the gangster movies, in Glasgow it was another matter. If you wanted something, then you had to take it. If you made a play and didn't get what you'd set out to achieve, then you either fought for it or lost face. Maybe it was because he had his team with him that he felt he had to take a stand, especially as I was effectively fighting single-handedly. Whatever Tommy's motive, it didn't come off for him, but I had the feeling there was pressure on him now to do something to show he was not prepared to let me get away with it.

By this stage, my family had made a bit of a reputation for themselves. We were the Shannons of Galloway Street. The McGoverns were down at Memel, so they became the competition, to an extent.

As a result of the stand-off, it became more difficult to do turns – indeed, anything – at the bottom end of Springburn; however, with our skills we managed to do a few of the shops down there, much to the annoyance of the McGoverns. Naturally, Tommy and his brothers, Steven and Tony, were not happy and I found myself constantly having to watch over my shoulder.

Despite my lawbreaking exploits, my thoughts about the army kept recurring and an incident in 1977 probably really planted the idea of joining up most firmly in my mind. At the start of that year, the Queen scheduled a number of visits to cities across the UK as part of her Silver Jubilee celebrations. It would be a whistle-stop tour of the kingdom, starting in Glasgow in May. Along with some of my mates, I'd been down in the city centre shoplifting and decided to find out what all the fuss was about. As part of her look at Glasgow, the Queen visited the City Chambers in George Square. I was sitting right by the barriers that were holding the crowds back and was just inches away from her. I really didn't appreciate the greatness of the occasion, or the fact I had been so close to her. To me, it was just the Queen.

Once the Queen left and the crowds started to disperse, my mates and I had a wander about, fascinated by all the excitement, colour and noise. There were lots of police and soldiers around, chatting and joking with each other as if they were relieved that the royal visit had gone off peacefully. The soldiers had been parading, marching through the city centre streets and then standing to attention very smartly, guarding the monarch. Now they could relax, and my mates and I followed them to see what they would be doing next. They were friendly, enquiring what we had been up to and whether we'd seen the Queen. When we asked where they were going, they told us it was time for them to have a break. Earlier we had seen long lines of buses parked in the surrounding streets guarded by police and had wondered why they were there. Now, we had found the answer, as the soldiers began climbing inside.

'Want a sandwich, wee man?' one of the soldiers asked and when I nodded he waved me into his coach, where lots of his mates were opening up their packed lunches. I wasn't really interested in getting food, I just wanted to see what the soldiers were like when they were off duty, what sort of things they did and talked about. Most of them just wanted a cigarette and when they saw me and my pals holding wee bags that we'd taken to go shoplifting started popping sandwiches, biscuits and apples inside. They were happy to let us have them and this was a real bonus. We would never have gone on the buses had we not been invited. After a few minutes, the soldiers told us it was time for them to go and we climbed down, our bags bulging with food. But for me what was even better than free food was that I'd been among these men, talked with them as though they were pals and had been treated with kindness. I had read about soldiers and had watched the army on television lots of times; now, I had seen soldiers at first hand. It was a great experience that left me feeling I'd been in the presence of heroes.

It turned out to be a wonderful day, but things did not always go so smoothly. At home, Mum discovered Jim Corrigan had disappeared. Theirs had been a pretty unsettled relationship and maybe Jim wasn't always on hand for Mum when she needed a comforting shoulder. Then one day he was there at home, the next he was gone. His decision to walk out didn't affect us; we just carried on with our own lives, wondering if he would suddenly reappear, but we weren't upset when there was no sign of him. If Mum was saddened that a relationship which had lasted about two years had suddenly ended, she didn't let it show.

In 1977, I was caught breaking into some shops. I had been picked up by the police in the past, when I was eight, but then I was judged too young to be criminally responsible and had got away with a severe ticking-off from a senior ranking officer, but the boys in blue had been watching me and others for a long time. They were sure we were up to no good, but, much to their annoyance, they'd never seemed able to catch us in the act. Now, it had finally happened and I found myself in front of a children's hearing in October that year. I faced three charges of theft: attempted theft with intent, housebreaking and opening lock-fast places with intent. That meant I'd been caught doing three shops.

It was a serious matter and I could have been sent off to an approved school. Instead, I was made the subject of a supervision order, which meant I had to be seen to be keeping my nose clean or I would be hauled back and given a more severe punishment.

Two months later, I was in front of the children's hearing on another attempted break-in. The break-in had been before my initial appearance, so all that happened was that I was placed under the same supervision order and told to behave or else.

At the time, none of this really meant a lot to me. I'd got a legal ticking-off and had been told that if I did not re-offend, then nothing more would come of it. In fact, that wasn't true.

The repercussions of those fairly minor infringements, or at least the consequences of being caught, could have been devastating, resulting in what amounted to a life sentence. I will explain why in a later chapter.

# CHAPTER FOUR

By now, I was nearing the age of 12 and it was around this time that I became very close friends with a cousin of the McGoverns, John Storrie, who lived close by. A few years later, I found myself caught in a really awkward situation when John was involved in a fight with another of my best mates, who sadly died. The trouble had broken out between groups from Springburn and Possilpark during a concert by Scheme, a local Glasgow group, at the old Pavilion Theatre. But that was for the future.

For now, I started to run around with John all the time, though he was not involved in any of the turns or fighting in which I was caught up. Due to our friendship, however, and despite the earlier run-in with Tommy, I would often end up down at the bottom half of Springburn with the McGovern brothers and John, all of us appearing to be the best of mates. At least that's how it looked. But all was not what it seemed.

One night, I was at a school disco in Albert primary with John when, out of the blue, about 20 members of the Memel Toi appeared, led by Tommy and Tony McGovern. At first I wasn't worried, thinking we were all good pals and everything would be OK, but within minutes it became obvious from the way they were staring and glaring in my direction that they weren't there for the dancing but instead for me. The odds were overwhelming, so I positioned myself at one of the exit doors and waited for it all to kick off. It did not take long.

After a few minutes, when nothing had kicked off, I wondered whether I had read the situation wrongly and that the evening would turn into a quiet affair. So, thinking all was well, I went off to the tuck shop and bought a cup of tea. But then my original suspicions turned out to be correct because as I went to sit on my chair, Tommy booted it away from underneath me. His crowd broke into gales of laughter. They clearly thought it was funny. I did not. Despite being massively outnumbered, and to everyone's surprise, especially Tommy's, I threw the cup of tea in his face. This gave me just enough time to make a fast exit while being chased by the angry Memel Toi. They had advantage in numbers, but I was good at running and knew I only needed to make it halfway up the hill to cross the dividing line that separated their territory from ours and reach safety. Once there I could count on the rest of my family and a whole crowd of friends from Galloway Street coming out to back me up. It wasn't just the McGoverns who were reluctant to enter the old end of Galloway Street where we stayed; even the police kept away, knowing there was only one way in and one way out. It was a virtual no-go area. If a police car showed up, it was bricked for the entire length of the street until it could escape. Tommy might have been more streetwise than the police, but there was no way he was going to risk a barrage of bricks and bottles.

I escaped, but the tea-throwing incident had me on my heels for a short time and I was being threatened on a daily basis. A message was sent, warning me I was not to go near the bottom half of Springburn. It obviously came from Tommy and his crew. This would severely restrict my movements, so I knew something had to be done.

One day, a couple of weeks later, I noticed a group of about 40 youths who had come from Memel Street right into Galloway Street to look for me. It showed how bold they were getting and how confident they were that their reputation would be enough to turn me into jelly. I happened to be standing with some of the older guys and thought the only way to resolve this was to walk straight into the middle of them all and put Tommy on the spot by inviting him to fight. It would be him and me, and we would both accept the outcome, no matter what it happened to be.

This might sound brave, but the reality was that I had little alternative. My oldest brother, Jamie, was in jail, and Tam was away. Only Pawny and me were left. I thought to myself, do I want to run away for the rest of my life? The answer to that, of course, was no. So I thought, I have to just go in there, walk right into the middle of them all, up to Tommy and challenge him. Once I do that, all the guys with him will look at him and say, 'Well, come on, he's asking you. You are going to take him on, aren't you?' If I do that, then I put him on the spot in front of all his mates and he daren't back down. I knew he wouldn't want to be seen to lose face in front of the older guys I'd been talking to because they would spread word about what had happened.

So, up I went to Tommy and said, 'Tell you what, Tommy. I'll take you on in a square-go and after that we shake hands and walk away.' To his credit, Tommy agreed and a few seconds later we went at it. It was pretty brutal, but I gave him quite a good kicking. I recall as I was doing it, because they were in my area, shouting, 'Young Springburn Peg', while the rest of them from Memel just stood by watching. When it was over, the two of us had a few cuts and bruises, but Tommy just got up, brushed some blood off his cut lip, shook my hand and said, 'That's it. It won't be mentioned again.'

To give Tommy his due, I walked right to the end of Galloway Street with him and his team, by which stage the older guys had gone and I was on my own. At any time he could have turned and waved his team in, but he didn't. Neither did he say a single bad word about me. I respected Tommy for that. He was brand new.

Despite the skirmishing, we were still good mates and I remained friends with his brothers. I could see their point of view. They were looking up to our end, seeing a family making a reputation and money. It was a case of them feeling they had to show their authority and let everybody know they were running the scheme.

There were conflicts like ours all over Glasgow, disputes over who controlled which area, but the tensions between us and the McGoverns never got out of hand. A lot of that was due to John Storrie being at our end of the street. He often acted as peacekeeper between us and his cousins. I don't know whether it was a case of John thinking, 'Well, I'm stuck up here with all of them. If I don't watch what I'm doing, I'll be on the receiving end.' John was well respected even then, so I'm sure nothing would have happened to him. John tended to make sure things remained happy between all of us, although there were instances when they were in danger of getting out of hand because I had a terrible temper. If I'm honest, every one of us did. I would just do things without thinking. If ever I was arguing with somebody and they said something to me that I regarded as confrontational, I'd flare up. This continued into my army days until there came a time when I knew I had to control my rages.

I suppose when we were younger we were all quite confrontational. We threw bottles and cans and attacked each other. There were no stabbings in those days, no shootings. Now and again somebody might get coshed over the head with a pole, drawing blood, but most of us looked on it mainly as fun. At least I did. Certainly, I was never scared.

The fight with Tommy seemed to clear the air and resolving the problem allowed me to go back to making money and developing another aspect of crime in which I was becoming increasingly adept. By the time I was 12, I was an accomplished car thief. I looked on this as a sort of hobby and could steal and drive just about every make of car on the road even though I was only just over four feet tall.

I also set about expanding my sphere of operations. Having started my first year at Albert secondary school, where Tam and Jamie were in classes ahead of me and had made their names and reputations, my area for good turns – good turns in the sense of thieving – now extended to Balornock and Barmulloch. I was able to do this because the local hoods from these parts of Glasgow attended the school as well. I made lots of new friends, including the Marr family from Balornock and a few other guys from Barmulloch. Everybody seemed to already know of the Shannons and our exploits, so we could now move about the north of Glasgow without any problems, almost doing as we wished.

As for stealing cars, I loved driving up and down Wallacewell

Road and Galloway Street at speed. To be honest, I'm surprised I didn't have an accident or kill someone; in retrospect, I realise just how stupid this was. I wouldn't advise anybody to follow me in this because innocent people – non-combatants, some might say – can easily die or be maimed.

Eventually, the time arrived for the Shannon team to split up. Tam was locked up on a theft charge, along with Jamie and Mairdo, and our friends the Dempseys, who had run with us, had moved to Maryhill while another family of our pals, the Mulgrews, moved to Rutherglen. Roseanne had emotional issues and left home to stay in a halfway house catering for young girls with problems. So it was Pawny and me, left to fend for ourselves and to make enough money to feed Mum. Things were about to change, however.

A few months earlier, Mum had gone to a party in Possilpark, where she was introduced to a merchant seaman named Jim Brannan. Almost from their first meeting, he fell head over heels in love with her. She brought him home and he quickly became part of the family. Initially, none of us took it well, as he was not much older than Jamie, my brother, but he provided us with some form of stability in our lives just at the period when we needed it. In what seemed no time at all, he and Mum had gone off to the registry office in Bath Street and married.

As it would turn out, Jim *was* good for us – but he had a fiery temper and was not scared of the established crew in Springburn, or any crew elsewhere in Glasgow, for that matter. I suppose he was just a regular guy whose attitude was live and let live.

The trouble started when Jim and Mum went off to Glasgow Green to watch the Orange Walk. At the walk that day was a man we'll call 'Charlie Davis' and his crew, who all lived up our way. They were the old school and thought they had the right to stop anybody moving into their area without first asking permission. Frankly speaking, they were the area bullies. When they met Jim for the first time that day, they tried to bully him. To their surprise – and fury – he was not having it and fought with them. The result was terrifying.

That night after the local bar, the Spring Inn on Springburn Road, emptied at closing time, Davis and his team came to our door tooled up with machetes, knives, bats and anything else that came to hand. They were looking for Jim. He and my mum had anticipated reprisals and were waiting. Immediately our door was kicked in, Jim began fighting with them all. As the intensity of the battle increased, somebody threw a knife down the corridor close to where I was standing; it thudded into the door about three inches above my head.

Like most bullies, however, Davis and his crew were cowards. Jim managed to get hold of a machete, coshed a few of them and then chased them down the stairs and back to where they came from. Of course we knew the matter would not end there. The police had been called and we were all taken to Baird Street police station and advised to stay there overnight. Initially, Jim was charged with attempted murder, as there had been a couple of serious injuries, but once all the facts became known this was soon dropped. Sadly, we could no longer go back to our home in Galloway Street, as there would certainly have been further reprisal attacks on Jim – attacks that would inevitably end in his murder. So, through no fault of our own and on police advice, we were forced to abandon our home. It meant losing everything – our clothing, furniture, personal papers, even keepsakes, including childhood photographs and family mementos. This is the reason why to this day there is only one photograph of me aged eleven, taken by a school photographer at Albert school. It might be the worst photograph you can imagine (the jumper I'm wearing is orange, the same colour as my hair, which is 1970s style, meaning it's a mess). In fact the photograph is so embarrassing that every time my youngest daughter, Nicole, brought her friends into the house, she would hide it in a drawer. It's all I have of my childhood, though.

The crew that turned up at my door that night would get payback in later years when I was in my mid-teens living in Possilpark. But that is for the future.

No longer having anywhere to stay, we were sent to a bed and breakfast for homeless people at Charing Cross. It went by the name of McLays and was run by a lovely Asian family. While Mum and Jim tried to come to terms with what had happened to them, Pawny and I had work to do. I needed clothes and money and knew how to get both.

McLays was handily situated for me, as it meant I did not have to hop on a bus into town to do my shoplifting because there were scores of shops around the guest house. It meant I could steal something for myself at every opportunity, and there were very many of them. Once we had found our way around, Pawny and I embarked on a mini crime wave, stretching from Charing Cross to the Kelvin Halls. The sun shone and we made hay.

Moving house also meant going to another school. This time it was Woodside secondary, the high school for Anderston primary. To my delight, I discovered I already knew many of the pupils from earlier days, including some I'd met at Dunclutha. I was also reunited with one of the girls with whom I used to play Doctors and Nurses. She had two brothers, who became firm friends. I also became great mates with Robert Taylor. Robert and his family lived in the west of the city and our friendship lasted many years. Tragically, Robert was jailed for 25 years in 1996 after admitting attempted murder. Charles Ballantyne was shot in the head and back during a football match, and while he survived, shots had been fired at some spectators. It turned out the intended target was somebody else, resulting in the wrong man almost being killed.

My main difficulty during this period was that I was being bullied by some of those who could remember the Shannons from years before. The family had been broken up, with the three eldest being in care or detention of some sort, and so old associates now decided they had a golden opportunity to pick on me. Just as Paul Ferris, when he was about my age, used to get terrible beatings from a local family, I too always got a good hiding. But, just like Paul, I would not let them see me cry and would keep going back for more. Of course, none of them had the balls to fight me one-on-one, irrespective of the outcome, which is typical of bullies.

A few years later I came across two of the main offenders when I was in the home of my future sister-in-law. Now the boot was on the other foot. I had my team of mates from

Possilpark around me, along with my best mate Mick Kenna. Mick was right up for stabbing the pair of rats, but I thought, no. Instead I'd let them know who I was in case they had forgotten. Mind games can have a devastating effect – more devastating even than physical violence, and it's certainly longer lasting. I determined to leave both of them with the knowledge that they had messed up – being a bully in your youth will always come back to haunt you one day. They were quaking and didn't know what was going to happen to them. I escorted them out the house, shook them both by the hand and said, 'Bye, bye. Just don't ever come back.'

After staying in McLays for about four months, we were moved on to a house in Finlass Street, in Possilpark, an area known as the Jungle. Going to a new district could be difficult if you knew nobody, but I was fortunate because a lot of my relations lived in the Jungle, from both my mother's side and my father's.

I started attending Possilpark secondary, where I fitted in and made some good friends. However, it was not to last. Mum and Jim went through a rough patch in their relationship where she began having second thoughts about the marriage. Her dilemma increased when she met up with Jim Corrigan again. Now she had to make a choice between the two men. In January 1980, Mum disappeared, leaving Pawny and me with Jim Brannan. One day, he just dropped us off at a social services office next to the Kelvin Halls, with a note explaining who we were, what had happened and that he could not cope. He told staff that we were now their responsibility. I knew yet another move was on the cards.

# CHAPTER FIVE

Pawny and I had done nothing wrong, or at least we hadn't been caught breaking the law. We had just been abandoned, almost like the proverbial newborn baby dumped on a doorstep. The social workers were largely sympathetic and begged us not to worry, that they were arranging for us to go somewhere nice, but soon we were put in a car and driven off to Falkland in Fife. There we were enrolled in St Ninian's Orphanage. Officially, it was termed a List D school, but in effect it was an approved school, with 50 pupils, many of whom had been sent there from children's hearings or court. I thought this was unfair. We seemed to be being punished because our mum had deserted us, while the man left to take care of us had opted out of that responsibility.

'Hey, what happened to the cushy home?' I asked the social worker with us.

'We were looking to put you into a care home under a Care Order in the future anyway, because of your criminal convictions and general behaviour,' she replied. It was no use protesting that it was over two years since the attempted housebreaking accusation.

In fact, St Ninian's would turn out to be the best move of my life. I was there for a year from 1980 and it gave me the stability I needed, while influencing key personal character traits, instilling in me values such as honesty, respect for others and loyalty. I'm not saying that I suddenly turned into an angel or ceased misbehaving, but as I grew older the attributes I picked up at the orphanage served me well.

My first impression on arriving at St Ninian's had been one of shock and horror. During the time I stayed there, I learned that the locals called it the Big House and many believed those who were kept there were animals – thieves, glue-sniffers and troublemakers. I am sorry to say that they were 100 per cent correct. As a result, Pawny and I fitted in perfectly! I was in my teens by then and it was filled with young boys like me from all over Scotland who came from similarly deprived backgrounds. But if I had any preconceived dreads about what to expect from a school run by a religious Order, these soon evaporated. I was able to play football, rugby and every other sport you could think of. The rural location of the orphanage meant I was breathing fresh, clean air into my lungs every day. There were hills, trees and fields to admire, no congested dirty streets with broken glass littering pavements and rubbish strewn in gardens. The daily routine suited my simple and basic lifestyle. There were three square meals a day, plus supper before bed. I had my own single bed with what I now know to be a duvet to keep me warm.

The Congregation of Christian Brothers in Scotland had opened the orphanage in 1951. The Brothers ran orphanages and homes all over the world, but not all the members of the Order had genuine Christian motives for joining, as I was to discover. During the time I was at St Ninian's and later, boys like me in similar orphanages from Australia to the United States to Ireland were being subjected to the most appalling sexual abuse by members of the Order. When these abuses came to light, the Order was forced to apologise for the sins of those who had done terrible wrongs and pay out huge sums of money in compensation to the victims. In many cases, the boys would never be able to forget what was done to them. The abuse they endured would affect them for the rest of their lives.

One experience at the orphanage left a very unpleasant memory. For a few months after arriving, I continued to bedwet. Back at home I'd often blamed Pawny for the state of the bedding in the morning, but he was in another room so I could no longer point the finger at him. After a time, though, I stopped, the turning point being a strange event that even now

I find hard to describe. Nevertheless, here we go.

Each morning the bedwetters – we used to call each other 'piss the beds' – would take a shower watched by one of the Brothers for any signs of infection caused by lying all night in urine. One morning, a Brother noticed spots and a rash on my behind and, as was his duty, reported it to one of his superiors – I'll simply call him 'P'; the man is long dead.

Now, there was considerable talk in the orphanage of sexual abuse; in fact, it was rife. We pupils obviously talked a lot to each other about what went on and there wasn't much that we missed. We realised some individuals were being victimised by the older men – even at that age we knew from the demeanour and behaviour of some boys that they were being bullied and taken advantage of. Remember, a lot of us were streetwise. We were, in a way, old beyond our years. We had known wrong, had often been without the comfort and protection of parents, and I suppose some of the boys there had already been victims of abuse at home. Maybe that was the reason why some were already at the orphanage. So it went on. At this stage, I believed my first duty was to my own – that meant looking after Pawny first, never mind anyone else.

My experience at the hands of P, however, would confirm that my suspicions and those of others were correct. I was one of the main altar boys at mass this particular morning and when it was over was taken to one side by P and told to report to his room that evening. He explained he wanted to see what he could do to sort out the rash on my behind. Now, that could, at a stretch, have sounded above board, but then he told me not to say anything to the other boys. When I asked him what time I had to go to his room, he said, 'Don't worry. Just go to sleep tonight as normal and I will come and wake you up when choir practice for the other Brothers is over.'

True to his word, at around eleven, he came quietly into my bedroom, woke me up and asked me to come to his room. It was just him and me, and on arrival at his room he told me to undress completely and turn round so my back was to him. I was very sceptical and suspicious, but did as he said, all the time keeping my hands over my private parts. I sensed him

THE UNDERWORLD CAPTAIN

come up beside me and then felt him starting to touch my behind where the spots were. Then he noticed my bum cheeks were as tight as I could get them, so he suggested I lie face down on the bed. This might relax me, he said, and allow him to put on the cream that he said would clear up the rash. I lay on the bed, but could not relax. I was scared and cold, wondering what was going to happen next. There was no way I was going to relax my bum cheeks. Nevertheless he spent about 20 minutes rubbing on cream, his hands moving over me very slowly, and all the time he was telling me to loosen up. 'There's no need to be so tense,' he said. 'Relax.' But I was too nervous and kept asking him if I could go back to bed.

Eventually, he gave in and asked me to stand up and get dressed. I did as he instructed, while all the time he watched. Then, just as I was about to leave, he told me to sit on his knee. I was too scared to disobey, and once on his knee he began moving me to the centre of his body between his legs. Now I could feel his erection with the sides of my legs. There was nothing else for me to do but to demand to be allowed to go back to bed. Reluctantly, he agreed.

Under the safety of my duvet I found it difficult to get warm. I lay awake throughout the night, all the time wondering if I would hear the door open and his steps come to the side of my bed. And I had another motive for desperately wanting to avoid falling off to sleep – by staying awake, I could make sure I did not wet the bed, so that come morning there would be no need for the dreaded shower with the watching Brother and the prospect of another cream-rubbing session in the privacy of P's room.

I was frightened that night and kept telling myself over and over: 'You're not going through that ever again.'

It worked, because I was never scared again, and after that night P got the message and, I'm willing to bet, told himself, 'Let him be.' From then on, I forced myself into a routine in which I would never drink any fluids after four o'clock in the afternoon, so my bladder was empty for the evening. It was a masterstroke. Never again did I wet the bed or be invited by P back to his room.

Nowadays, what he did is termed grooming. I was always a strong character and I believe P recognised that but decided to take a chance. For him, it was hit or miss, but he very quickly learned I wasn't up for it. He had tried again before I left his room on the off chance I might relent, only to find my resolve not to give in was stronger than ever.

It was commonly known that there were boys who were going into the Brothers' rooms and staying. They tended to be weak individuals, those who were generally picked on. The majority of guys in the orphanage were pure street chavs, as bad as Pawny and me, whose attitude was, if it isn't bolted down, then we're off with it. Most of us would speak together, stick together, sniff glue together, all that kind of stuff, and then keep the rest at arm's length. That included the Brothers and those who were actually or potentially getting abused, to some extent. I know, looking back, that I tended to turn a blind eye to some things or ignore them on purpose, taking the attitude that if it hasn't happened to you, then stay quiet and do nothing.

Like a lot of young guys of my age, I'd sniffed glue. Nowadays, I suppose, young people use drugs instead, but at the orphanage it was glue. It was evil stuff, but you could get hold of it more easily than you could alcohol, for instance. When we stayed in Galloway Street and there was no money to buy glue, we discovered you could get an amazing high from fire extinguishers. From Galloway Street, you could cross a wasteland and get onto the railway line to the sidings at Cowlairs. There were often trains standing there, waiting to go into repair sheds. We used to break into the trains, steal the fire extinguishers and take them back to the waste ground, where we would burst them open and spray the contents into a can. Then we'd sniff it. It was mental. I wouldn't advise anybody to try it. One of our friends sniffed the contents of an extinguisher one day and it knocked him out. He fell and hit his head on a paving stone and died.

Happily, sniffing glue didn't seem to affect me, and at St Ninian's I excelled in sport, education and singing. I had always been a good footballer, but my money-making turns in the real world meant that while my pals were playing I was doing other things. Even so, at Albert primary and secondary I played for both school teams. Once I got to the orphanage, though, I was being noticed by scouts from some of the main football clubs in the area. Every week we would play the local schools and clubs at rugby and football and I was captain of both teams, and regarded as a very good player with a lot of talent. Word of this got about to the extent that one day, whilst I was walking down the aisle in my full altar boy regalia, the priest, Father Burns, stepped out and took a photograph of me. He told me that if I ever ended up playing for Glasgow Rangers, he would embarrass me by sending the photograph to the *Daily Record*. I still have the photograph to this day; however, it tends to get hidden on occasions, along with the orange jumper snapshot.

I made a lot of friends at St Ninian's and was made team captain for our House, but unfortunately in life there always seems to be a dark cloud around every corner and now one appeared on the horizon, heading in my direction.

I found myself joined by three guys from Springburn. We knew each other and I had done turns with them in the past. However, I was determined not to drift back into my old lawless routine because I was content with life; I was focused on doing what I was told and had decided to join the army. Things rarely work out the way we plan, though.

Pawny was starting to go off the rails, running away only to be brought back by the police. The sight of him standing by the roadside, thumbing lifts, became frequent. He was trying to get back to Glasgow and always had some story to tell anyone asking where he was going. The local pubs and shops were regarded as fair game to those in the orphanage, with the result that drink and cigarettes would often be passed around for free. I dreaded being accused of being responsible, knowing that would have almost inevitably meant another summons to the room of P, his excuse being that I needed to explain my actions to him.

# CHAPTER SIX

After a year at St Ninian's, I got the news I had always dreaded: we were leaving. Mum had appeared back on the scene and had been allocated another house, and we were moving in there with her and Jim Brannan. I had loved being at St Ninian's and was not looking forward to returning to Glasgow, but there was nothing I could do.

Our new home was in Burmola Street, Possilpark, at the top end, at Wester Common. At first I was apprehensive, thinking of what had gone on in the past and wondering if the rows would recur, but my fears were soon overcome when I saw that Mum and Jim appeared to have got their act together. The house was smartened up and we had our own rooms. It was like being back in Galloway Street because outside was a street full of people my age, only this time they were mainly females. Suddenly, things were looking good.

I returned to Possilpark Secondary School and met all my old friends from my last stint there. Things were definitely looking a lot better. I began moving from one girlfriend to another, which brought me into closer contact with the family of Robert O'Hara, who, when he grew into adulthood, would regrettably be sentenced to life imprisonment for murder. Pawny and I and our girlfriends would spend a fair bit of time babysitting him for his parents during weekdays and weekends.

Eventually, I moved on from babysitting and, like so many of my friends of that time, I started experimenting with all sorts of stimulants such as acid tablets and, of course, alcohol. Tiny squares of acid, the hallucogenic drug LSD, also known as tabs and blotters, were all the rage. I read one day that they took you on a trip during which the entire universe could turn wobbly, the intensity of colours changed, your senses were confused and disoriented and everyday objects took on bizarre and terrifying forms. Absolutely right.

Pawny, meantime, maintained his friendship with Robert, who was given the nickname 'Birdman' because he developed a really keen interest in birds, especially pigeons.

* * *

Despite his friendship with other girls, Alex continued to hanker after Angie. Their meetings were rare, and often her comments towards Alex would seem terse, almost offhand, but slowly she was starting to quite like him.

The Shannon brothers knew another local boy by this stage, named William 'Gibby' Lobban. As the years passed, Lobban would be given many other nicknames, including 'Billy', 'Tootsie' and, more sinister perhaps, 'Judas'. Like the Shannon brothers, Lobban had known hardship and came from a deprived background. In a sense, his life was mapped out for him from the first day he entered the world, when his mother, a member of the Manson family, gave birth to him in Exeter prison on 21 February 1968. She was serving a prison sentence for her part in a robbery that had gone wrong. The baby was sent north to Glasgow to be raised by his grandparents before his mother was able to rejoin them and take over the task of raising her son.

As other youngsters drifted into the company of the Shannons, Lobban tagged along with them. He liked to think of himself as one of the Shannon gang and the brothers became aware of the increasing frequency of his visits to their home. Most of the others had already had at least one run-in with the police, and Lobban liked to claim he too had had his brief moment of infamy. He boasted of how he had decided to exact his own youthful form of justice when his grandparents became embroiled in an argument with their neighbours. His version of events, one intended to impress, was that he had stolen money from home and gone to a gun shop in the east end of the city where he persuaded someone he knew to go in and buy him a slug gun capable of firing pellets. His idea was to shoot out the windows of the neighbours who were upsetting his grandparents. He took up position on the other side of the road to begin his onslaught, but at that point the neighbours' son appeared and so he switched his aim to the boy's leg and fired. The police were called but because of his age Lobban was merely given a similar dressing-down from a senior officer as that dished out to Alex following his earlier arrest for burglary.

It was around this time that the name Arthur Thompson was being whispered in criminal circles in Glasgow. He knew all about life in the tough east end, having been raised by his mother Catherine and steel worker dad Edward in the same Springburn streets as those in which the Shannons and McGoverns faced each other. He learned a trade as a joiner and then as soon as he was old enough earned cash as a bouncer in dance halls and clubs. His barrel chest and broad shoulders then brought him to the attention of entrepreneur Morris Mendel, who ran a string of pubs and clubs, and a lucrative bookmaking racket. Mendel kept a step ahead of the law, but Arthur was not so lucky. He was jailed for three years in 1951 for assault and robbery, and not long after being released was back inside, this time serving an eighteen-month stretch for extortion. In 1966, he was badly injured when a bomb exploded under his car as he was giving his mother-in-law a lift. The device killed her. Not long after he had recovered Arthur was driving near his home when he spotted two men he suspected of being behind the bomb plot. He forced their van to smash into a lamppost, killing them both. On the same day at the High Court in Glasgow, he was first cleared of their murder and then went into the witness box himself to claim he could not identify three men standing in the dock accused of planting the car bomb. They walked free.

Arthur expanded into money lending. It was said he crucified at least one customer for not paying him back on time. He ran protection rackets, sold guns and then moved into the drugs business. He worked for the Kray twins in London and counted among his trusted friends the likes of London gangster Ronnie Knight, later to become the husband of *Carry On* and *EastEnders* star Barbara Windsor. In 1968, Arthur was arrested on suspicion of being involved in a £3,000 warehouse robbery after a suspicious policeman discovered stolen clothing in one of his cars. While he waited for his trial, anticipating a heavy sentence, it was rumoured he was visited by undercover officers from the intelligence services who were interested in his arms dealings in England and Ireland. No one knows what transpired, but shortly after the visit Arthur was jailed for just four years and walked free after serving only two.

As his underworld reputation grew, he became known as the Godfather of Glasgow. Arthur always denied having any involvement in crime, protesting he was nothing more than a legitimate businessman, but his role as a feared capo in succession to the hoods who had gone before him was not disputed until the emergence of others, in particular Tam McGraw and Paul Ferris. Neither sought the title, but notoriety was thrust upon them, particularly by the media.

If Arthur had hoped his thriving businesses would be safe in the hands of his oldest son Arthur (known cruelly as 'Fatboy' or the 'Mars Bar Kid' due to a liking for chocolate treats), then he was disappointed. Arty was a wizard with things mechanical – cars and especially guns – but he had a habit of using his father's name to threaten anyone crossing him.

By the early 1980s, he was making an increasing number of enemies due to his participation in the high-risk drug-dealing business. His activities in this field were also bringing him to the notice of the police.

Arthur kept McGraw, whose Barlanark Team was going from strength to strength, at a distance. The men had no desire to encroach on the territory of one another; such trespassing would only bring trouble. He was devoted to Arty, but, conscious of his son's weaknesses, looked elsewhere for young men who would do work he could not entrust to his eldest son. He cast his eyes in the direction of Ferris, Tam Bagan and Ian 'Blink' McDonald. The former two would, for a time, work for him as enforcers: collectors of debts and exactors of punishment. The latter decided that if Arthur had dirty work to be done, then he should do it himself.

Being asked to join the Thompson camp was a feather in the cap of any up-and-coming gangster. The Godfather was thought to be indestructible and fearless. However, it was said that there was one man for whom he would step from the pavement in order to allow him to pass – Bobby Dempster.

Another who had begun life in the east end of Glasgow, Dempster had become a leading light in the young gangs running the streets of Possil, known locally as Posso, but knew bigger things awaited him. Big, strong and clever, he would go on to run a highly successful company supplying security to the likes of clubs and building companies. His principal attribute was his discretion. Few knew his business and fewer were bold enough to ask questions. He moved away from the east end, but his mother remained, living close to the Shannons in Possilpark. Bobby regularly returned to see his mother and those visits were watched by a young man who seemed especially curious.

* * *

Lobban hung around us and our house so much that he became a sort of stepbrother. We'd go home and find him already there. When we went out, he'd appear out of the blue and join us. He particularly attached himself to Pawny, who had his own gang by this time and was doing very well. We had no problem then with Lobban, but one thing that always sticks in my mind about him growing up is his fascination for Bobby Dempster. As soon as Bobby's car appeared outside his mother's house, Gibby would be down there asking, 'Is everything OK, Bobby? Do you need anything done? How's your ma, Bobby?' It was as if they were the best of mates. Maybe it was his ambition to follow in Bobby's footsteps by being successful that resulted in Lobban going down the path he did in later life.

Posso was one of the roughest areas of Glasgow and was home to many families with big reputations, including that of Jamie Daniel. Jamie had known my family for many years. He was especially friendly with Tam and they had a great mutual respect for one another. Jamie was a good guy who stuck by his friends and we knew that if we should ever need his help it would be there for us. My cousin George Masterton stayed and worked with Annette Daniel. They lived across the road from us when we were in Finlass Street and are still together. I don't want to mention too many names, but there have been scores of people involved in murders and major crimes who have lived in this part of Glasgow over the years. Perhaps it was the hard upbringing most of us had, the lack of money and food that made us cling onto what we had and refuse to give in to anybody who tried to take what was ours away from us. If that meant fighting to hang onto our own, then we would fight. The Jungle was well named.

Around this time, a face from the past came back to haunt me, the man I'm calling Charlie Davis. I have always believed that every bully gets his just deserts and now his dawn had broken. With a few of my mates at my heels, I followed him up to his home in the Wester Common flats. Before he could reach the safety of the lift, he had been caught and retribution dished out. There were other occasions where he could have been punished for his part in that terrible night in Galloway Street, but I left it at the one reminder. He truly got what he deserved, but every other day he would walk by me at Saracen Cross and I felt nothing but hatred for him. To me, he was the reason I'd had to leave Springburn and endure all that had happened to me after that. Other factors came into it, of course, but we lost everything because of him and I cannot help how I felt and what I thought at the time. I never said another word to him again.

Heroin had taken its toll on our area. There seemed to be junkies everywhere and a couple of our friends were dabbling in the drug that has taken so many lives. Eventually, one of our mates, who was just 15, overdosed and died. At the time, he was said to have been the youngest drug user in Glasgow to have lost his life. This shocked me into thinking about sorting out my own life.

After leaving St Ninian's, I had tried to be more reserved in what I was doing, but times were hard and I still needed money.

I was occasionally burgling the odd shop to keep my pockets jangling, but I no longer went out at night to screw a shop just for the sake of doing so. I would leave it until I was skint and then go and tan somewhere. I was being more selective, but all the same I was taking chances. I was known to the police, so I was being lifted and caught on a regular basis, and sometimes the methods the police used went beyond the bounds of reason.

Constantly in the back of my mind was my determination to join the army, but while I was honestly doing my best to stay trouble-free, temptation can be difficult to resist. That was how it was in the case of the man from the Provvy, the Provident Financial.

The principle of the Provident Financial was that you took out a loan in the form of a Provvy cheque which you could use in shops, then paid interest on the cheque until it was repaid. One evening I was in Barmulloch, where Mr Singh, a teacher from Albert primary, ran a shop. I saw him quite often and he would always say, 'I hope you're keeping out of trouble. I know you can do it.' He made the same comment that fateful night and I was very proud to say to him: 'I haven't been in trouble for six months. I'm going to keep my nose clean. I'm going to join the army.' Later that same night I found myself in Baird Street police station facing prison. It all went wrong for me after talking to Mr Singh.

A mate and I had followed the Provvy representative and watched his movements. We tailed his car until he got to a particular house, where we knew he was collecting money. We waited until he had put all his money in the car, then left to see his customer in the next house. While he was inside, the pair of us went over to his motor, smashed the window and ripped off all the money and the Provident cheques. We didn't rob him; we wouldn't do that. We robbed the car. I stashed the cheques, along with some of the money, and the two of us set off for home.

How did I get caught? Well, it was mental.

I could have run, but my pockets were full of money and so we were walking along when a police van drove up to us. It was a routine stop, so I said to myself: no need to run. The cheques and a lot of the money were safely out of the way. OK, I had £180 in my pocket, but in those days it was up to the police to prove that the money was stolen – you didn't have to show where it had come from. So the police searched me, found the cash and asked where it had come from. I told them I'd been saving it up, but unfortunately they decided not to believe me or my friend. Next thing, they put us in the van and took us to Baird Street police station.

The police took me up to the first level. There were four of them, all holding the old-fashioned black truncheons, and they just began hammering my legs as I was made to stand. This wasn't the first time I'd encountered police brutality, but this particular time they really gave me a good hiding. I knew they only had six hours to get anything out of me before the law ruled that because of my age I had to be charged or released. And they knew that, too. So for six hours I didn't say a word. Eventually, they locked me in a cell.

They did the same to my mate. He came from a well-known Barmulloch family and they got stuck into him too, giving him similar treatment. To his credit, he held out for about five hours, but then he gave in and said we had screwed the car, stashed all the money and the Provvy cheques, thousands of pounds worth. For good measure, after he had broken, the police came back down into the cells, took me back again and set about me once more with truncheons.

I have told this story to ex-servicemen I know who are now policemen, and I'm sure they believe me, but they still tell me that it wouldn't happen now. But I wonder. The fact was that this beating was just one of many. I used to get hammered all the time.

The outcome in this instance, however, was that I was charged with fraud. Everything, the cheques and cash, had been recovered and when it went to court I was fined £15 and told to pay £40 for breaking the car window.

Three months later I was back in court, this time Glasgow Sheriff Court, accused of a break-in at a shop. I was fined £20 and ordered to pay compensation. I used to defend myself, but it was never any use. You got the feeling that even before any of the evidence had been heard, a guilty decision had already been made.

That was also the case when I was accused of mobbing and rioting. It all started off in the aftermath of the 1981 riots in Brixton and the Toxteth area of Liverpool. In Brixton, the trouble had been caused when a crowd felt the police were not getting medical help fast enough for a black youth who had been stabbed. Three months later, in July, long-standing ill feeling between the local community in Toxteth and the police reached boiling point. The result was an outbreak of mob violence.

In both cases, gangs who would normally have been battering each other joined together and set about attacking anybody or anything they felt had any association with the police or authority. It was a case of if you weren't with them, then they took it that you were against them. The media had a field day and there were pages and pages of dramatic coverage in the newspapers. What the rioters really loved was the fact that television cameras followed every petrol bomb, brick and burnt-out car. The troublemakers revelled in their moment of glory.

Naturally, once the footage appeared on national television, others elsewhere decided to get in on the act. There were outbreaks of lawlessness across the country, mainly in areas of cities where there was high unemployment. In Toxteth, the trouble was ignited by two things: the loss of thousands of jobs at the docks due to containerisation, and strong-arm tactics by the police in the arrest of a black man. Elsewhere trouble kicked off simply because young men had nothing else to do and fancied a bit of excitement.

After the Brixton Riots in April, it was as if young people just waited until the summer months and then, out of sheer boredom, decided to try getting themselves on television again. There was more rioting the following year, although not on the same scale as 1981, but one of the spots where there was trouble was Glasgow. Sometimes it was no more than a crowd gathering to taunt the police, who retaliated by indiscriminately arresting anybody who happened to be in the area at the time of the bother. I know, because I was one of the victims and, for me, the consequences could have been dire.

With Mick Kenna and a few of my mates, I wandered over to Wester Common flats, where trouble had kicked off. It was just a case of the wee mob rioting. We were curious to see what happened and had even taken a carryout with us. I can honestly say we had no intention of getting involved – as far as we were concerned, we were only there to watch and maybe have a bit of fun. We didn't want to get into trouble and, in fact, I remember thinking we were beyond all that, even though we were only in our mid-teens. I had left school while we were all making money from a variety of enterprises and we would have been crazy to do something stupid that could have got us arrested and stopped us earning. But when the police came along – twice – and said, 'Right, you mob move on,' we felt they were picking on us. We were doing nothing wrong. Maybe it was because we were older, or maybe it was approaching their tea break and they fancied getting back to the police station and needed an excuse in the form of having to take prisoners with them. Whatever it was, next thing they seemed to be saying to themselves, 'Right, let's lift the nearest ones we can find.' And that's exactly what they did.

We were standing doing absolutely nothing when they drove up alongside us. Out jumped five policemen and lifted seven of us. 'In you get,' they told us.

We were pushed into a police van and taken off. Before I knew it, we were all charged with a breach of the peace, and mobbing and rioting. When it eventually went to court, I was charged with a breach of the peace. I pleaded not guilty and tried to defend myself, but at 16 you are not going to get anywhere, so I was convicted.

In all honesty, we did nothing wrong. I was asked what I intended to do with my life and said I was going to join the army. Of course, anyone could say that to make him sound impressive and so the bench decided to see if I was telling the truth. The sentence was deferred for a year – I would have to go back and if I didn't turn up in uniform, I'd be for it.

These early experiences have made me sceptical – not just about the police, but about the justice system in general. A minor conviction like this can have a lasting effect and close doors to potential opportunities. I had committed no crime but because there were seven policemen against me I had no chance. In their version I was the troublemaker, so I was deemed to be one. Worse was that it would be on my record for the rest of my life, all because of something petty. What happens when it comes to serious things? People get fitted up just because the police think they might be guilty and worry that without additional evidence they won't get a result. I know of many cases where men have gone to prison to serve life sentences for crimes they have not committed. These things follow you for the rest of your life. Forget all this Rehabilitation of Offenders Act. Once you have been convicted of even the most minor offence, even if you are innocent, and later you want to try and turn your life around by joining one of the armed services, the police, the prison service or whatever, don't bother. One strike and you are out forever. In deprived areas of Glasgow such as Possil, Springburn, Castlemilk and Easterhouse, I think the police and others, certainly in the 1980s and possibly these days, simply see all those young boys with no job and nothing to do as scum, lowlifes, and if they can get some of them off the streets, then who cares? Nobody cares. That's the way I believe they saw it. I still feel sad looking back on it all.

# CHAPTER SEVEN

Despite my troubles, Angie was never far from my thoughts. One day, as I was standing at Saracen Cross, a face I recognised from the past walked by. I realised right away who it was: Adam Scullion, Angie's brother. I knew he stayed in Galloway Street, so I used the excuse of asking how things were in our old stomping ground to get talking to him and then turned the conversation to his sister.

Angie was 18 months my senior and I knew she felt she was too old for me. Such a difference is much more noticeable at that age than when you get older, and she had tried setting me up on dates with her school pals. None of them really interested me; my heart was set on Angie. Adam told me she was working in a chemist's shop in Bishopbriggs. He said if I went to see her, she might slip me some uppers or downers. Needless to say, this wasn't the case, but then Adam had been known to be a bit of a storyteller in his time. It didn't bother me, though. Just the fact that he had mentioned her name and where she was got me wondering how she was keeping. I persuaded Mick Kenna to go with me to Bishopbriggs and, sure enough, when I got there and found the shop I could see Angie through the window. She was beautiful, but I was too scared to go inside and so I persuaded Mick to try breaking the ice.

Angie remembers that she saw Mick and me outside talking, and then Mick coming in and asking if she was Angie. For a laugh, she told him she was called Sharleen. Mick wasn't sure, so came outside. I knew she'd told a fib, so we just hung around outside the shop until she eventually came out and asked us to move on. I couldn't refuse – by that time, I was head over heels in love with her and knew I would see her again, one way or another.

* * *

When school broke up for Easter in 1982, I knew I would not be going back. The time had come for me to leave and decide what I wanted to do with my life. As far as I was concerned, I had made that decision a long time ago. I was going to join the army.

Just a few days before I left school, Argentine forces had invaded the Falkland Islands in the South Atlantic. Stories and photographs of troops landing on the Falklands and a tiny British Army force having to surrender filled the newspapers and dominated television channels. It was an event I followed with avid interest. I kept wishing I had been older so I could have joined the task force sent to overthrow the invaders. The Argentine forces were no match for our own, but by the time they surrendered on 14 June and the Falklands, South Georgia and South Sandwich Islands returned to British control, 255 British and 649 Argentine soldiers, sailors and airmen had lost their lives, along with three civilian Falklanders. I did not know it then, but the Falkland Islands would loom large in my life.

While my heart had been set on joining up long before that war, the dispute, with its dangers and excitement, had given me an extra buzz; however, because of my age, I knew my application papers would have to be signed by my mum. And that would be easier said than done. My oldest brother, James, had been in the army, but things hadn't worked out for him and he had left. Mum had been upset by this and would have her heart set against another of her sons going down the same route. I would have about a year to wait, in any case, which would give me time to work on her.

For the meantime, I was put on a government Youth Training Scheme, YTS. I worked as a welder at Hawthorn workshops off Balmore Road and loved it. I was 16 and getting to meet all sorts of people from different schemes across Glasgow. It meant I could go into the schemes and do whatever I wanted, getting to know more people all the time. I would go partying in places like Ruchill. The guy training me was ex-army. He knew I wanted to join up and was forever encouraging me.

One of the girls who worked with me had also gone to my school. Her boyfriend was Robert Fleck, who was a few months older than me and was about to become a star striker for Glasgow Rangers and Scotland. He scored 29 goals for the Gers in 85 games before being transferred to Norwich City. He came down to meet her every day. His younger brother, Alan, had been in the same class as me, and Alan's boy John now plays for Rangers. I knew the Flecks well but would be disappointed by something that happened when I met Robert a few years later.

Being on the YTS was good because it meant I was earning legitimate money. It was only £25 a week, mind you, so I had to subsidise my income with some turns. But even better was the fact that I could now afford to go into the Brothers bar on Saracen Street. Even though it was in the middle of Posso, it was one of the most popular pubs in Glasgow, but make no mistake it had more than its fair share of tough customers. A few years later Birdman O'Hara staggered in there, near death, after being the victim of a drive-by shooting.

At weekends young people from all over the city headed to the Brothers. I would often join them, but I had to keep on my toes. As I was getting older, I was becoming a police target more and more. I knew I had to get into the army as soon as possible before it was prison.

I went to the army careers office in Glasgow to begin the process, but initially there were a couple of obstacles – Mum's reluctance to sign the papers and my weight.

As long as I was under 18, I would need her consent. I could have waited until 1984 but believed I might have blotted my copybook too much by then, so I pestered her. Initially, she refused, having preconceived ideas that I would not be able to cope. She kept mentioning James, who had been based in Ballykinler in Northern Ireland but had spent a stretch in the glasshouse, leaving her to try to resolve and deal with the problems resulting from his imprisonment and ultimate departure from the army. I think she assumed that would happen to me, but I knew differently. I remember explaining to her, 'Look, Mum. I've been lifted a couple of times by the police and there's nothing for me here, so I just want to get away, give myself a chance to stay out of prison.' It worked because after a time she agreed to sign the necessary forms.

I was five foot two and weighed eight stone, half a stone under the minimum needed to enlist. I did serious training, started boxing and was really fit, but you can imagine my horror when I went for my army medical and failed because I was still underweight. So I set about beefing up.

My determination to get fitter, stronger and bigger did not curtail my visits to the Brothers bar, where two of my favourite acts were Scheme and the Radio Clyde DJ Mr Superbad. His real name was Freddie Mack. He had grown up on a cotton plantation in South Carolina and one of his friends was the world heavyweight boxing champion Floyd Patterson, who had encouraged Freddie to take up the sport. And he did, with so much courage and skill as a light heavyweight that he reached No. 3 in the world rankings. He turned to acting after meeting Richard Burton and got a job in *Cleopatra* as one of the slaves who carried Elizabeth Taylor's sedan chair around. When he moved to Britain, he landed an acting part in *Taggart* and became a rhythm and blues singer, then in 1979 moved to Glasgow with his wife Jan and became a disc jockey. He was a really well-liked guy and his gigs were always packed.

We youngsters were capable of looking after ourselves, but there was one person who had us all petrified at the time. Legal reasons prevent me from mentioning his name, though he has been in prison for a long time. He was known to cruise the streets of Posso and Maryhill looking for young good-looking guys he could take away and do whatever he wanted with, whether they liked it or not. Some of them were my friends, and none of them liked what happened but they were too scared to say anything to anyone. Everyone knew, though, that as soon as you saw him or his car you should make a fast escape. I personally never had any dealings with him, but some of the stories that came back to us either first or second hand were frightening; they made you watch what you said, and where you went, in case you were next. Maybe the fact that Tam, Pawny and me tended to stick together and we had a reputation for not allowing anyone to mess us about saved us from this man.

One of the questions the army had asked when I applied to join was whether I had any convictions. Of course I had, but I was so desperate to become a soldier that I said nothing about them, hoping nobody would find out. I was sure that had I been truthful I would have been rejected, so I decided there was no need to let anyone know about my past problems. What would I have done had the army found out there and then that I had a criminal record and turned me down? Someone suggested I might have tried joining the police. Well, there would be one occasion when I made an approach about becoming a police officer, but at the age of 16, living in the east end of Glasgow, such a prospect was never going to become a reality.

Next, I had to wait until I could pass the medical. I think the guy in charge at the careers office got fed up with me because I regularly rang up and asked, 'Can I come up and get weighed? I think I've put on the half stone.' Of course, I hadn't. I couldn't believe it. I had even started eating porridge!

I was elated the day I went along, stood on the scales and was told, 'Congratulations, Shannon! You have finally made eight and a half stone.'

Now I was ready to take the Oath of Allegiance, doing so in a fairly informal ceremony in which I promised 'I, Alex Shannon, swear by Almighty God that I will be faithful and bear true allegiance to Her Majesty Queen Elizabeth II, her heirs and successors, and that I will, as in duty bound, honestly and faithfully defend Her Majesty, her heirs and successors in person, crown and dignity against all enemies and will observe and obey all orders of Her Majesty, her heirs and successors, and of the generals and officers set over me.' That done, I took the Queen's shilling, although I think it was a fiver in those days. Formalities completed, I waited to be given a joining-up date.

* * *

While all this was going on, to my astonishment one night Angie came to see me. I was like putty in her hands, and she knew it.

She had begun visiting my mum's house at the end of the night with a few of her pals for a few drinks and we would talk for hours about everyday things, like what we had been doing over the previous few days. I was too shy to let her know how I felt, and as 1982 wore on I had another problem. Two warrants had been issued for me in respect of unpaid fines. If I was arrested, it would almost certainly end my chances with the army, so I went back off to Springburn to lie low and stay with my dad. It meant I was unable to get to see my mates or Angie as much as I would have liked. Then, to make matters worse, she met someone she really liked in the Brothers bar. It turned out to be one of my mates and she was fairly serious about him, but heroin was taking over his life. He was already a part-time addict. I knew he was stringing her along – he had a few girls on the go at the same time and I was sure Angie didn't see what he was up to. I couldn't get involved, though. To do so would have appeared selfish on my part, and it was more than likely that I would have done or said something out of jealousy. I decided I had to let things take their course, but I tried to let her know I was there for her if she ever needed me.

Angie and I would still see one another at house parties. I loved bumping into her but realised that at some stage I had to let her know how I felt. Finally, my enlistment papers came through and I knew I would be leaving Glasgow in January 1983.

At the end of 1982 my friends decided we should all go to the Penthouse discotheque on Christmas Eve as a farewell occasion. The night turned out to be even better than I could have hoped when Angie turned up. We found ourselves together and sat talking the entire night about life and the past. And I plucked up the courage to tell her how I felt about her. When it was time to go, we said our goodbyes, but before she left she gave me her work telephone number and told me to keep in touch while I was away at basic training. That was one order I was always going to obey.

# CHAPTER EIGHT

The Royal Scots (The Royal Regiment) is Scotland's infantry regiment. Its soldiers have proudly honoured the regimental motto *Nemo me impune lacessit*, meaning nobody touches me with impunity, on dozens of battlefields from Western Europe to the Far East. The oldest regiment in the British Army, it was raised in 1633 when 1,200 Scots were recruited under a Royal Warrant from King Charles I. Seventeen years later, it won its first battle honour at Tangier. Since then soldiers from the regiment have appeared in almost every campaign fought by the British Army, acting with courage and skill at Malplaquet, Inkerman, Mons, Ypres, the Somme, Menin Road and Gallipoli, to name but a few, up to the start of the Second World War, when it was part of the British Expeditionary Force. Twenty of its men were massacred by Nazis in a murderous and cowardly incident at Le Paradis in May 1940. The war saw the regiment in Italy, France and the Rhineland, and it also took part in the Burma campaign. It featured, too, in the 1991 Gulf War. Now, it was about to recruit a delinquent from the deprived streets of the east end of Glasgow.

The start of any new career remains memorable for many varied reasons in the mind of any young man or woman. So, as he waited for his train on the morning of Monday, 10 January 1983, Alex Shannon had more reason than most to be nervous. The warrants for his arrest for not paying his fines were still in force; it needed only a policeman who knew his face and who was aware of their existence to recognise him and a tap on the shoulder would end ambitions he had harboured for years. The army was aware neither of the warrants nor of the past convictions of the young recruit, otherwise the door to his entry would have been shut in his face. Since he had left St Ninian's little more than a year before the interviews, it was assumed he was telling the truth. Further, as he was joining the infantry, background checks tended to be less rigorous.

* * *

I thought the day would never come, but then I was given my train ticket to get from Glasgow Queen Street to Aberdeen. I noticed there were a lot of young boys on the same train as it headed north and guessed they were travelling for the same reason as me, but I didn't bother speaking to anybody else. The ultimate destination was the camp at the Bridge of Don, and when the train pulled into Aberdeen and we all piled out, there was this big, tall corporal, at least six feet six inches tall, dressed in combats and wearing glasses, shouting in a broad Glaswegian accent, 'All those for the army training establishment at the Bridge of Don follow me, follow me.' He led us in the direction of the waiting buses. The other guys were mostly dressed in suits, wearing ties, carrying bags and suitcases. I had on a jumper and a pair of jeans and was holding a plastic Co-op bag. Inside was a towel, a bar of soap, a toothbrush, toothpaste, a pair of socks and a pair of underpants. That was all I had. Even worse, I had no money and had had hardly anything to eat for the previous few days, as I was too scared to leave my dad's house in case the police were watching and arrested me. When we arrived at the side of the buses, the others were all lined up, standing with the gear beside them, waiting for instructions.

As I stood there next to them, the corporal stopped me, looked down and asked, 'Where are your bags?' When I told him that was all I had, he looked staggered. 'You were supposed to bring a big bag or a case with spare clothes, underwear, coat hangers, shoe polish and that kind of stuff,' he told me. 'Well, I've got none of those,' I said. He then turned to one of his colleagues who was helping to organise the buses and said, 'Fucking hell, we've got a real one here.'

The platoon sergeant came marching up and was asking people where they had come from and what they had brought with them. When he reached me, he had a quiet word with the corporal. There was a kind of laugh and chuckle between the two of them and then the sergeant said, 'And what have you got?' I repeated what I'd told the corporal. He looked at me and said, 'Well, we've got a right one here. Straight off the streets of Glasgow.'

I had been conscious on the journey there that because I was joining what was basically an east coast regiment there would probably not be a lot of Glaswegians with me.

'Look, we'll need to get him sorted. Get him some stuff,' the sergeant told the corporal.

Because I didn't have money, he asked the other trainees if they would help buy me coat hangers and polish, and all the guys chipped in to help. They weren't ordered to hand over money, but as soon as they were asked, they offered it.

Our destination was the Gordon Barracks, which would house us for a year while we trained as junior soldiers. When we arrived, I was in my element. I had never been that far north in Scotland before, while I think the majority of the other trainees hadn't been away from home for any length of time. I fitted in right away because, to me, it was just like going to another children's home, especially as it was filled with guys – and I had spent enough time in homes to be able to handle the sort of regime I met at the barracks. Not once was I homesick, though sadly some of the others found, for a variety of reasons, that they couldn't handle the life. I think my section started off with a dozen men, but by the time we completed our training it was down to five or six. The platoon I was in had begun with something like 48 recruits and when it came to Passing Out there were just 18 remaining. It seemed that almost every week somebody left because of injury or illness, or simply because they missed their mothers. It was a shame when the others dropped away, but it didn't bother me. I loved it. I felt comfortable and safe. I knew the police wouldn't look for me at the barracks and so the fear of being arrested began to evaporate, but it could never disappear. I knew there would have to be a day of reckoning.

I occasionally thought about jail. I knew that, had I been sent there, as had some of my friends, I would almost certainly have met up with guys I had known in the children's homes. Just as the barracks was another sort of home, so was prison. Guys left children's homes with no prospects and nowhere to go and just drifted into crime. They ended up in approved schools, borstals or the young offenders' units, along with others from the same background. It was like a merry-go-round, except you only got off when a prison officer allowed you to. It happened a lot then, and it is still happening now. Lonely backgrounds, maybe a history of abuse, children's homes, young offenders, prison, and on it goes. You get out of prison, enter a hostel, commit a crime, sometimes because you have no money or maybe because you just want to be back in the environment you know, then you are back in and the whole process begins all over again.

Just as I was settling into life in the army, a cloud appeared on the horizon. In March 1983, when I had appeared before Glasgow District Court for the mobbing and rioting incident, my sentence had been deferred after I said I was joining the army. Now, I had to go back to court to show that I had kept my word. The arrest warrants had been discharged.

During my second month at the Gordon Barracks, I had been allowed a short leave and had gone home. I wanted to see Angie – I was missing her. One day as I was travelling in a taxi it was stopped by a policeman who recognised me. He opened the door, stuck his head inside and said, 'Alex! Your fines! Go in and pay them. I know you have money now.' Then he wished me well. I had army wages, so I did just that.

He was ex-forces, and I thought back to the beating I was given by the CID people. There were good cops and bad cops.

Paying off the fine meant I could go about freely, but as the court appearance neared my worries increased. Then the citation arrived, ordering me to show up. There was nothing for it but to tell the sergeant major. He went mental and informed me that I would be automatically discharged on the grounds of Defect in Enlistment for not owning up to having been in trouble with the law. During the interviews before joining up, I was asked whether I had a criminal record. I knew I should have come clean, but was desperate to enlist so had made out I had never been in trouble, had never been lifted by the police. Now, it was all going pear-shaped. There was no way I could have sneaked off to court in Glasgow without anybody knowing, so my career looked to be heading for a sudden end. It was a terrible blow.

I went before the officer commanding (OC), who told me another officer would accompany me to court. He advised me to totally come clean about my past. It would have been silly to try to hide anything because the probability was that my record was going to be read out in court anyway. And so I gave a full account. After a while I was summoned back by the OC and told that because I had made a full admission I was going to be given a second chance. I was allowed to stay on provided the court hearing went OK.

An officer from the Black Watch spoke on my behalf during the hearing in April 1983, saying I was fitting into training well, I had knuckled down and there was a future for me. As a result, I was admonished. I knew I had been lucky and was told, 'Had it not been for your doing well in the army, you were facing a custodial sentence.'

I returned to the Gordon Barracks knowing I now had nothing to hide. The OC was informed of the outcome and I was given another severe warning, but told I could soldier on. As I marched out of his office, I knew that had I not been forced to go to court, frankly I wouldn't have said anything.

Back in training, I worked harder than ever. I knew I had to remain on my very best behaviour. Throughout my life, when something like that has happened, when I've had a close shave, I have always learned from it and moved on. It was a hard year, trying to keep my nose clean. Every time I went down to Glasgow on leave, I had to tell myself to stay out of trouble. And every time I was home, something seemed to happen, but whether by good luck or just coincidence I managed to keep out of it.

By the time summer came around, we were entitled to six weeks' leave, which coincided with the school holidays. I went off to rejoin all my mates and see Angie. It was a very enjoyable time. We used to go out drinking and enjoying ourselves, and because I had a few hundred pounds' pay in my pocket I could afford to get rigged out with the best gear. Yet despite the fun and freedom, I missed the soldiering and used to pine to get back to it. It is just how I lived, plus I was conscious that while I was in the barracks I had less chance of getting into trouble.

I knew I had to keep my guard up while I was training. I was among guys who were fully developed physically, while I was still this tiny wee thing. But while I might have been the smallest, I think I terrified the rest of them. In such situations, there develops a pecking order and you have to decide on your place and then fit into it. You need to let others know you are not going to be messed about, either physically or mentally. I was really sharp mentally and found I could reduce the biggest of the other guys to tears. I wasn't a bully, because I don't like bullies, but I made sure everyone knew they had to stay away from me and couldn't mess me about.

During my leaves, I'd meet up with Pawny and William Lobban, who told me they had been doing some turns together. They kept to themselves one particular turn they had in mind, which involved screwing the Balmore bar in Saracen Street, Glasgow. They had come up with a pretty remarkable idea for getting in. Next to the bar were some shops, including one in which you could play the puggies, the slot machines. It was a popular gathering place for young people, but Pawny and Gibby needed to be alone so they arranged to stay in the shop throughout the weekend. Their plan was to get under the floor of this shop, then cut through the basements of the intervening shops until they reached the cellar of the Balmore bar. Having done so, they would smash their way in. They promised a third party, who was helping, a share of anything they managed to steal and went ahead.

The raid itself was a spectacular success, with everything going precisely as they had hoped. They emptied the cellar of its entire stock of beer, spirits and cigarettes and carried it back to a nearby house where most of it was hidden in the crawl space beneath the floorboards. Naturally, the police were called in and began looking for likely culprits. As a matter of routine, they concentrated their enquiries on locals with criminal records for stealing or with reputations for thieving. There was also a suspicion that someone may have tipped off the police who was behind the raid. As a result, they began looking for Pawny and Gibby, and they called at the house to which the stock had been taken. The suspects weren't there, but, even so, the police made a cursory search for signs of stolen property. Fortunately, they did not lift the floorboards, so the haul remained in place, gradually being distributed to customers and friends; however, another man who had helped with the robbery eventually caved in to police pressure, confessed and implicated Pawny and Gibby, who were arrested.

I was at the Gordon Barracks when all this took place and I heard what had happened during a phone call home. On my next leave, I was told the full story and called at the house, where I was presented with a couple of dusty bottles of rum. I put these in my bag, thinking they might come in handy some time, and took them back with me to Bridge of Don.

Pawny and Gibby, meanwhile, were charged and when they appeared in court were both sentenced to borstal training at Glenochil in Clackmannanshire, Pawny for a year and Gibby for two. The third party was older and got 18 months' imprisonment, which was harsh considering he had never been in trouble before.

# CHAPTER NINE

I remember one particular exercise during my training which involved taking part in a survival course on Ben Macdui, the second highest mountain in Britain after Ben Nevis, and the highest in the Cairngorms. It is said to be haunted by the big, grey man of Ben Macdui. One evening, as we were lying about, trying to fight off the cold, I said I had something to warm everybody up. I reached into my Bergen and produced the two bottles of rum. I was asked where they had come from and simply told them a friend had advised me to carry them with me for occasions just like this. The rum came in very useful and I silently murmured thanks to Pawny.

I had been promoted to junior corporal and was just four weeks away from completing basic training and Passing Out in December 1983. Then I would be a fully fledged infantryman and would formally join the regiment. This would be a big moment and one to be very proud of. However, one of my problems remained my inability to curb my emotions. Everyone knew I had a quick temper, and as some had found to their cost in the boxing ring, I was not someone to be messed about. But true to my word, I was never a bully.

During another training exercise, the sergeant tasked me to move ammunition boxes from one place to another. It was a menial task, but I was a junior NCO, in a position of authority with about eight other junior soldiers under my command. This was the first time I'd been experiencing leadership. Off we went, and about halfway through the job I gave an instruction to a guy from Dumfries who was slightly bigger than me to pick up some boxes. He came back with a bit of an attitude and told me to fuck off. Without thinking, I gave him a Glasgow kiss – a head butt – catching him squarely on the mouth, causing his front two teeth to rip through his upper lip. Blood spattered everywhere.

I told him to wait while I fetched medical help and found the platoon sergeant to tell him what I had done. He listened, then all hell broke loose. I was convinced by his angry reaction that my life and career in the army were over. Luckily for me, the victim was a good guy and not the sort to grass on a colleague. By the time we reached him, he had been cleaned up and was waiting to go to hospital. He gave a very different version of what had happened to the platoon sergeant. 'I tripped over one of the ammunition boxes, and fell and banged my face. My teeth went through my lip,' he said. When he was asked if I had been responsible, he said it had been nothing to do with me; it was a complete accident. The platoon sergeant was an old hand who knew the man was covering up for me but had to accept his version. It meant he could do nothing against me officially, but all the same I was taken before the OC, who told me in detail that the army would not accept any form of bullying or harassment by any rank or individual. He made it plain I should count myself lucky because had it not been for the soldier blaming himself and putting the incident down as an accident I would have been stripped of my uniform and found myself back in Glasgow within 24 hours. 'You are on your last legs,' he told me as I left his office.

So, I was on my final warning. I knew I had to be extra careful now, almost walking on eggshells until I Passed Out. Controlling aggression was difficult for me, but somehow I managed to do so.

\* \* \*

Angie had finally made up her mind and decided I would be her boyfriend. Our relationship was still in the very early days, but one evening when I was on leave and we were together in my mum's house, the conversation swung around to the future. I was aware Angie was still very unsure about what she wanted to do, so the time we spent together was sometimes stressful, but as we talked I said, 'Well, would you think about getting married?' I was only 17, which shows how immature I was. It was said almost as a joke, but I remember her response: 'Yes, I suppose I'd think about it'. There was never an outright, 'Will you marry me?' but by the end of the evening it was mutually agreed that we were getting married.

The next day we met outside Boots in Argyle Street and bought an engagement ring. It cost £40. We were both young. We had probably made a decision based on our situation at the time, not how it would be in the future, and it wasn't really thought through properly. Almost from the moment the ring was slipped on her finger, Angie was having doubts about the wisdom of our plans.

My first posting was to be to the Falklands. We had more or less decided we would get married before I left, but then we had second thoughts. I felt I was too young – I was still going out, enjoying myself. I kept asking myself, 'What happens when you marry? Does all of this stop?' So I felt maybe I didn't want to go ahead. Everyone kept telling me I was too young, that it wouldn't last.

\* \* \*

I kept my nose clean and Passed Out on 12 December 1983. It was a great moment for me, not least because I had managed to swell myself out to nine stone and had grown a couple of inches. However, no one from my family was there to see it, nor was Angie about to travel. The only person able to get there was Jim Brannan's brother, John.

I went home for Christmas and New Year with mixed emotions. I was a fully fledged soldier and had lots of money to spend, but I knew I had to report back on 3 January and in late February would be off again, away from Angie, and this time not to another part of Scotland but to the South Atlantic.

I wanted to make the most of our time together and to show my feelings for her by getting her a really special present. I did my best by selecting a gorgeous Pringle sweater. It looked terrific, but I bought one for someone around a size 20! Angie was size 8. She gave me a beautiful chain and we also swapped envelopes containing money. Once again, I felt I messed up: Angie gave me £40; I gave her £20.

I went to a party in Possil for New Year, but it turned out to be disappointing and ended in the place being raided by the police. There had been a break-in at a nearby shop – it turned out that's where the people holding the party got the drink. The police arrested a few of us, accusing us of having broken into the shop, and carted us off to a police station. I got picked up for no other reason than I happened to be in the wrong place at the wrong time. I was released and never charged, but I was totally astonished by the whole thing. I didn't even know there had been a break-in.

The arrest was bad news for me. When any member of the armed forces is arrested, the police contact the Royal Military Police and provide them with all the details. In those days, as far as the army was concerned, you were considered guilty until you could prove yourself innocent. A few days after I was released, I returned to the barracks. When I appeared in the guardroom, a corporal told me to report to Bravo Company, giving me directions on how to find them. Off I marched, with all my kit, to find the whole company, 120 men, on parade. The Company Sergeant Major (CSM) asked who I was and I replied, 'Private Shannon.' Saying my name was the equivalent of showing a red rag to a bull.

'So, it's you. It's you, is it.' He went mental shouting. I wondered what was going on, but before I could ask he had pulled me to the centre of the Company and ordered it to about-turn so that everyone had their back to us. They did this in one very smart drill movement. Next thing I was being punched and kicked all about the place until I was decked. I had to take it for three painful minutes. He was knocking fuck out of me, shouting, 'You're the thief. You're the one who broke into the shop.' It was no use trying to tell him I was innocent. This was my introduction to the battalion.

When the blows ceased, the CSM shouted at me to stand up. He said, 'That's for getting caught. Now, get your kit and follow the corporal. He'll show you your room and give you a brief tour of the camp.'

It turned out the corporal, an older guy, had known my brother Jamie, who had spent a few years in the same regiment and had been a popular guy. That was before he got into trouble by going AWOL and was discharged. I was different from Jamie – I loved the army – but it didn't prevent others tarring me with the same brush. They thought they could goad and bully me to the point where I, too, could no longer soldier, but in my case it didn't work. Thankfully, this kind of tormenting disappeared from the armed forces about 20 years ago.

I started to settle in and got my head down. From the first day, I was nicknamed 'Del' after the pop singer, Del Shannon. It was the same tag that had been given to Jamie when he joined. I was popular from the beginning but noted how some soldiers thought it was clever to slag off me or my brother. I remembered who they were and, as time went by, like Charlie Davis, they would come to pay for their impertinence.

There were around ten Glaswegians in the Royal Scots, but since the regiment was largely composed of men from the east coast of Scotland, some were frequently picked out for special treatment. I tended to be left alone, but my mate Steven Fox, from Craigend, was the victim of particularly cowardly attacks from morons who went out night after night boozing, couldn't hold their liquor and came back fighting drunk. I felt so sorry for him, but there was not much I could do, as I had to look after myself for now and could not afford to be seen to step out of line again.

We were in what had been a Close Observation Company (COP) that had only recently returned from a two-year tour of Ballykinler in Northern Ireland. In this company were the best soldiers in the regiment. They were ruthless but professional, and made sure there was no bullying, insisting instead on character building, stressing the importance of this as we continued to train for the Falklands. In order to get us prepared for the dreadful terrain and weather we would encounter on the Falklands, we were made to go hillwalking every day throughout January and February, carrying our full kit over the

Pentland Hills to the south-west of Edinburgh. Day after day, torrential rain battered us, and we bent our backs against freezing blasts of gale-force winds that froze every part of our aching bodies. The idea was to build us up for what was to come. We were the new kids on the block and had to expect this sort of treatment. Maybe it was because I was small, or perhaps the CSM was still wreaking his vengeance on me for what he saw as me having brought the company into disrepute by being arrested, even though I was declared wholly innocent, but I was always given the man-portable multi-role recoilless rifle produced by Saab in Sweden and known popularly as the Carl Gustav 84 mm. It weighed eight and a half kilos – but after lugging it around the Pentlands in downpours and hurricane winds for most of each day I was convinced it weighed the same as me. It wasn't worth complaining. Nobody cared. It was a case of survival and every man for himself. My one consolation was knowing that each weekend I could return to Glasgow to meet up with Angie. But as the weekends passed, the day when I would set sail for the south raced nearer.

# CHAPTER TEN

The battle for the Falkland Islands was long over, but the diplomatic fighting continued and, while the talking dragged on and the threat of another invasion attempt hung over the bleak landscapes, British troops remained there in strength. There were vast areas to patrol, including fields, beaches and peat moors holding the unseen and ever-present danger of thousands of deadly land mines left by the Argentine invaders. Alex had known during his training that once he joined the regiment he would soon be on his way to the South Atlantic. For months he and his colleagues had read about and familiarised themselves with locations such as San Carlos, Bomb Alley, Goose Green, Mount Tumbledown and the town of Stanley. Now, they were about to see them at first hand. He had been ordered to deploy on 5 March 1984.

* * *

I would see Angie every weekend until I left for the Falklands. On our last night together it was soul destroying knowing it would be months before I could hold her again.

Next morning, as I was boarding one of the buses taking us to the Royal Air Force base at Brize Norton in Oxfordshire, I heard a call and turned to see the wife of the company sergeant major. She asked if she could have a word, and when I joined her she gave me a teddy bear. It was meant as a good luck mascot.

'Look after him while you are away and give him back when you return safely,' she said. I promised I would, but frankly I was embarrassed when I joined the other soldiers carrying the cuddly toy.

From Brize Norton, we boarded an RAF jet that took us – and the teddy bear – to the Ascension Islands, south of the equator. That flight seemed to take hours, and when we arrived and disembarked it felt as though we were walking into a fire. The heat was merciless. But the journey was far from over. We had each been allocated a muster area to which we now marched and waited to be called forward to board helicopters transferring us onto the SS *Uganda*. It was to take us on the final leg of our long trip.

The *Uganda* started life as a passenger liner between London and East Africa before being converted into an educational cruise ship operating mainly in Scandinavia and the Mediterranean. In 1982, she was used as a hospital ship during the Falklands conflict before a refit made her ready to shuttle troops between the Ascensions and the Falklands.

Once on board, we were shown our accommodation: four-high tiered bunks, with twenty men to a cabin. It was grim, but this was to be our home for the next two weeks until we disembarked at Port Stanley. It was my first experience of a cruise and for the first few days everything was fine. We stuck to the same sort of programme as on land – keep-fit sessions, weapons training, signals and anything else the officers could think up to keep us occupied. There were other diversions, such as trying to scrounge food to make up for the appalling stuff dished up to us. Watching the antics of the staff entertained us as well. They were mostly merchant seamen, some of them openly gay and on the lookout for company, and with the arrival of hundreds of fit young soldiers they must have thought all their Christmases had come at once. I don't know if there were any takers, but at least you could share a good laugh with them.

\* \* \*

During the voyage, the soldiers would often be found in a shop selling small personal electrical items such as portable music players and digital clocks. They were expensive and so were kept in a glass-fronted case with sliding glass doors held in place by an alarmed lock. One enterprising Scot with a history of thieving was confident that by applying pressure to one of the doors it would be possible to ease the door past the lock without setting off the alarm. Surrounded by mates who hid what was going on from the eyes of staff, he was endeavouring to carry out this manoeuvre when the glass shattered and the alarm went off. In a second, with the hand of a practised shoplifter, he snatched a digital clock and secreted it in his combat jacket. Chaos ensued. A cursory glance revealed the clock had vanished and staff demanded to know who had been near the cabinet. There would have to be an inquiry.

Officers were summoned, but when an initial investigation turned up neither clock nor thief, the matter was put in the hands of the Royal Military Police. They decided to wait before pouncing.

The culprit, meantime, fearing a search of every man and his equipment, realised he had to get rid of the offending item for the time being. Sneaking off to the engine room, he hid it behind an array of pipe work, intending to retrieve it on the homeward voyage, hoping that by then the hunting hounds would have been called off. To this day, the clock sits in a house in the north end of Glasgow.

\* \* \*

Midway through the voyage, the Atlantic weather took over. For a week, I was constantly seasick. Initially, I had been unwilling to sample the food; now, I simply could not keep anything down. When the Falklands finally hove into view, I felt relieved, but weakened. On first sight, I thought Port Stanley looked like Legoland. It was surreal: small houses, all painted in different colours, and in the background a cold, drab landscape. My initial impression was 'Oh God, what's this?' My fears were compounded when we began chatting with the outgoing members of the Royal Regiment of Fusiliers, whom we were relieving. As they stepped off the same helicopters that would take us ashore, they wished us luck, warning us we'd need it!

In the distance, I could see the Coastels, floating

accommodation ships normally used by oil rig workers. We would be living on board them for the next five months. They looked cold and uncomfortable. When we climbed into them, however, we discovered they were fantastic – better than our army quarters at home. Once we settled in we were given instructions as to what our routine would entail. There were to be three platoons, each rotating in three six-day cycles, comprising patrols, when you stayed out for the full cycle, relying on having supplies dropped by helicopter; sangar duties around Port Stanley airfield; and fatigues combined with being part of a Quick Reaction Force based at the Coastels.

My favourite cycle was going on patrol around the outskirts of Port Stanley, climbing Mount Tumbledown, Mount Longdon (where Platoon Sergeant Ian McKay of 4 Platoon, B Company, 3rd Battalion, The Parachute Regiment won a Victoria Cross for a heroic charge on enemy positions in June 1982 that cost him his life), Wireless Ridge and Two Sisters Ridge. I was 18 years old and walking in the footsteps of heroes.

The war had been over for almost two years, yet it was as if we existed in a time warp. The enemy had long since disappeared, but everything was still in place, seemingly waiting for them to return. At the same time, danger lurked everywhere. We had been warned to be on the lookout for minefields, yet still managed to walk into them without knowing it. Fortunately, none of us was injured because there were a lot of brave people working there at the time trying to find them. It was slow, risky work, but in the meantime the patrols had to continue.

One day as we walked from Tumbledown to Longdon, we crossed a peaty area. Reaching the other side, we climbed a fence and, looking back, saw a sign showing red triangles marking the site of a minefield. Had we come from the other direction we would have spotted the sign. As it was, we had walked right through the field and emerged unscathed. The odds against one surviving were high; for the whole squad to escape injury or death the odds must have been phenomenal.

I was never scared of being blown up by a mine. My attitude then was that the only time you thought about the chances of being blown up was not before it happened but after. Soldiers tend to tell themselves, 'It'll be somebody else, it won't be me.' If it does happen to somebody right next to you, then maybe it can get to you, but your attitude is more likely to be, thank fuck it was him and not me. That's not being callous, just realistic. After it happens, you simply crack on. When tragedy occurs, soldiers usually turn to black humour as an antidote to fear or worry, and it is this that keeps them going.

There were other dangers. We were constantly finding live grenades too, and when we did our orders were just to mark them and then move away, leaving disposal experts to make them safe. Some areas were like Second World War battlefields, with weapons and equipment abandoned everywhere. There was never any temptation to take any of it because ours was superior. Despite the risks and the need to be ultra careful, this was heaven to me. I was able to walk along all these routes where troops had marched to battle, examine the battlefields themselves, discover where the various positions of both sides had been and imagine the fighting through the minds of both attacker and defender. I had pictured Tumbledown as a mountain of the nature of Ben Macdui, but it turned out to be not much steeper than Balgrayhill. Here were locations I had seen on television news programmes; now, I was standing on them, feeling glorious, almost as though the battle still raged. I saw things from the Argentine viewpoint, in particular the defences they had placed around Stanley, and all I can say is thank God we had not been there to attack the city. It was one of the best defended locations I've ever seen. They were sometimes dug in five or six feet down, like underground houses. Seeing them reminded me that we were patrolling because we were on an operational tour; we were expecting Argentine forces to return and attack at any time, so there was an ever-present need for vigilance.

As my career in the army developed, I would become increasingly familiar with the term 'sangar'. This is a small, temporary fortified position, sometimes made of blocks or bricks, or even sandbags. Sangar duty in the Falklands meant spending six days inside, watching the area around the vital airfield at Stanley and heading out to patrol the perimeter, while always being on the ready for a surprise enemy attack.

Least popular of the cycles were fatigues. I tried getting my head down and gave maximum effort to everything, but I just did not like fatigues. Sometimes you had to peel potatoes for five hours on end, and once that was done you were given any rubbish jobs someone in authority could think up. During one of these fatigue cycles, I was told to go and paint oil drums outside the CSM's office. So, at about nine in the evening, along with another young guy, I headed down there to start painting. It was pissing with rain and we were using water-based blue and white paint, so every time we put the paint on it would just run. Around midnight, I went into the CSM's office and explained the problem to an NCO. His response was to slap me around the ear and order me back outside.

We continued painting for another couple of hours and then thought, 'Fuck this,' and went back to the NCO.

'We've been out all day, it is raining non-stop, we haven't been fed and we need to go over to the accommodation unit and get someone to take over,' I told him.

This clearly did not go down well.

He pulled me over a table and smashed a couple of good uppercuts to my chin.

Reeling, I thought, 'I don't believe the NCO is too keen on me.' I headed back outside and continued painting until I was told to stop. When I returned to the accommodation section, I explained to my closest mates what had happened and we decided to try and do something that would get us into this man's good books.

One of my pals had noticed he had often been seen in the NAAFI admiring a particular Nikon camera and lens but had never bought it, so we came up with a plan to get it for him. Obviously, we had no intention of paying because the camera and lens were around £300.

A few days later it was discovered that the camera and lens had disappeared from the NAAFI. Staff were frequently complaining that the locks to glass-fronted cabinets displaying merchandise were regularly being opened. The young soldier customers were a friendly bunch who would group around the assistants long enough for a drawer holding the keys to the locks to be slid open, the keys removed, cabinets opened and locked, and the keys replaced. It took only a minute or so. Nobody knew who the thief was and that night there was a knock on the door of the NCO. The caller told him, 'Sir, I have something for you,' and handed over the camera and lens. He was naturally suspicious, but in a jocular way asked whether it was stolen. He was assured it wasn't and was told, 'The lads had a whip round because we knew you would like it.' He could not have known about the robbery from the store a few hours earlier. As far as he was concerned, we'd presented him with a gift because we liked him and after that he was brilliant with us. He knew we were just streetwise young guys trying to get on in life.

But we also had hidden talents, especially me, and I became known as the person who could get things. It did not matter what it was or where it came from or how much it cost or what shop it was in, if I was asked then I would arrange to get it. I was a scrounger, and it reached the stage where I was so prolific in getting my hands on items that I was selling stuff to the other companies in Goose Green and Fox Bay.

* * *

Alex Shannon had discovered a problem when he arrived in the Falklands: he missed Angie and worried about her. Before leaving they had settled on a date for the marriage later that year – 14 September, her birthday. While he was away, she had been left to plan and make arrangements for the big day. She wrote, regularly at first, but then her letters suggested that what faint enthusiasm she had shown for marrying young was beginning to wane. Soldiers could telephone home from the Falklands, but few did because a call had to be made by BBC satellite link, which cost £7.50 per 90 seconds. When he wanted to speak to her, he had to call the shop, but sometimes she was unable to speak and at other times he had to wait for her to be brought to the telephone, all the time the cost rocketing. He was being paid £60 a fortnight as pocket money, with the rest of his army pay going directly into a savings account. He needed to speak with Angie to find out what her true feelings were, and he did not want a brief hurried few words with her. It was going to be expensive. When he was young, living in Glasgow, and had faced the problem of where to get cash, he had resolved it by stealing.

In Glasgow, shops had at least been fairly securely locked at night, if they were not alarmed, that was. But Stanley was a thief's paradise. Before the invasion, the town's people had lived largely in the same trusting way as many rural communities did back home, even neighbourhoods in big city schemes where everyone knew everyone else and could leave doors unlocked without fear of being robbed as they slept or shopped. Shops such as the Philomel Store, to Stanley what Harrods was to London, despite being made out of corrugated iron, had had no reason to contemplate being the victim of a break-in prior to Argentine, then British forces' arrival on the islands. Now, the back door of the Philomel, already almost literally falling off its hinges, was kicked in and the building rifled for expensive Barbour and Gore-tex clothing. The thief knew these would fetch good prices and be much in demand by those soldiers who had flown and sailed to the Falklands unaware of the harsh weather conditions that soaked and froze a man within minutes of his stepping into the outdoors. Now, as night fell, he would silently creep into the shop, pick up a basket and load it with whatever he could carry. Much later he would boast 'I screwed every shop in Stanley.'

The NAAFI was a favourite target. It was well secured, but there was no need to use force to steal. Security was lax, staff trusting. Watches costing £180 a time disappeared and were soon afterwards found on the wrists of soldiers who had paid £50 for them. There was never a shortage of customers, whether the items were Mars Bars or Barbour coats. The thief realised, however, that real profits were to be made from the sale of cigarettes.

The NAAFI was supplied by boat and when supplies arrived the thief was always among the first to volunteer to help. From the boats, trucks would carry the goods to the store, where helpers would carry them up four flights of stairs, each item being checked as it arrived by staff. For some reason, the thief always seemed to wear bulky full combat gear and have his Bergen rucksack on his back. By the end of unloading, the bag was packed with cigarettes and sweets, with more cartons of cigarettes and drinks stuffed into his combat wear.

After one unloading operation, an NCO came into the thief's room in a state of panic. 'Fucking hell! Somebody stole 20,000 fags. They're going mental.'

'I know,' said his host. 'It was me.'

'What have you done with them?' he was asked.

'They're in my Bergen.'

'Well, just get rid of them. Take them away and bury them. Just get them out of the way.'

The thief scrambled to find his accomplices and with Bergens packed to bursting point they passed curious groups waiting for the arrival of the Royal Military Police and officers from its Special Investigation Branch. The men headed in the direction of the main road and then towards the airfield, where, out of sight, they found trenches into which they tumbled. Drinking the beer and smoking furiously, they did their best to use up as much of their booty as possible. What remained was hidden and then the culprits returned, claiming they had been for a training run in full kit. A week later they returned, recovered their haul and sold it.

It didn't go unnoticed that Private Alex Shannon seemed to be able to afford to use the expensive telephone link whenever he pleased. Sometimes his calls went on for 20 minutes and he never had any trouble paying his bill. Curious squaddies wondered where his money came from. He was also regularly becoming embroiled in fights – he didn't quickly forget the insults he had been forced to suffer when he had first joined the battalion, especially the cruel and unnecessary remarks about his brother. He had sworn there would be a payback time and, sure enough, once in the Falklands the offenders found themselves on the end of beatings. Rumours abounded, not only in Stanley, about Del Shannon, who was running around knocking men out. People whispered that if anything of value was not nailed down he would disappear with it. His reputation as someone not to mess with reached other areas such as Fox Bay and he was treated with wariness and suspicion. From time to time, the rumours would reach the ears of military police, who would turn up unannounced in the Coastel and search his room and belongings for signs of stolen property. They always left empty handed. An examination of the roof space, however, would have been more fruitful. Military policemen grumbled they were hunting a proverbial magpie, and wondered how the soldier from Glasgow who had appeared penniless with his few belongings in a plastic bag to begin his training had managed to acquire such apparent wealth.

# CHAPTER ELEVEN

Everybody has heard of the Great Train Robbery. The Great Spud Rustling Scam never made it into the record books, but for sheer audacity and invention it deserves special mention. I was an occasional visitor to the Globe Tavern in Stanley and on my way back to the Coastel would often look in on the city's only fish and chip shop. To my great disappointment, it was nearly always closed. I was puzzled as to why a chippy on an island surrounded by water and fish never seemed to be in business.

One day when I was in the Globe with a group of mates, I asked one of the islanders why the chip shop appeared to be permanently shut. He said it was due to a shortage of potatoes. I was astonished to hear this. 'There's plenty of land, why not grow them?' I asked.

The islander began laughing and told me, 'It's obvious you're no gardener. We're just a massive peat bog here with a few mountains. The islands will support sheep, but you can't grow potatoes in peat.'

'Does the chippy ever open then?' I asked him.

'It does,' he said, 'but only for a few months at a time. The potatoes have to be shipped in and once they are used up, then the chippy shuts down again until the next cargo arrives.'

His remark set me thinking and I remembered a very recent fatigue when we had sat outside the cookhouse for hour after hour peeling potatoes, fetching them from a huge mound made up of sacks of spuds. It must have been five feet high and one hundred and twenty metres long. I thought to myself,

'Who is going to notice if a few sacks disappear?'

While I had been having the conversation about growing potatoes, I realised the man who ran the fish and chip shop had walked in. I walked over, introduced myself and told him I hadn't realised there was a potato supply problem. 'I know where there are a lot of potatoes,' I said.

'You sure?' he asked.

'Definitely. How much would you be willing to pay?'

'These things are like gold dust to people here. Where would you get them?'

'Oh, I can get them, don't worry. And it would all be above board. Are you interested in buying?'

'Sure, and so would a few others. I could give you a list of names.'

'That's great, but how much?'

'How about £8 a sackful?' suggested the man.

'Done.'

Within a few minutes, we had made a list of potential customers, together with the number of sacks each would need. I did a few quick mental sums and realised the deal was worth around £1,000.

'Leave this with me, I'll be in touch,' I said.

I knew I was on to a good thing, but humping more than 100 sacks of potatoes into the city would need help. So I roped in a few of my closest friends, explained the arrangement and what was in it for each of them.

One of my friends asked how we were going to get them there. I had already thought this over. 'We'll need transport. We'll ask one of the NCOs for the loan of a truck, but we'll tell him why we want it.' So I went to see the NCO, but as I was about to explain why I wanted the truck he stopped me.

'I don't want to know what you are up to, but if you are asking me whether you can borrow a truck to get to Stanley, you can have one. Do whatever you have to do, but just make sure when you're finished it's clean and back in place loaded up with fuel.'

Then he told me where I could find a truck and the ignition keys.

We went off to collect it and drove to the rear of the Coastel, close to the cookhouse and the huge stash of spuds. We had a look around just to make sure the mound wasn't being guarded and, satisfied the coast was clear, carried the sacks to the truck. It was dirty, dusty work. We had humped about ten sacks onto the truck when I rounded the corner of the cookhouse and saw a bag of spuds dumped on the ground. I instinctively knew something was wrong and my worst fears were about to be confirmed.

I peeped round the corner and could see the master chef holding my mate, Pete, by the throat, shaking him vigorously. We'd been rumbled. I wondered what had gone wrong. 'Time for a quick exit,' I thought, and ran all the way around the Coastel to our accommodation area. By the time I reached it, the master chef already had one of my mates, known as Rents, in front of the NCO who had agreed to let us borrow the lorry. The chef was telling him that somebody had asked the poor young boy to do this. 'It's not his fault. Let's get the spuds put back and we'll leave it at that. Nothing more will be said,' I heard him say.

He marched off and I heard the NCO bark the names of the others in our band. We immediately ran down the corridor of the Coastel, calling, 'Yes sir,' desperate to keep him happy.

'Go and help Pete put the spuds back where the master chef wants them,' he ordered, 'and then come back and see me.' Off we went, furious with ourselves for what had happened.

We replaced the sacks on the mound and then returned to the NCO, who lined us up, tallest at one end, shortest at the other, and spent five minutes punching and kicking each one of us in turn. We had to stand there and take it, despite cut lips and swollen eyes. In those days, it was known as in-house discipline, and we accepted it without complaint because we had screwed up. When the beatings stopped, we got the usual pep talk, but this one was different in that he was more upset that we had not thought it through properly nor done enough reconnaissance. Had we done so, we would have known that the chefs were having a function in the cookhouse that night. The glass in the windows there was smoked, so it was possible to see out but not in. The result was that as we were marching past, humping sacks of potatoes, the astonished chefs were watching and wondering what we were up to. From that day, whenever any of us went into the cookhouse at meal times shouts would ring out: 'Here come the spud rustlers.' It was one more lesson learned – one we would not be allowed to forget for many years.

* * *

I had settled quickly into the Falklands routine, but more importantly I was also well accepted as a member of the platoon and 'B' Company. My reputation for acquiring goods had helped, but I was regarded as an excellent soldier and was looking at being put on the next promotion course. I'd been caught rustling and had settled old scores. Now, I was determined to do some serious soldiering without getting into any further trouble.

One day I was ordered to carry out a cadre course at Fox Bay. On the voyage south, months earlier, we had been told the best of the best soldiers would be given the chance to take part in this. The idea was to form a really top-class reconnaissance platoon for service in Germany. I didn't think much about this, as a necessary requirement for applicants was at least three years' service and I was a new recruit. The new platoon would form a type of Special Forces unit, pounding hills and monitoring enemy positions and movements. It was the sort of work the SAS had done with such skill and efficiency before the British forces had landed on the Falklands to retake the islands.

When I was told I was going on the course, I was filled with both pride and dread. I was proud to have been chosen to potentially be part of a very elite unit, but at the same time joining it would pretty certainly mean having to stay longer on the Falklands and delay even further my reunion with Angie and that filled me with dread. It was a difficult time and I was still young, but I went on the course, run by the best soldiers in the world, came through and found the experience valuable in the future.

* * *

Alex determined to keep his mind on his work, but emotionally his mind was in turmoil. He had always looked forward to reading Angie's letters, but gradually they diminished and by late July when the tour was over and it was time to return to Scotland he opened a letter to read she had decided she no longer wanted to marry. He was shocked, as he knew she had been hard at work planning. There was nothing he could do but wait until their reunion. He had been looking forward to meeting up again with his friends and family, to dressing up and going around his old haunts in Glasgow, but Angie's change of mind meant he had an extra reason for longing to be home.

As the Ascension Islands drew near, he decided he would like to return home with a tan. The heat would also make a pleasant change from the cold and wet of the Falklands. He made the same mistake so many had before, and still do. After downing a few beers, he fell asleep on deck under a blazing sun. When he awoke, his skin resembled the colour of a lobster. Medical staff had to put him in an ice bath to try to reduce his burning temperature.

*   *   *

The thief was anxious to get on board the SS *Uganda* for the return voyage to the Ascension Islands. Had the stolen clock hidden in the engine room been discovered? The answer was no, but crafty military police had guessed the culprit would have the stolen item with him and reckoned that by now his guard was probably down. The clock was hidden in the sausage-shaped bag holding most of his clothing. As the *Uganda* was about to dock at the Ascensions, he saw police searching everyone.

'Hell, this is it,' he thought and went to seek his bag, intending to ditch the clock into the sea. To his delight, he discovered the bags had already been taken off and loaded into helicopters. His gamble in deciding to retrieve the clock had paid off, but only just. Discovery would have meant ignominious discharge and possibly prison.

Finally arriving back in Glasgow, having first returned the teddy bear to its happy owner, Alex was anxious to look his best when he called to see Angie. He went for a hair cut in the city centre. The pretty hairdresser took one look at his bright red complexion and asked him if he had been in a fire. He explained what had happened and she advised him to get a bottle of baby oil and rub it into the areas that had begun peeling. It worked a treat. He felt up to facing Angie and whatever bad news she might give him.

# CHAPTER TWELVE

Alex arrived back in Glasgow at a time when simmering tensions had boiled over into terrible violence. There had always been disputes over who had the right to operate ice-cream vans on lucrative routes through the various housing schemes. Verbal threats or a bout of fisticuffs were usually enough to sort out boundaries, but some routes could be extremely valuable and once money came into the equation nastiness turned to evil.

In April 1984, just five weeks after Alex had journeyed south, someone set fire to the home of a young van driver at Ruchazie in the north-east of the city. The inferno that ensued cost him his life and those of five other family members, among them a baby. Outrage and a demand for an end to the Ice Cream Wars, as they became known, followed.

Police made a series of arrests, but nervousness had gripped the underworld. The killings were an indication that the gloves were off and, in future, gangland arguments would be settled not by beatings, slashings and shootings but by murder. Alex had kept up with events at home through phone calls and news passed around by other Scots, but he had his own problems to resolve.

* * *

Angie and I had spent the previous five months 8,000 miles apart. During that time, our relationship had gone from high to low. Now I was back home, determined to mend the tear that was ripping us apart. The Falklands had been a profitable tour for me in lots of ways and I arrived back in Glasgow with around £5,000, a lot of money for a young man of just 18, and headed for the city centre and the clothes shops. But not the run of the mill stores where everyone else went; I wanted nothing but the best. I had always loved top-of-the-range gear and now I could afford it. When I met up with Angie again, I wanted to be looking my best because I needed to make a good impression. I was still unsure where we stood as a couple and admit I was pretty nervous when I made my way up to her house. Her young brother, Paddy, let me in, but warned me, 'She's in bed, drunk.' It was around two in the afternoon, but when I went in to see her, sure enough, she was lying on her bed, a bottle of vodka beside her. I tried speaking to her but got nowhere, so I took the vodka, poured it down the sink and left. I set off to walk back down the road to Posso, thinking, 'That's it. It's over.' It was a dreadful feeling.

I started to make plans with all my mates for that evening's activities. It was back to the old routine of my house first for a few drinks, then nip along to the Brothers and finally on to the dancing. Part one was going along fine until I heard someone at the door and my mum shouting down the corridor, 'Ally, it's that Angie Scullion for you.'

When I went out to see her, she looked stunning in bleached jeans and blue boots. Best of all, she was sober. She said she was sorry and asked to come in. Well, immediately the words were out of her mouth, I was helpless. It was a case of come into my house, and my room, and into my heart. I knew then that I loved her more than life.

That night we sat by ourselves, talking over what had gone wrong and how we could repair the cracks in our relationship and get our lives back on track. We decided not to get married on her birthday in September as we had originally planned, but on my 19th birthday the following February. We were young and scared, and in reality this was the first time we had both really been 100 per cent serious about the future. She stayed with me throughout the night, the first time we had been together like that. I was blown away, overwhelmed with love and passion.

Next morning I was walking on air as I made my way to

Ritchie Camp, in Kirknewton, West Lothian, a former RAF station and one-time prisoner of war camp for German officers. I still had a week to go before I was due some leave, but I felt the previous night had more than made up for all the hurt, heartache and worry I'd endured while I had been in the Falklands.

It had been a year since Angie and I had first dated, and I know others had been telling her to wait before making a commitment, but now she had, and it was to me. During the years that have gone by since then, I have come to realise that often her reticence is simply shyness. She has always put others first but has a severe lack of confidence in her looks and ability. This has resulted in her suffering from severe bi-polar depression. Yet, to me, she has looks that would take her from the kitchen to the catwalk.

Over the next few months we began planning our future engagement and marriage. I was still serving in 5 Platoon, Bravo Company and we were now beginning training in preparation for our transfer to West Germany in March 1985. Compared with the excitement of the Falklands and the ever present threat of another Argentine attack, hanging around in the barracks and the routine of training was pretty boring, but at least the number of guys in our contingent from the west coast had risen. It meant having more of my own around me, plus each night we could drive one another home.

Following a rift with my own mum, I had moved in with Angie's mum, Margaret. She was brilliant with me. I became her confidant and punch bag, willing to do any job she had for me. While she believed I was good for Angie, she continued to have this image in her head of the Shannons of years gone by. Whenever she introduced me to her friends, she would tell them, 'This is Ally Shannon, but he is one of the good ones, not like the rest of them.' I just laughed it off. Throughout my time there, I was made to sleep on the settee. Often when it came to 10 p.m. I would be thrown out of Angie's room and told to get to bed in the lounge.

Just when I thought army life was getting boring, something happened that would leave a terrible stain on the history of the great regiment in which I was privileged to serve. Each morning, a couple of mates from the Stepps area of Glasgow would pick me up and together we would head to Kirknewton. One day, during parade, I noticed a strange face. The man was a corporal – he stood out like a sore thumb. He was standing, arms folded, with the look of someone who had a complete attitude problem. I wondered who he was exactly. Later that day I found out. A friend told me he was called Andy Walker and had just returned from training recruits. He advised me, 'I know you can handle yourself, but give him a wide berth. He has a reputation as a bit of a bully and can be very handy with his fists.' I wasn't worried. It was well known that 5 Platoon had all the regimental hard men in it. Andy had clearly got wind of the fact that there were so many characters in the platoon and it was best for him to give us a wide berth!

Walker also had a reputation as a cadger – always borrowing money, never seeming to spend any. 'Give me a tenner. I promise you'll get it back,' he would say. He was known to be forever short.

I thought nothing more of Walker – strangers were always turning up, some of them staying on, others leaving. He didn't interest me any more than anybody else. But, as the weeks passed, and Christmas and New Year went by and our wedding day in February 1985 drew nearer, I found myself seeing more and more of him. This was largely due to the company as a whole participating in weapons training and other activities in preparation for going to Germany. As a weapons instructor, Walker had been moving between Glencorse Barracks near Penicuik, to the south-west of Edinburgh, and the Royal Scots base at Kirknewton, where we were ordered to do guard and sentry duties, basically guarding the camp.

On Thursday, 17 January 1985, I was in 5 Platoon on duty at the main gate. It had been a cold night, the ground was frost-covered and we were stamping our feet to keep warm. There was snow in the air. That morning I had been manning the vehicle barrier and remember a familiar car passing through. I knew right away who was driving. I had been doing that same duty for a few days and had become used to seeing the car. Its colour made it distinctive. It belonged to one of the camp storemen, who had loaned it to Walker. After a quick check to make sure all was in order, I opened the barrier and gave the thumbs up to wave on Walker, who was wearing combat clothing. He nodded, as if to say, 'I'll see you later,' and disappeared. There was no reason to think any more of it. I would have every reason to remember this seemingly trivial meeting. It would later transpire that Walker was on a very personal and deadly mission.

Everything seemed to go crazy the next evening when it came through on radio and television news broadcasts that three soldiers had been killed in an armed robbery. By the time I got back to work the following morning, there were all sorts of stories going about as to what had happened and who was responsible.

The rumour mill was having a field day. Suggestions as to the identity of who was behind the massacre ranged from a team of London gangsters to an undercover unit of the IRA. At the time it was widely believed that the IRA was building up to mainland attacks, beliefs that were shown to be well founded later in the year. Groups of men sat around in the NAAFI at Ritchie Barracks that day discussing the murders and trying to ascertain precisely what had happened. Guesswork abounded, but I was conscious that one man was especially vociferous in his condemnation of those behind the horror. Most men in 'B' Company had an opinion, but Walker was louder than any other in expressing his disgust.

\* \* \*

The day Alex had seen Walker drive off in the yellow motor, paymaster Major David Cunningham, aged 56, Staff Sergeant Terence Hosker, 39, and married dad-of-one Private John Thomson, 25, all from the Royal Scots, had called by appointment at the Royal Bank of Scotland in Penicuik and collected a £19,000 payroll. They then set off in a Land-Rover to drive back through falling snow to Glencorse Barracks, where all were based. At this stage, they were joined by evil. Walker, then aged 30, had been waiting as they left the bank and had

# THE UNDERWORLD CAPTAIN

asked for a lift. He was armed with a sub-machine gun, which he had signed out from the barracks armoury, and as soon as they drove away he aimed it at his three colleagues. They immediately realised they were being held up and knew what their probable fate would be.

Walker knew that in all likelihood one or more of the men had recognised him. He had decided their fate long before they had even drawn the money from the bank.

Hosker was determined not to give up without a fight, and as they drove along the town's Mauricewood Road he struggled to wrest the weapon away from the robber. He was shot twice, then the gun was turned on Cunningham, who died with a bullet through his head. Thomson, petrified and convinced, despite Walker's denials, that he too was about to die, was made to drive three miles to Loganlea Reservoir, where his fears were realised. To make sure all three were dead, Walker fired into their bodies. He then took the Land-Rover back to the spot at Penicuik where he had left the yellow car. En route he skidded and crashed and had to abandon the army vehicle – his carefully worked out plan would now have to be changed. Instead of driving to get the borrowed motor, he now had to walk.

His fury at the accident turned to rage when he looked into the bags carrying the money. He had expected to find between £70,000 and £80,000. The murderer had already ordered a new £8,000 MC Maestro, intending to use some of the proceeds to pay for it.

The bulk of the money was hidden somewhere between the abandoned Land-Rover and Penicuik, and the killer took some of it home, telling his wife he had found it hidden under a drystone dyke.

Meanwhile, when the payroll team were late back, Colonel Clive Fairweather, commanding officer at Glencorse, called the police and joined the search himself. He wondered, at one point, whether they might have stopped for a beer on the way back at the Flotterstone Inn near Penicuik, but a trail of blood in the snow led them to the bodies. The hunt for the triple slayer began.

* * *

109

Rumours soon emerged that it may have been a soldier or a team of soldiers who had carried out this terrible act. Before long, we were all confined to camp, which was surrounded by the police while everyone was questioned, searched and investigated. Then the police came in and scanned all our clothing for traces of blood using ultraviolet light. That went on right through the night. We were ordered to stay in our rooms overnight. Eventually, they whittled the suspects down to someone or a group from 'B' Company.

The next day, everything changed. We were all paraded and told to go to certain areas around the camp to ensure no one entered or left. I was ordered to stand on guard, facing battalion headquarters, which meant I was able to see all the comings and goings. Once, I saw Andy standing outside headquarters with his tam-o'-shanter on the back of his head; on another occasion, he looked over to me and shouted, 'Del, got any smokes?' So over I went and gave him a cigarette and a light. I asked him what was going on, if everything was OK. He laughed and said, 'These fuckers are trying to stitch me up for this robbery.' Just then a couple of detectives emerged and asked him back inside. That was the last I would see of him until a few years later, when I came across him during a prison visit.

Three days after the slaughter, Walker was arrested and charged with the murders of the three soldiers and robbery. During his brief spell of freedom following the killings, word reached the camp that on the night of the robbery he had been seen in a pub in Kirknewton on the other side of the Pentlands from Penicuik throwing money about.

We all knew about that, even when we were talking about the murders the next day. Of course we realised it could have been somebody in the army, and once we began suggesting that, we all started looking at one another. The day before Walker was lifted, fingers were being pointed and comments passed like, 'Hang on, he's suddenly been cutting about with quite a bit of money.' He was even throwing it about the night before his arrest.

Walker was charged because an investigation showed that on the day the three men died, he had taken the sub-machine gun used in the crime from the armoury. He claimed it was to give a lesson to another soldier, but the pupil knew nothing about it.

While he was on remand, he shared a cell with a teenager who told police the corporal blackmailed him into carrying a letter blaming the murders on the Provisional IRA.

Walker pleaded not guilty at his trial but was convicted and jailed for 30 years, at the time the longest sentence ever passed in a Scottish court. It was later reduced to 27 years on appeal.

Although I know the whole story about how he got the sub-machine gun under the pretence that our armourer was away somewhere, he had signed it out to 'D' Company instead of 'B', his own. Then, normally when a weapon is cleaned, you lightly soak it in oil and then wipe off the oil so you barely see it. When he returned, he more or less dipped the gun in some sort of oil drum and stuck it in a locker with no doors on it.

Whatever the truth about what actually happened that terrible day, I can never forget it was me who let him out of the camp to carry out the robbery and murders. We continued to wonder what had happened to the missing money. He knew the Pentlands like the back of his hand because he was up there every day training the Glencorse recruits. Mind you, so did many of us because of our pre-Falklands training, going up there once a month to tab 18 miles over the hills carrying our full kit. Rumours continued to float about as to how he was up to his ears in debt, he owed money all over and the cash was still buried in the Pentlands waiting for the day when he was released from prison.

Andy had a lot of pals, he was right good mates with some of them, and after he was locked up they kept in touch.

\* \* \*

By the time Walker was safely in prison, Alex was a married man and had deployed to Germany. But the marriage, already called off once, came close to ending in disaster and yet again his army career faced ruin.

The big day was to be 16 February 1985 at Colston Wellpark Church, Springburn, followed by a reception at St George's

Cross. Pawny would be best man. All had not gone well in the lead-up to the wedding, but then such occasions created for the joining of couples are notorious for also being the cause of bitter splits and arguments among those closest to them. With the wedding a week off, Angie and Alex headed into Glasgow for their respective hen and stag nights.

Friction between one of the girls and Angie had been mounting in the run-up to the big day and at the end of the evening, as the various groups spilled out onto Sauchiehall Street, the women found themselves next to one another. Trouble was inevitable. A fight started and all hell broke loose, with the two women rolling around on the ground. There were a lot of people with them and, as more joined in, it became a free-for-all. William Lobban was with Alex. Neither of them got involved, but they both found themselves in jail.

\* \* \*

I had on a suit and tie, and Angie had given me her handbag and shoes to hold when the fighting began. I thought: 'Women! Just let them crack on. Stay out of it,' so I was just standing at the side, holding a woman's handbag and shoes, while they were rolling around, going at each other. Somebody had called the police, who soon arrived, broke it up and proceeded to arrest anybody who happened to be nearby. That included me.

There were so many of us that there weren't enough seats, so I was shoved into the back of a police van and told to sit down among a whole load of traffic cones and road signs. There I was looking out of the window as we went along Sauchiehall Street still hanging onto the handbag and shoes, wondering what was going on. I was still holding onto them when we reached the police station. And I was still standing with the bag and shoes when they lined us up and started pointing at us and shouting, 'Police assault. Two police assaults. Breach of the peace. Two police assaults.' It seemed a bit hit-or-miss to me.

I don't have anything to hide about that night. I had done nothing wrong. I was a bystander, but again it demonstrated to me how the police could get things wrong. But what chance have you got? The police, they are always right.

We were bailed and allowed home. I had explained I was a serving soldier and, with my wedding just a few days off, here I was with charges over me that could ruin my career, and Angie in trouble, too.

When the wedding day arrived, everything was ready, all the arrangements made, but as we waited for a car to take us to the church, I had to tell Pawny to stop smoking hash. He was sparking them up one after another. I didn't want our special day to be messed up, but he didn't want to stop smoking. When the white Mercedes limousine drew up, the pair of us were all ready in our top hats and tails. I had been prepared for the traditional Scottish wedding scramble, where coins are thrown as you are getting into the car taking you to church. In some areas it is the bride's father who scatters the money, an action meant to bring the happy couple financial good luck. In our case, I had the bag of coins ready, but when we looked around for the customary crowd of youngsters there was only one wee boy waiting. Whether it was in the hope of getting some money, I will never know. I told him to just take it all. There was no point in scattering the coppers. He couldn't believe his good fortune. His luck was better than ours.

After driving through Possil up to Springburn to Colston Church, we discovered the gates were locked. Despite my hired suit and hat, I clambered over, managed to find the door into the vestry and asked the minister to open the gates. The wedding was at half past three and it was quarter past already. He told me to calm down, that everything would be all right. And it was. He opened the gates, everyone walked in and the wedding went off perfectly. Afterwards, at the reception, in my speech I said, 'I know a lot of you don't get on with each other, but for my sake can we just have this one night without any trouble?' And that was it. I sat down and everybody did as they were asked.

The day after the wedding we were to travel to Gourock, where we had paid £400 to spend our honeymoon in a really nice hotel. But we both woke up the next morning hungover and decided not to go. To be honest, I think we were still shy with one another and apprehensive about how we would feel being alone together for a few days in strange surroundings. We had never been away before and so instead stayed with Angie's mum. She pushed two single beds together for us and laughed as she said to me, 'Now you may stay in the room after ten o'clock. I'll be the one to sleep on the settee.'

# CHAPTER THIRTEEN

In early 1985, Alex was deployed to West Germany. He left behind a city in which drugs were spreading like an epidemic. Heroin was rearing its foul head and leaving an increasing number of casualties in its wake. As the death toll among the young mounted, police had limited success in tracking down distributors – it would be some time before they were geared up to the size of the challenge. They relied for much of their information on a network of informants, most of whom were themselves involved in the trade. One high-profile arrest was that of Arty Thompson. He was given a heavy sentence for heroin dealing, and while in jail he made himself unpopular by making threats against not only other inmates but also former associates on the outside – one of whom was Paul Ferris. A target himself with the police, Ferris had been making a profitable living through his work for Arty's father, Arthur Thompson. During one brief spell of incarceration, Ferris also met up with William Lobban.

* * *

Alex and Angie had talked over their long-term plans and decided that after his posting to Germany was completed Alex would leave the army and the couple would settle in Glasgow. Angie was to remain in Scotland with her mum while he did his soldiering, their reunions limited to whenever he was able to get leave. However, hanging over them were the potential consequences of the charges following the Sauchiehall Street brawl. And Alex was about to continue his flirtation with crime, not content to have just escaped career-ending punishment for his Falkland Islands scams.

Alex was posted to West Germany in March, but within a few days he realised he was missing Angie and wanted her by his side. He discussed his unhappiness with her in a series of telephone calls and discovered, to his secret delight, that she felt the same, so the young couple agreed to change their plans and he began the process of applying to his superiors for married quarters. During a short leave home, he was able to tell Angie these would be ready for them a fortnight after he returned, giving her time to arrange to quit work and join him.

On the return journey, Alex found himself surrounded by Liverpool supporters on their way to the Heysel Stadium in Brussels for the 1985 European Cup final against the Italian stars Juventus.

\* \* \*

I travelled by bus and train right through Germany to Zeebrugge in Belgium, where I caught a ferry to Dover, then used bus and train back to Glasgow, doing the same in reverse when it was time to report back. I had stayed too long in Glasgow with Angie and knew I would be in trouble when I got back to base for being a couple of days overdue. I was thinking about her and what I would say when I reported back, and probably daydreaming a bit on the ferry when I realised I was surrounded by crowds of Reds supporters. Glaswegians and Liverpudlians usually relate well to one another and I was wishing them the best of luck for the final. I got on especially well with a couple of Scousers – I could tell straight away they were a pair of scallywags, the sort I would run about with back home. I was 19 then, and they were slightly older than me, probably in their mid-20s. I was a really keen footballer, a centre-forward, but didn't know about football in England. One of the things that made them laugh was that I didn't even know Everton was a team from Liverpool! Everton could have been in London, for all I knew. As you can imagine, that went down a treat with them – the equivalent of an Englishman telling Rangers fans he thought Celtic were from Edinburgh or Dundee.

These guys, though, were not Reds but Everton supporters. They were going to the Heysel all right, but seemed to have thought up a bizarre way of getting revenge on their rivals from across Liverpool by stealing from them. They admitted they were basically a pair of pickpockets and had already made a few hundred pounds. They were hoping to make more and thought the whole scam was hilarious. They reckoned they'd pull a few final tickets as well, leaving Liverpool fans looking glum and ticketless. We sat drinking for virtually the whole of the crossing and when we docked in Belgium I discovered my train wasn't until half three in the morning, with theirs slightly later. So, rather than waste time hanging about, off we went in search of some more pubs and it wasn't long before we ended up starting to pickpocket as a team of three. Since I had already been at this in Glasgow when I was younger, I knew what I was doing. So I did the stalling, acting as the diversion, while they were in and out of the pockets of victims.

They must have done about ten guys in Zeebrugge and made a fortune. They kept handing things to me and I found myself holding something like nine tickets to get into the game. I actually wasn't doing it for money or to be able to get to the final, it was just because I thought they were good guys. At the end of it, they had a lot of money and tried to give some of it to me. I told them no thanks, so they said to come along with them to the stadium. Unfortunately, I was already overdue returning from leave, so going to the match would just make it worse. One of the guys – Dave, as I remember – and I exchanged addresses and off they went to the game.

It's well known what happened. An hour before kick-off a concrete wall separating the two sets of fans collapsed, killing 39 people, most of them from Italy but including a Liverpool fan from Northern Ireland. More than 600 were left injured. Fearing violence if the match was called off, the authorities allowed it to go ahead and Juventus won 1–0. In the aftermath, Belgium was banned from hosting a major European final for ten years, while English clubs were banned for five years from European club competitions.

Back at camp, I was given seven days' Restriction of Privileges, which basically meant I was fucked about from dusk until dawn, given any crappy task that happened to come into the mind of my superiors, in particular the provost sergeant, who seemed to have a downer on me for some reason. For example, I had to parade at the guardroom at seven in the morning, twelve in the afternoon and six at night, basically just to get messed about. And then I ended up getting another seven days added to my original seven because somebody wrecked the provost sergeant's car. Word got back to him that I had done it and for the next seven to ten days I was going down there every day and getting set about by him. I just had to stand there and take it, and he kept adding days on and adding days on. I was waiting for Angie, who was coming over in a few days, and I couldn't afford for her to arrive with me still on some form of discipline, so I couldn't say or do anything. Every day I was getting mucked about by that arsehole. He was quite a tall, well-built guy, with a bit of a reputation, but I hadn't touched his car at all. Somebody had tanned it simply because they didn't like him and I got the blame.

I was in the Officers' Mess one night, as part of my Restriction of Privileges, cleaning silver but also watching the big game on television when the horror of Heysel unfolded in front of me. All I could think about was Dave and his mate. Next day, I fired off a note to Dave at the address in Liverpool he had scribbled down for me to see if he was OK, asking him to drop me a line. I was relieved a couple of weeks later when I got a letter from them, saying they were all right. They were a pair of brilliant guys.

Angie found it tough going when she first arrived in Germany. We had nothing when we moved into married quarters – nothing except what she was able to carry in three suitcases. We had even lost our wedding presents by giving them to a friend to look after. She had got involved in drugs and had sold them. The army had provided a settee and some cutlery, but we had to build everything else up from scratch. It took a while, and yet we got there eventually. We had no help from anyone, and in a way I'm glad because that meant I didn't have to thank anybody.

We quickly settled into a routine, finding the social life vibrant and fun. There were bars in camp but most soldiers and their wives preferred going into nearby towns, where there were discos and dances, and prices were cheap. I soon found myself in demand as a footballer, playing twice a week and being called on to take the field against visiting teams, including Hibs, when a pre-season tour took them to Germany. But there was even bigger news around the corner.

Angie had only been in Germany a couple of months when she discovered she was expecting our first child. We were young and newly married and realised everything had to change. So as soon as we found out she was pregnant, we made a vow that we would ensure any kids we had now or in the future would not suffer in the way we had at times in our childhood. This was a new start for us, our lives would never again be the same, and we wanted to get the decks cleared of any past problems. I wanted to prove myself one of the best soldiers in the regiment and be taken seriously.

One problem looming on the horizon was my pending appearance before Glasgow Sheriff Court to answer charges following the street fracas. The case had been delayed because we were living in Germany, but I had indicated to the authorities in Glasgow that we could get leave shortly before Christmas and would travel over.

We had no money to pay for a solicitor, so when we appeared in court on 19 December 1985, it fell to me to defend us. I was charged with a breach of the peace and assault, and Angie with a breach of the peace. I had no experience or knowledge in this field, but knew I was innocent. I wanted to show I had done nothing wrong and that the police had charged the wrong person, but, like so many before me and since, I learned that when it comes to a policeman's word against that of a civilian, there is always going to be one winner, regardless of whether the civilian is innocent or guilty.

We pleaded not guilty but were convicted of all charges; however, the sheriff took a shine to me and told me he was impressed with my defence and the fact that we had travelled all the way from Germany, paying for our flight from our own pockets. In addition, I made sure the court could see Angie was showing how heavily pregnant she was. He admonished us on all charges, to the very obvious dismay and disgust of some of the police officers I was supposed to have assaulted. Of course, I didn't point out that the army had flown us back to the United Kingdom for annual leave over the Christmas period. It all ended well, but I had yet another conviction to add to my list.

After Christmas, we headed back to Germany. The next 18 months were demanding on both of us. Our son, Thomas, was born on 3 April 1986.

In hindsight, I would say this period of time was to be the foundation block on which I built my career as a soldier. It began with me doing a course at Warminster, near the great army training area of Salisbury Plain in Wiltshire. It lasted eight weeks and the content was military communications and Morse code. I excelled in both and felt I had taken my first tentative steps onto the promotion ladder – and was over the moon when I was promoted to lance corporal. News that our next deployment would be to Northern Ireland came in 1987. I had known that at some stage we would be going there; now it was confirmed.

Angie and I made every effort to get back to Glasgow when time or money would allow it. It was always good to be home, but I stayed well clear of criminal friends, with the exception, of course, of Tam and Pawny.

William Lobban had been jailed for six years for his part in an armed robbery on a Group 4 security van. He was a model prisoner, realising that keeping his head down and obeying the rules was the surest way of guaranteeing maximum remission of the sentence.

Tam had been out of the scene for a while after being jailed in 1984 for possessing a shotgun. Now he was out and had immediately linked back up with Pawny, who was starting to get more involved in things, mainly on the drugs scene. They were both earning names for themselves as young men who could be trusted, and their reliability brought them to the notice of major players in London, who reckoned they were a steady team with whom to do business.

Sometimes when we'd gone for a drink while I was on leave, their London friends would show up. I never really knew who all of them were, but it was clear from the way they behaved that they were in some way involved in crime. For instance, they were so wary of strangers, wanting to know the name of anybody who showed up unexpectedly. They spoke little and softly, making sure nobody could overhear, and had a hard look about them. These were men who had chosen a life that constantly put their freedom at risk, so it was hardly surprising they were so distrustful. It was only in later years I learned their names. I was only being drawn in on the social side but was conscious that when we went out, people would stare and whisper questions about me. Who was I? What was I doing? When they learned I was in the army, I guess they wondered just how proficient a man I was with weapons. I merely stayed in the background.

By mid-1987, the regiment was preparing for the forthcoming tour of West Belfast in November. I had hardly seen my wife for much of the year. In between courses, we were on exercise or training, and because I represented the regiment at football, most weekends were spent playing in competitions all over Germany. Looking back, I suppose it was unfair on Angie.

That summer, Glasgow Rangers visited the region and when I realised Robert Fleck was in the party, I kept going on about my mate who played for Rangers. It was clear those around me were sceptical; I was sure they thought I was simply boasting to make a good impression on them. Eventually, however, I persuaded them to travel and watch Fleck and the others in action. It was a journey that took several hours deep into Germany.

As Fleck was coming off the team bus at the stadium, I was shouting, 'Rab! Rab!' but he just nodded his head and walked straight by me. I was raging. He'd embarrassed me in front of all my pals, yet the two of us had been good mates. I used to go and play five-a-side with him. Even though he was playing for Rangers, we'd go into the ash parks at Possilpark secondary school, so we kind of grew up together. He stayed on Sunnylaw Street and I lived in Burmola Street. Then I'd seen him every day with his then girlfriend when I was working on the YTS scheme. We knew each other really well. I felt snubbed.

\* \* \*

With West Belfast looming fast, I was instructed, at short notice, to return to Warminster, this time to complete a communications instructor's course. It would last six weeks, and two days later I was on my way with the rest of the regiment to Ulster. The date was 14 November 1987.

Six days earlier, during a Remembrance Day ceremony at the war memorial in Enniskillen, County Fermanagh, a bomb planted by the Provisional IRA exploded, killing 11 people and injuring more than 60 others, some seriously. News of the outrage caused worldwide horror and revulsion, while the moving story of how Gordon Wilson held the hand of his daughter Marie as she lay dying beneath the rubble led to intense feeling against the Provos. Partly due to the hatred engendered by the bombing, on the day the regiment arrived and made its way to its base in North Howard Street, James Molyneaux, then leader of the Ulster Unionist Party, and Ian Paisley, then head of the Democratic Unionist Party, were attending a protest rally against the Anglo-Irish Agreement in Hillsborough. It was a bad omen for the new arrivals. To outsiders, nobody seemed to want peace in the province and the soldiers were in the middle of it all.

# CHAPTER FOURTEEN

My first experience of Belfast left me wondering just how crazy the black humour of soldiers could be. On one of my earliest patrols, we had left a police station in a team of four. I don't know whether the other guys were winding me up, but we were heading up the Falls Road away from the police station when they disappeared left down an alleyway and left me walking alone in the street. I turned around, wondering where they were, and heard cars beeping their horns.

'Where the fuck are they off to?' I asked myself. I had to run across the Falls Road and down a lane, shouting, 'Where are you? Where the fuck are you?' I eventually found them after seeing them about 300 metres away. When I caught up with them and asked where they were, they looked at me as if to say, 'Who's he?' They were like, 'What's up, mate? What's the matter?' I reckon they had been playing a game with me.

\* \* \*

Maybe his attitude to soldiering in Northern Ireland at a time when civilians and troops were being blown up and needlessly slaughtered on a near daily basis had made colleagues decide to put his apparent indifference to danger to the test. In fact, his hard upbringing and his scrapes on the tough streets of Glasgow had equipped him well for patrolling the deprived Belfast estates where Republicanism and a hatred of the British thrived. It was simply that neither he nor Angie showed the worry that lurked within.

\* \* \*

In the early days in particular, I would telephone Angie every day. If I could phone twice a day, I would do so. Angie worried about me all the time when I wasn't at home. During the times when I was in Ireland and it came over on the radio or television that a soldier had been killed, her heart would skip a beat. When something happened in Northern Ireland, the soldiers' phones tended to go down, so nobody could ring their family until that of the casualty had been informed, which added to the uncertainty.

We never made a big scene when I was leaving to go on a tour. I'd just go into Angie at night, give her a kiss and say, 'Cheerio.' I would never do the big dramatic thing, with tears and histrionics and 'I don't want to go.' I've always done it as though I was going to be back the next morning. That's the way Angie used to deal with it as well otherwise she couldn't handle it. It was always done almost as a matter of fact. It's how the two of us would cope with it and we didn't like it any other way.

Even when I used to come back, even though we would make a bit of an effort between us to show how glad we were to be together again, we didn't go out of our way and do the sort of dramatics you see in *An Officer and a Gentleman*. I always tried to fit back in as soon as I could. My thoughts were: 'Don't make a fuss of anybody. Don't make out as if I've been away for a long time. No matter what's happened, don't go on about it. Just crack on and get back to normal as quickly as you can.'

In all, I did six tours to Northern Ireland and my feeling on the last was precisely the same as on the first: I loved it. I loved the adrenaline rush, the challenge, the whole lot. I thrived on being put in situations that were adverse or dangerous. Never did I feel fear. I used to see guys greeting at the prospect of going out there or over things that they saw or experienced, but not me. It didn't frighten me in the slightest and I never, ever worried about it. But I did read up as much as I could before I went on what was happening out there.

I admit that my first tour in West Belfast was an eye opener and a couple of times when I was on patrol it was scary, but I never really thought it was my time to be injured or killed. It was always somebody else's. I kept telling myself, 'I'm never going to get it. If somebody else is going to get it, then I'm not so much happy, but I'm happy it's not me.' That's the way the majority of soldiers look at it.

* * *

There was a particular reason for there to be special interest in the arrival of the regiment as it sat in four-ton trucks for the journey from Aldergrove airport just outside Belfast to the base at North Howard Street Mill in the great city. They were the first troops to be equipped with the SA80 firearm. For a start, it had a sight that could magnify a target four times. There were rumours that terrorists thought this was some kind of super gun, but, as any soldier knew, the weapon was only as good as the individual in whose hands it lay. In fact, had the Provos known that in each truck only one man carried ammunition – and, at that, just ten rounds – the welcome might not have been so muted. Alex wondered about the wisdom of the arming arrangements as, for instance, they drove past the notorious but now demolished Divis Flats complex. While the army had established an observation post on the top of the Divis Tower, which dominated the housing scheme, there was considerable resentment in the area towards the armed forces and police. Locals had not forgotten the tragedy in August 1969, when little Patrick Rooney, aged only nine, was killed as the Royal Ulster Constabulary fired a Browning machine gun into the Tower from an armoured car. The RUC later justified its action by claiming its officers had come under sniper fire.

Alex's regiment had been told it would be based at the Mill for the length of the tour, which was to be five months. It turned out to be one of the bloodiest and bitterest periods of the whole Ulster troubles.

Initially, things were relatively quiet. Alex began in the Battalion Operations Room and Intelligence Cell, where a continuous flow of information from men on the ground enabled the secret watchers and listeners to see and hear all that was being played out by the IRA and army on a daily basis. He thought it to be a good education on the military doctrine of both sides and in the use of high- and low-level intelligence by the army. But around Christmas, the terrorists struck.

\* \* \*

I was walking up the stairs in the Mill towards the cookhouse on the level above me, where the rest of the guys from 'B' company were. Suddenly, there was a massive bang and I seemed to be covered in soup. We had been told that if anything happened, we were to run straight to our rooms and cover our bodies with our mattresses in case debris fell on us. And that's what we did. I remember running in and throwing the mattress over me, and then the second explosion went off. It turned out we had been hit by a rocket-launched grenade and a Mark 12 or 13 mortar fitted into the back of a blue Hiace van. One of the devices exploded over an area known as Falls Court. Neither actually hit the Mill, nor did the damage result in the massacre of troops, which had been the intention of the amateur artillerymen responsible, but the sheer size of the bombs ripped off tiles and shattered windows. In fact, the attack backfired on its perpetrators. There were no military casualties, but houses in North Howard Street suffered damage and a number of residents received minor injuries.

It was my first experience of a mortar and it was one I'd never forget. A few weeks later the bombers tried again, and this time fired a Russian-manufactured RPG-7, a portable shoulder-launched anti-tank rocket-propelled grenade, into the gymnasium. Again, it was relatively ineffectual.

These incidents had the effect of ensuring troops were kept on their toes, but if their principal effect was to cause discomfort to eardrums, they were as nothing compared with what was to come.

\* \* \*

Alex remembers January and February of 1988 as being busy with the usual riots, petrol bombings and attempted killings of the so-called soft targets, such as off-duty members of the RUC or UDR and any other civilians who happened to get in the way of the various terrorist groups.

# THE UNDERWORLD CAPTAIN

It was the Loyalists who suffered the first setbacks. On 8 January, a routine search by the RUC of a three-car convoy in County Armagh uncovered a vast array of firearms on their way to the Ulster Defence Association, and a week later two members of the Ulster Defence Regiment, a British Army infantry regiment, were murdered in separate incidents. More murders followed before the month was out, a Catholic civilian dying in County Down and a policeman in Belfast.

There was obvious hatred toward the army in Belfast, and likewise towards the politicians who had put the troops on the streets and commanded them to remain. This anger, compounded by the belief that soldiers and police were under orders to kill without warning, became fury when it was announced that for reasons of national security nobody would be prosecuted following the Stalker Sampson Inquiry into allegations that the British government had operated a shoot-to-kill policy in the province. John Stalker, a former senior policeman, reported that the Royal Ulster Constabulary had carried out such a policy. His findings embarrassed both the RUC and the government, which was desperately trying to soothe Irish nationalists angered both by the presence of British soldiers on the streets and by claims of brutality by the troops. This hatred within the community was inevitably vented on soldiers such as Alex Shannon.

The temperature of the rage increased when judges in London threw out appeals by the group known as the Birmingham Six, who had been in jail since being convicted of pub bombings in the Midlands in 1974. New forensic evidence suggested the men were innocent, but back to prison they went and they would remain there until being released in 1991, declared victims of miscarriages of justice.

February was no better. Private Ian Thain of the Light Infantry had been convicted of murdering Thomas 'Kidso' Reilly, a road manager with the all-girl pop group Bananarama, and jailed for life in 1984. Now it was revealed he had been released and had returned to his regiment, a development the terrorists used to their considerable advantage in the crucial public relations war. The following day the IRA blew up and killed two members of the UDR. Five days later, the IRA lost two of its own when a bomb they were planting went off prematurely. But the worst was still to come.

* * *

While I was working in the Battalion Operations Room, all sorts of specialists would call in from time to time. One of these was Corporal Derek Wood of the Royal Corps of Signals, who usually arrived to fix and maintain radios and install measures to ensure that communications between us and men elsewhere remained secret. He frequently turned up in civilian clothing, a woolly hat or rolled-up balaclava on his head. I asked him why he dressed that way because frankly I felt his appearance made him stick out as though he was some undercover operator. Naturally, the terrorist organisations, in particular the IRA and PIRA, made particular efforts to track down and identify members of the SAS and undercover teams. Corporal Wood laughed this off as if I was joking with him, but I was deadly serious. Our exchanges about his appearance preyed on my mind for the rest of my career, especially in light of the tragic events that were about to take place.

On Sunday, 6 March 1988, three members of a PIRA active service unit were in Gibraltar. Their intention was to explode a car bomb at the spot where a band from the Royal Anglian Regiment would be parading for the weekly changing of the guard at the governor's residence. British security experts had been tipped off about the bomb plot and mounted Operation Flavius to identify and arrest the trio, Danny McCann, Sean Savage and Mairead Farrell. The task was put in the hands of the SAS. These elite troops believed – wrongly, as it turned out – that the bomb was already in place. As a result, when three of their members, armed with 9 mm Browning high-powered pistols, confronted the terrorists and saw McCann reach into a bag, they shot him, thinking he was about to remotely detonate the bomb. Farrell died in the same way, apparently moving to open her handbag, and when Savage made a movement to his pocket he too was killed. An examination of the bodies revealed all were unarmed. McCann had been shot five times, Farrell eight, and at least sixteen bullets had hit Savage. The set of car keys in Farrell's handbag led police to a vehicle parked in Marbella containing Semtex. The shootings, reported as 'Death on the Rock', sparked a wave of condemnation of the SAS action and the threat of retaliation by the dead terrorists' masters.

When I saw and read about the incident, I immediately recognised volunteer Danny McCann, who was 30 when he died. He was a well-known IRA terrorist who had been jailed twice and was part of the West Belfast Brigade at a senior level. When I was out patrolling, I would stop him and check his details, searching him at every opportunity. He was not singled out for any special treatment; this was the routine with all known terrorists whether Republican or Loyalist.

McCann had told me during these searches that he was a butcher by trade and that his father owned a butcher's shop on the Falls Road. It was said that after his son's death McCann's father was having brochures advertising holidays in Gibraltar put through the door of his shop on a daily basis, supposedly by the resident infantry battalion – my regiment, the Royal Scots.

As you can imagine, the whole regiment had been on a high because we'd managed to successfully deal with all the IRA could throw at us over the previous few months in Northern Ireland, but the events in Gibraltar sent the province spiralling almost out of control.

On 14 March, Volunteer Kevin McCracken, aged 31, set out to guard the home of the Savage family, who were preparing for the funeral of Sean. A committed member of the IRA since 1975, he had been jailed for 13 years in 1977. He had helped in the September 1983 mass escape of 38 members of the Provisionals from 'H' Block of the Maze prison and had been released in 1985. There are conflicting versions of what happened on 14 March.

According to IRA sympathisers, McCracken was shot in the back by an army sniper and, in the 15 minutes it took for an ambulance to arrive, was beaten up. He was pronounced dead on arrival at the hospital. My version, from conversations with other troops, is this.

A patrol from our 'A' Company was behind some shops having a quick smoke break when one of the team spotted some movement that looked suspicious down a lane next to the shops. He told a superior, who was and is one of my closest friends, what he had seen and they began to investigate. As the superior walked into the lane, he noticed a boiler-suited individual wearing a balaclava and carrying an AK47 rifle. It was Kevin McCracken. He was shot with the superior's SA80 rifle. As McCracken lay on the ground, the soldier tried to save him, even though he realised that his patrol had probably been the dying Volunteer's target.

Ten days after they were killed, the bodies of McCann, Savage and Farrell were taken for burial to Milltown Cemetery in Belfast. Feelings against the security forces were so strong that it was decided, after discussions with Republicans, that the army and RUC would stay away from the funeral. After a service and requiem mass, the cortege, carrying coffins draped in the Irish tricolour, arrived at the cemetery, where gunfire was heard. Many thought this was the traditional IRA salute to dead Volunteers; in fact, it was the start of a horrific attack by UDA fanatic Michael Stone.

Hiding hand grenades, a Browning semi-automatic pistol and a Magnum revolver, Stone had infiltrated the mourners intent on murdering IRA commanders. As he launched his onslaught, the crowd surged after him, defying the grenades and pistol shots. Stone was caught by enraged mourners, but, as he was about to be taken away by the IRA for execution, he was intercepted and arrested by the RUC and 'A' Company of the Royal Scots. He had killed three people – Caoimhin Mac Bradaigh, John Murray and Thomas McErlean – and wounded more than sixty others. Badly injured, Stone was taken to Musgrave Park Hospital for his own safety, where he was guarded around the clock by RUC officers. As his condition improved, he began receiving gifts and get well cards from around the world. He would eventually be jailed for a total of 682 years.

Three days later came more tragedy, and once again I knew one of the victims. Corporal Derek Wood and his friend

Corporal David Robert Howes were driving in a silver Volkswagen Passat along the Andersonstown Road towards Milltown Cemetery when they found themselves mixed up in the cortege carrying the body of Caoimhin Mac Bradaigh. They realised they had taken a wrong turn, but their efforts to extricate themselves led mourners to believe the two men, in civilian dress, were Loyalists hell-bent on another Stone-type attack. The car was surrounded and Wood, who was carrying a pistol, shot into the air. As television cameras recorded the horrific scenes, both were dragged into a taxi. They were then taken to a waste ground, stripped, tortured and murdered. Wood was shot six times and stabbed four times.

On the day both these soldiers were killed, I was waiting to be picked up from Belfast City airport by members of the Motor Transport Platoon in a covert vehicle. I watched the whole terrible event live on television in the airport bar. I realised I too was about to head back into the area of the tragedy in an unmarked car. As you can imagine, what I had just watched freaked me out to the extent that when the vehicle came to pick me up I went straight into the weapons bag and took out the SA80, loaded it and made ready with a magazine of 20-plus rounds. I sat with the rifle on my lap all the way back to the Mill, saying to myself, 'If you're coming to get me, then there are nineteen bullets for you and the last one for me.'

I can't criticise the two dead corporals because I don't know how or why they ended up in the middle of the funeral gathering, but I am aware that at this time it was common for some individuals who had access to civilian vehicles to go out cruising, mainly in Republican areas, that were completely out of bounds at all times to these vehicles. How do I know that? I had done it myself once in early January. I found the experience strange and thought at the time that I wouldn't be doing it again. It was too dangerous. The guy I was with kept telling me to stop worrying, but he taught me a lesson that I used later on in my military career: don't take risks with other people's lives.

I would point out to any individuals I happened to be training that by their dress the corporals had made themselves stick out like sore thumbs, attracting attention. I often referred to Derek Wood and would stress the difference between Special Forces and Specialist Forces, pointing out that the two were totally different. It was dangerous for the latter to believe or act as though it were the former and vice versa.

I have come across many Walter Mitty characters during my service, particularly in Northern Ireland – men who believed that because they were posted to Special Forces they had remarkable abilities and became overconfident. Often they would be no more than drivers, medics or storemen. These beliefs in themselves could be dangerous and on occasions could lead to death. There were many lessons learned from the tragedy of the corporals, as I discovered when I went on a Close Observation Platoon course as a team commander.

# CHAPTER FIFTEEN

Alex's first tour of Northern Ireland was coming to an end in May 1988, but the killings went on. A bomb hidden in a gas canister killed Royal Artilleryman Lyndon Morgan, aged just 20, as he was on foot patrol at Carrickmore, County Tyrone, in April. Elsewhere there were regular attacks on RUC officers. What caused concern to many service families were the killings by the IRA of three members of the RAF in the Netherlands on 1 May, one by a sniper, the two others as a result of a bomb attached to their car. It meant the terrorists were spreading their murderous talons into the European mainland where the wives and children of many troops on duty in Ulster lived. Among them were Angie and Thomas, now aged two. Undermining the morale of the vulnerable was part of the IRA strategy, of course. Realising their families were now living in fear could cause troops to lose concentration and put themselves and colleagues at greater risk. Apart from occasional leaves when Alex could join her and Thomas, Angie had been on her own. She was looking forward to her husband coming home, but when he did he had news that meant she was about to be alone yet again.

* * *

Towards the end of the tour I was informed I had been chosen to go on Pre-Selection for my Section Commanders' Battle Course, which was to begin as soon as we returned. I was up for it because completing this course successfully would enable me to carry out a long-held ambition to train recruits. I was also conscious of there being a good many hurdles to climb and there would be strong competition for places on the actual course; fifteen of the best lance corporals and corporals in the regiment would compete for just three vacancies.

After a tough four weeks, I was told I had made it into that top three. Now, I would be expected to spend three months at Brecon Barracks, headquarters of the army in Wales. I had been back from Belfast for seven weeks, had spent four of those in the pre-selection contest and now had to tell Angie I would be going off once more.

I knew she was being put under pressure and realise it must have been very lonely for her at times. She had Thomas to look after and not long after I came home from Northern Ireland we discovered she was expecting our second child. The main driving force for me at this stage was financial. Each step up in the ranks meant a consequent increase in pay. At the same time, I suppose the professional soldier in me wanted to lead others rather than be led. There was a price to pay if this ambition was to be realised. It wasn't just that I went on course after course, but I had to be able to pass them. The army is no different from any big business in the respect that rarely do you get a second bite at the cherry. But I missed Angie as much as she missed me; she was the rock upon which I leaned and on whom I relied. There were many times when she must have felt down and exhausted, yet she would put her own cares to one side to pick me up when fatigue left me feeling low.

The Battle Course was one of the toughest in the army. Only selection for the coveted 22 SAS is harder and I found myself alongside 12 members of 22 SAS.

This SAS company has an astonishing record, having been involved in covert reconnaissance and surveillance operations in many parts of the world. It took part in the raid on Pebble Island during the Falklands campaign and was involved in Operation Flavius in Gibraltar; everyone knew a mere rumour that the SAS was in town was enough to send shivers down the spines of the Provos, while its most highly publicised operation – ending the siege at the Iranian Embassy in London in 1980 – had been seen by millions live on television. Being with these soldiers and talking to them candidly helped me to understand the regiment better. Despite the aura surrounding it, I came to realise that there are no differences between infantry regiments in the army, whether Paratroopers, Guards, the Scottish Division or Special Air Service for the simple reason that all Junior and Senior NCOs are trained to the same high level. The British Army was then, and still is, the best in the world. The only difference between soldiers is their level of leadership, capability and ability.

The course went really well for me. I loved learning about tactics, live firing and pushing myself to the limit to gain extreme fitness. I was testing myself against the best of the best and doing well. However, my old Glasgow temper almost brought a premature end to my ambitions when I came close to being thrown off for fighting with another guy in my section.

We were doing a realistic exercise in woodland and he was supposed to turn up for sentry duty at two in the morning but was half an hour late. I wasn't happy about this and told him so. One thing led to another and after a fairly short debate he ended up with a burst nose. I thought no one knew what had transpired, but of course word reached the ears of the platoon commander, who was given a briefing on the incident. Next morning he hauled both of us in front of him and grilled us on the previous night's activities. Much to his credit, the other soldier said we had simply clashed into each other due to the lack of ambient light in the woods. He was grilled pretty fiercely over the details but stuck to his story, with the result that the officer accepted his version; however, it was pretty obvious the officer had suspicions as to what had really happened and he warned me that from that moment on he would be watching me closely and if I did anything wrong in the remaining three weeks of the course I would immediately be sent back to Germany. It was a lucky escape this time, but as my career developed the Brecons would serve up more unpleasant surprises for me.

The warning acted as a spur and I kept my nose clean. When the course ended, I was told I had a very strong pass and so I was feeling good as I headed back to Germany to rejoin Thomas and now four months pregnant Angie. After the stresses of Northern Ireland, the challenge of making it through pre-selection and then the Battle Course itself, I felt I needed quality time at home, but the lure of the football pitch tempted me out.

I had settled back into the old soccer routine of 'have boots, will play anywhere'. During the pre-season, Hibernian stayed at our camp for a couple of weeks and I was lucky enough to play a series of games against them. It was a great thrill to challenge Scottish Premier Division stars, but – no offence, Hibs – so many times during those games I wished the opponents had been Rangers.

I kept the memory of that incident with Fleck in Germany in the back of my mind. What I didn't realise at the time was there would come a night when he would regret making a fool of me. The old saying 'everything comes to he who waits' was spot on about a year later. During the four and a half years I spent in Germany, Angie and I would return to Glasgow at least twice each year and on each occasion stay with her sister Lizzie and mum Margaret in the St George's Cross area. I knew Angie enjoyed being with her family and did not mind the fact that I liked to meet up with and spend time with my brothers. Whenever we could Tam, Pawny and I would head out into the city centre or around some of our old haunts for a few drinks, but Angie and Thomas were always the most important people in my life and I would try to be home for ten o'clock, so I could spend some time with them before Thomas went off to sleep.

One night when I was back in Glasgow, Pawny and I were at the dancing in the Savoy and who should be there but Fleck with another footballer. There was a whole gang of us, including a big crowd from the Milton area, many of them associates of the Lyons family. My good pal George Redmond was with us and there must have been about 40 of us. It was like some underworld reunion. I noticed Robert Fleck chatting in the corner to the other player and when he spotted me he came over.

'Oh, aye. How's it going?' he asked.

Pawny knew about the incident in Germany and before I could say anything had jumped up and told him, 'You better get away from here or I'll end up shooting you.' He was kidding, of course, but Fleck didn't know that. 'My brother tried to speak to you in Germany and you just fobbed him off and you think because you're some kind of football player you're some kind of star, get yourself away. Beat it.'

Everybody was staring at him. There were some hard-looking guys with us and it must have been pretty scary. He and his friend left the Savoy immediately and didn't come back.

Back in Germany, on St Valentine's Day 1989, my second child, a daughter Danielle, was born. It felt as if life was good for us all. I was waiting to be promoted to corporal and was hoping for a posting to train recruits in Edinburgh in the near future.

Clouds were forming on the horizon, however.

# CHAPTER SIXTEEN

As I had hoped, my posting back to Scotland came through and in August 1989 we returned home. It was to be a two-year deployment and I would be based at Glencorse Barracks. I was over the moon at getting this new job, but it turned out to be a double-edged sword.

Before leaving Germany, I had been assured I would have a dual role, initially to trial, deliver and instruct recruits on current communications systems being used in the army, then revert back to being an infantry tactics and weapons instructor, a task I had wanted to do ever since joining the forces. However, as is so often the case, things never go to plan and as a result I was left in the training wing with too much time on my hands and every weekend off. I was soon travelling through to Glasgow during the week and most weekends going out drinking or just visiting family and friends.

By now, Pawny and Tam had really made a reputation for themselves – no mean feat, considering the number of tough up-and-coming crews operating in and around the city. They had been accused of an armed robbery in Glasgow, a charge that was ultimately dismissed through lack of evidence, but news filtered 400 miles south to a former resident of the city now living in the capital and directing operations from there. He was always on the lookout to recruit good men and had invited Tam and Pawny to meet up with him. From there, they were told the head of another team with major gangland links had asked for an introduction. The one-time Glaswegian had vouched for the brothers, and now Tam in particular was effectively being interviewed by the leader of this team, a stranger, as a prospective foot soldier. But Tam was his own man.

He had listened carefully and politely as the stranger ran through Tam's recent past in the course of which stabbings, shootings and robberies were mentioned, but then said, 'Look, wait a minute. I've come all the way to fucking London and I've only met you today. I've never met you before, but you know all about me, what I've done in the past couple of months and all the rest of it. What the fuck are you all about?' The stranger realised his mistake. He had been prying into Tam's background without asking consent and, while it was frequently done, it was generally done discreetly – you didn't tell someone you had been checking up on him. Not wishing to further offend this hard-looking man from the east end of a city he had never visited, he held up his hands in apology. 'I understand why you are upset, maybe we should just leave it at that.' It had been a case of the Glaswegian forgetting his roots, assuming he could just pass over someone he believed would be useful to one of his cronies. It was not the done thing.

\* \* \*

Tam Shannon was still violent and was a bit of a loose cannon, while police suspected Pawny of being the most prolific drug dealer in Scotland. This was a time when drugs were really swamping the schemes and clubs. A group who became known as the Happy Dust Gang had pioneered a thriving trade in cocaine from Europe until an informer caused their demise in the early 1980s. The leaders had been jailed, but their success had not gone unnoticed and there were plenty of others ready and willing to take over the mantle of the supplier, despite the prospect of a long prison sentence.

As time went on, more routes were opened up. More money was invested by businessmen who ensured their own security by staying away from Glasgow and paying others to take risks. Ever increasing quantities of heroin were finding their way into the veins of the young, causing premature death and misery. Ecstasy tablets were changing hands for up to £20 a time, while temazepams, better known as yellow jellies, may have been less potent but their price tag was cheaper. Some felt the move to harder drugs was partially the fault of the police, who had used considerable resources to track down those smuggling in less destructive drugs such as hash usually hidden in cars driven from Spain. An example of that was the arrest of Pawny late one afternoon.

Almost certainly through a tip-off from an informer keen to remove competition, the police believed that Pawny had established a very straightforward supply route. He would fly to London, do his deal and return, carrying a substantial amount of drugs, sometimes heroin, sometimes cocaine, sometimes pills, sometimes hashish. And so they placed in position a very expensive surveillance operation. Pawny was watched. When he flew to London, it was noted. When he returned, he was followed to see whom he met. He usually simply went home or visited another family member. It was decided that on his return from his next trek south, he would be arrested. Police waited to see whom he met when he arrived at the Glasgow airport terminal, wondering if it might be a courier who would take whatever package he had on to dealers. They were surprised to see him drive off alone and assumed the bag at his side contained drugs. As he headed onto the Kingston Bridge, amongst the rush-hour traffic, chaos ensued. It was suddenly blocked off and onlookers noticed a helicopter hovering overhead. Armed men shouting, 'Police,' ran from unmarked cars and arrested him; however, a search of his person and property revealed nothing incriminating.

As he sat in a comfortable coach heading back from London to Glasgow, Tam had no inkling of the drama unfolding many miles to the north. He could allow himself an occasional smile. In the locker above him was a holdall containing a selection of drugs. He and Pawny operated a simple routine. They would travel south separately, Pawny by air, Tam in a coach or train, then they would meet up in London once Pawny had concluded his business and Tam would return home with whatever his brother had bought.

Alex knew his brothers' business. He was not part of their

activities, but as they would be there for him should he need help, he was just as fiercely loyal to them, even at immense risk to himself. While he was based at Glencorse Barracks, he found himself becoming increasingly heavily involved with them, a development that was slowly beginning to concern Angie. After leaving Germany, she and Alex had set up home in Lasswade, Midlothian, close to Rosslyn Chapel, the inspiration for the film *The Da Vinci Code*. They had moved there on the recommendation of a friend, but Angie was a Glasgow girl and she felt increasingly out of place and gradually depression began setting in. Alex's excursions into Glasgow, with their potential for trouble, were becoming more frequent and adding to her worry. Her moods only lifted when Alex suggested he might leave the army, as he was becoming more and more disillusioned at what he saw as a lack of progress up the ladder.

* * *

Tam and I used to go out all the time and were looked on by the majority of people as two of the main troublemakers, when in truth this was not the case. I was something of a dark horse, with those outside our immediate circle wondering what I did for a living. I simply wanted to enjoy myself with my brothers. In many of the pubs and clubs we frequented, drugs and drink were not only in abundance but also free because we found ourselves mingling with the main crooks of the time. Money was no object. We were still good friends with the McGoverns, who were making a name for themselves as a force to be reckoned with.

Once, I went with Pawny and one of his mates to a rave at Ferguslie Park in Paisley. It had been set up in a huge tent by the McGoverns and Grant McIntosh, known as 'Mr Paisley' because he was said to control the town. Grant was friendly and generous.

As we stood at the back of the marquee, I noticed a large group of individuals all dressed in suits and black overcoats heading straight towards us. I wondered what was happening, but by this time Pawny, alert as ever, had noticed something was up and could see it was Tony and Tommy McGovern with their crew. As soon as they reached us, Tony stuck out his hand and asked how I was getting on. He invited me to meet up with him, Tommy and their brother Steven for a few drinks in the forthcoming weeks. I was happy to agree, but thought, 'There's more to this than meets the eye.' It was true, I was good friends with the McGoverns, but for them to have me, Tam and Pawny on board would have made a formidable team. Tony joked to Pawny, 'Are you still running about daft trying to shoot everyone? You and Tommy would be brilliant together.' And that was a fact.

The next occasion on which I saw the McGoverns was a tragic one. By 1989, drugs had taken Steven's life. He had been a great friend of Pawny and after the funeral Tony asked us back to the Eagle Lodge in Sandyhills for something to eat with the rest of the immediate family. We were deeply moved by this kind gesture and by the warmth with which we were welcomed and made to feel part of the family. Sometimes, even now, Pawny will make a pilgrimage to Steven's grave to lay a few flowers and have a word with his friend.

Around this sad time my best mate, Mick Kenna from Posso, appeared at the High Court in Glasgow for two attempted murders and was sentenced to seven years. During my time at home, the pair of us had had some good nights out. I had often visited him in the house he shared with his girlfriend, but then a couple of weeks after he was jailed I was at the dancing with Tam and a crowd from Maryhill when I noticed her seemingly out with some guy. She didn't seem bothered by the fact we'd spotted her, so I went over and had it out with her in front of the stranger. I soon figured out from his accent that he was a Scouser up in Glasgow for the weekend. She was left in no doubt that I felt Mick deserved better. When the Scouser intervened, an argument started between us. At that, Tam came over and told me to leave it, that we'd get him outside. I knew what Tam meant – we would wait until they left and teach him a lesson – so I agreed. When we went outside, though, the pair of them were nowhere in sight. Thinking they'd probably worked out what we were up to and had done a runner, we decided to go and get a bag of chips round the corner.

As I walked into the chippy, I lifted my head just in time to be caught square on the jaw with a set of knuckledusters. It was a tremendous blow and just about knocked me out. By the time I orientated myself, Tam already had the perpetrator – the Scouser, of course – in a neck lock. Others joined in and from nowhere a knife appeared. Within seconds, the Scouser's legs and behind were saturated in blood. Still he would not go down. You had to hand it to him, he was a real go-ahead with no fear. Even when he was thrown through the chip shop window, covered in blood from head to toe, he wouldn't give up. Instead, he got to his feet, picked up a piece of smashed glass about a metre square and tried to attack me and Tam with it. By now, it was time to go. Somebody had called the police, who were appearing from all over, and so we made a fast exit.

None of us knew then that the fight was going to have very serious repercussions the following day, but we soon realised that when friends told us the Liverpudlian was a well-known gangster who had been up in Glasgow for the weekend to do business with a heavy team from Blackhill, Paul Ferris's home territory. We had already had a few run-ins with this crew because their main player spent a lot of time in Posso and at one time William Lobban had given him a hiding in a square-go. It was claimed that during this fight the guy had set his Alsatian dog on Lobban and when it started ripping at his legs, Tam had stabbed it. So, as you can imagine, this player was not at all keen on us.

When the telephone rang and I picked it up, Pawny was going mental about the fight. By now, word had shot around Glasgow about the struggle in the chippy and how the shop and street outside had run with blood.

I could hardly speak for a few weeks and thought my jaw had been broken. At one stage, as part of the peacemaking process, I had to go to a telephone meeting in Posso with Pawny in which the phone was put on loudspeaker. At the other end were the Scouser and the guy who headed the mob from Blackhill. The idea of the meeting was basically to come to an agreement to leave things as they were and for both sides to agree not to retaliate any further. The Scouser said, 'Yes, I have a few cuts or stab wounds to my arse and legs, but I'm happy with that since I've broken your brother's jaw.' Pawny cut in, 'Sorry, but you haven't. He's sitting here now. Do you want a word?' Clearly, the guy at the other end of the line was too astonished to ask me to speak. I was glad because I would have struggled to get a word out.

Captain Alex Shannon wearing Service Dress against the backdrop of the streets of north and east Glasgow, where he grew up. (© Brian Anderson)

Alex as an altar boy at St Ninian's, Fife, in 1979.

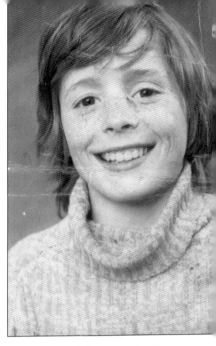

Alex aged about 11, when he was a pupil at Albert primary school.

Alex's best mate, Mick Kenna, and close pal Tam Fraser at the Brothers bar in 1983.

Young soldier Alex aged 18 at Port Stanley, the Falkland Islands, in March 1984.

Alex returning from the ship's medical room after being badly burned as a result of falling asleep on deck en route home from the Falklands in 1984.

Alex and Angie on their wedding day at Springburn in February 1985.

The family at a wedding in 1989. From left to right: standing, Jamie and Tam; sitting, Pawny, mum Ellen and Alex.

Alex knew butcher Danny McCann, who was shot during an SAS operation in Gibraltar in March 1988.

Ian 'Blink' McDonald who ran the Talisman bar and was a trusted friend of the Shannons. (© Brian Anderson)

Alex (left) and colleagues Pete and Peter test their weapons at the firing range at Ballykinler, Northern Ireland, in 1993.

Alex's favourite photograph of
Angie, taken in December 1995.

Alex (right) pauses briefly while on patrol
with two team members in highly dangerous
Crossmaglen, South Armagh, in 1993.

Heavily camouflaged Alex (right) gives orders during a live field firing
attack at Otterburn range in Northumberland in 1994.

Alex is presented with his Long Service and Good Conduct
Medal by Major General Mark Strudwick at Otterburn.

Alex liked and respected
Tony McGovern, who was
murdered in 2000.

Left to right: William Lobban,
Tam, Alex and Jamie at a New Year
party in Hartlepool in 2000.

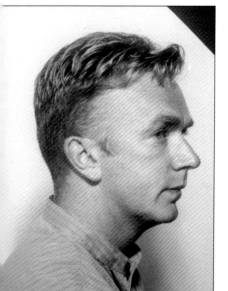

The Shannon family celebrated New year 2000 at Hartlepool with
William Lobban and friend. Standing left to right are Ellen
and her sons Jamie and Alex with Lobban, while kneeling are
Tam Shannon and Alex's son Thomas.

A treasured photograph at Edinburgh Castle after Alex and Angie
renewed their wedding vows in 2005. Left to right are:
Angie's sister Babs, Ellen, Alex, his late dad, Thomas, and Angie.

Alex (centre) with his immediate family at the silver wedding anniversary party in February 2010: (l to r) Nicole, Thomas, Alex, Angie and Danielle.

Alex takes a journey down memory lane in 2010, revisiting St Ninian's.

# CHAPTER SEVENTEEN

Ian 'Blink' McDonald was well known and liked in the Glasgow underworld. Some said his nickname was the result of a temporary childhood eye affliction; others that it had stuck because he could slash a rival faster than a victim could blink. He had carried out his share of slashings – Mars Bars, they were known in some circles, caused by deft use of a razor, a Hugh Fraser. Tall and impressive, he had at one time teamed up with Paul Ferris to raid jewellery shops and had been jailed for the theft of expensive clothing in Carlisle. He was a friend of the Thompsons and an admirer of young Arty's ability with guns, and he was trusted by the Shannons.

His mum and his wife Sheila had taken over a bar in the north end of Glasgow that had previously been the base from which a leading crime family ran their operations. The women were standing for no nonsense. It was their place now, and they made the rules, and the gang had effectively been kicked out.

The business was built up and then Sheila decided to run a place of her own. She talked it over with Blink and the decision was made to move into the Talisman bar on Balgrayhill Road, Springburn. It was a rough, tough joint that had been going downhill fast, but Sheila and Blink turned it round and good drinkers, the half and half men who were the bread and butter of any bar business, began returning.

As, of course, did men from the heart of gangland.

Tam Bagan and Paul Ferris would occasionally visit Blink and Sheila. The McGovern family sometimes called in for a drink or two, along with their friend Jamie Stevenson, who was

145

rapidly becoming a man to be reckoned with. One of his closest friends was Tony McGovern. Although not the eldest of the family, he was regarded by most as the brains and mastermind of their operations. The McIntyres, Duncan and Joe, were also customers. They ran with the McGoverns and Jamie Stevenson. The McIntyres knew the Shannons well, having lived in the same area of Springburn as youngsters, but for reasons best known to themselves allied themselves with the McGovern faction. The feeling at the time was that if you took on the McIntyres, you took on their army of associates as well.

Notorious hard man Frank Ward, a bodybuilding fanatic and thug, decided to use the Tally as his drinking hole when he was released from a stretch in prison, and sometimes the door would open and in would stride George 'Goofy' Docherty, a small-time hoodlum who liked to play the part of a gangster by wearing dark glasses and gloves that he said were necessary to prevent his hands sweating up in case he was needed to use a weapon at short notice. Most thought his antics over the top, but nobody said so to his face.

Then there were the Shannons: Tam, with his disregard for danger and notorious for his quick temper; Pawny, known to run one of, if not the most, thriving drugs rackets in the city; and Alex, cloaked in mystery.

One day at the Tally, Duncan McIntyre wandered over and asked about Alex's position within the army. At the mention of 'weapons instructor' in Alex's reply, McIntyre's eyes lit up. 'Is that so? God's sake.' He wandered off, evidently deep in thought.

The McGoverns tended to be wary of bars as a result of a particularly nasty incident when Steven had been alive. As was so often the case, silly words led to bullets. Someone close to the family had got into an argument in another pub in the district with a punter over a woman. A casual aside had become a full-scale shouting match and the woman's escort had left feeling insulted. Not long afterwards, Steven and his brother James were in the same pub, Thomson's Bar in Springburn, when a man entered by a side door and blasted them in the face. The odd thing was that he wasn't a regular street player, just someone who wasn't prepared to lie down and be walked over. The McGovern family would later own that same pub.

There were all sorts of customers at the Talisman bar. Sheila ran the place and made no bones about her being the boss. Generally, if she issued an instruction, it was obeyed. One thing that seemed to worry Blink, though, was the number of people who smoked hash inside. Eventually, it got so bad that some of the older regulars began complaining, joking it was a deliberate move to make sure their throats were always dry so they'd keep on drinking. Something had to be done. The solution was that a pool table was installed in one of the side rooms and the hash smokers were told, 'If you want to smoke that stuff, do it in the pool room where you won't be seen. But nowhere else.' They thought this was great and there was never any trouble after that.

Blink had been friends with the Shannons, Pawny and Tam in particular, for a long time. He would very occasionally see Alex coming in with his brothers and knew people wondered about him. Apart from the fact he was a soldier, no one was sure what he did in the army. A lot of rumours would float around the Tally, especially about his ability with and access to weapons, and because of the mystery surrounding him people tended to be wary of him. Blink kept a shotgun stashed away at the bar in case of bother, and the Shannon brothers knew where it was. No one else.

About this time, the McGoverns were making a real name for themselves. When Frank Ward was released, he looked up Blink and asked who the McGoverns were. Blink told him to stay away, but Frank was having none of it. He was determined to show them who ran the east end. He had been used to having things his own way and failed to realise that while he was in jail the balance of power in the east end, and Springburn especially, where he lived, had shifted in the McGoverns' favour.

Frank had an argument with Tony McGovern and was not the type to let a matter like that end there. Tony and his family were asleep in their home when it was firebombed. It was a cowardly attack that could have led to a major tragedy and even Tony was shaken. Some weeks later Ward was shot in both legs. He was recovering in hospital when Blink visited him. Ward evidently listened to Blink's good sense – there was no way Frank was going to win the fight. Neither side took the dispute further. While Ward remained a feared presence, he would never be a match for the McGovern family.

Alex was worried about his brothers. When Tam was locked up, it had left Pawny on his own, running his drugs trade, his success fetching jealous looks from others who fancied a hostile takeover. Major crews were selling at opposite ends of Springburn. These were allied but not averse to doing deals behind the back of the other. Neither was aware that they bought their gear from the same third party nor that he relied for his supplies on Pawny, who in addition to being a type of wholesaler had his own network of dealers. The two crews knew he was operating as a freelance but were reluctant to try chasing him out of a territory that they regarded as their own. But to have rivals coming at you from two sides could be dangerous. One of the McIntyre allies was a man we are calling 'Michael McKay', with whom Alex had already had a series of run-ins.

* * *

I never liked Michael McKay. I'd attacked him a couple of times while I was in the army and put a bottle over his head. I don't know why I had no time for him; there was just something about him I hated. I loathed him with a passion. He thought he was smart, possibly because his brother worked in the police force. He ended up especially close to the McIntyres, and as a result of their association with the McGoverns, plus the fact Tam had been doing a prison sentence, I couldn't really get to him. I had been waiting for Tam to be released in order to have back-up. Now, he was finally out.

McKay had at one time gone about with Jackie, who would become Pawny's wife. She had obviously decided she preferred Pawny and so this caused friction between the men. On top of that was the fact that I'd battered him with a bottle, while all the time there was the simmering anger by him and his cronies over our disregard for any territorial claims the McIntyres might have. It was a slap in the face to them that we just went about and did our own thing. Even Tam would punt whatever he wanted and they just wouldn't have a say in it. They found that quite annoying, plus they felt we were intimidating. They must have asked themselves time after time, 'How can they get away with all of this?' but nobody said anything to us, not even the McGoverns, and that must have riled the McIntyres even more. The attitude of the McGoverns was that we were pals. It was more 'Let them do what they want – unless something happens.'

So, the McIntyres and McKay decided to test which way the McGoverns would jump if it came to the crunch. They needed a flashpoint so that they could turn to the McGoverns and ask them to enter on their side. But trouble would not begin of its own accord; it had to be instigated. They needed to set off the fighting between us and once it began would put the onus on the McGoverns to intervene by simply saying: 'Look, they are fighting us, and you and we are all the one firm here.' It was a highly dangerous situation.

They decided the trigger would be McKay.

While training recruits at Glencorse, I continued to play football for army sides and after taking part in a match in Germany one weekend arrived home to disturbing news from Angie. She told me she had been in the Talisman on the Saturday night with a crowd that included Pawny and Tam when McKay walked in. It was busy, people were enjoying themselves and having a good time, but without warning he suddenly pulled out a big machete and began waving it about. This had been brewing for some time. It seemed they had deliberately planned an argument with Pawny that night. They had come all tooled up with knives and had attacked Pawny and Tam.

Blink was caught between a rock and a hard place. It was his wife's bar and now he would have to step in and sort things. He was a very close friend of ours, but he had to think of his other customers. We had always promised ourselves that if anything kicked off in the Talisman, then we'd be backing him, and we knew he would never let us down. He also knew our family would not take any rubbish from these clowns. McKay didn't hit anyone, but Tam pulled out a knife, then other knives were produced, and everybody was trying to stab each other. The fight then spilled out onto the main road, stopping traffic, while Pawny and Tam went ahead and took on McKay and the McIntyres.

Next day, it flared up again. Tam had lots of friends, among them Jamie Daniel and Derek 'Deco' Ferguson, two men with plenty of gangland pull, but he preferred not to involve anyone outside the family circle. Tam chased the McIntyres and their hangers-on all the way down Galloway Street and even tried to shoot a few of them. Pawny drove the car round to collect Tam halfway down the street and as Tam jumped in, he pulled the trigger again and took off the top of his shoes. He was very lucky not to have lost his toes. Now, the gloves were off. This was the start of a long feud that would go on for years.

When Angie told me the news, I knew it had been deliberately kicked off to bring in the McGoverns, so I began trying to get to them to ask whom they were backing. Reaching them would prove not as easy as it sounded, and a good deal of unpleasantness and danger followed.

While this was kicking off, William Lobban had been moved to Dungavel open prison on the outskirts of Glasgow to serve the remainder of his six-year sentence. Previously the Duke of Hamilton's hunting lodge, it was the spot where Adolf Hitler's deputy Rudolf Hess was heading in 1941 when he made his astonishing flight from Germany seeking to end the Second World War.

After the battle at the Tally, we all went up to see Lobban to let him know what had been going on. Prison staff had to keep a detailed record of all visitors and who they met. It turned out to be sheer good fortune that Tam and I were down to visit one of Tam's mates from Govan who was doing a lifer. Pawny and a pal called Ronnie Curry were on the visiting order to see Lobban, but we all took the opportunity to brief him on our problems.

We had a long conversation with Gibby and it turned out following the chat that he had decided he was going on the run so he could help us out. One thing I will say for him, he had no fear.

He might have been offering to do us a good turn then, but in later years we would come to hate him and he us. Some say he is the devil personified and I would now tend to agree with this. When he asked to be interviewed by the *News of the World* in 2005, Lobban said the reason he had absconded from Dungavel was because of his mother's illness. He said he had been a model prisoner, but after a couple of weekend leaves he got a pass to visit a hospital to have tattoos removed and did not go back. He also said Arthur Thompson had offered him work. But I know it was because of us, we who had knocked around with him through his adolescence, that he did a runner.

Lobban didn't tell us how he was escaping or when he would do it. After the prison realised he was gone, and apparently wasn't coming back, the police were contacted and asked to find him. People went missing from open prisons regularly and there was a routine to be followed. The police visited his family first and, discovering he was clearly not there, looked up who his latest visitors had been. As a result, they called at and searched the homes of Pawny and Ronnie, but found nothing. They would continue occasional searches of this sort for some considerable time afterwards and I would have very special cause to be thankful that I had been down as visiting someone else that night in Dungavel.

* * *

Meanwhile, my days as a soldier were rapidly coming to an end and I felt my discharge could not come quickly enough. Too many things were going on in Glasgow and I felt I needed to be there. Much as I had been exhilarated by my spell in Northern Ireland, I had been unable to shake off the feeling that I needed a change. Because I had been in the army from such a young age, I had done the entire career course and yet people kept commenting that I was still young. At times, my youth made others believe I was a recruit, so I felt a bit of a burnout. Maybe I peaked too soon and needed a complete break, something totally different to recharge the batteries. I had believed you rose up the promotion ladder depending on your abilities, but

I found that wasn't the case. I had reached the rank of corporal but was effectively living the life of a civilian. Anyway, I simply made up my mind to get out and I did.

We had a beautiful home and I thought a job would be guaranteed. Friends tried talking me out of it, and a lot of high-ranking officers told me I was on a fast career path and I would definitely go to the Royal Military Academy at Sandhurst, the elite British Army officers' training centre, but the truth was I was living a double life. During the working week, I was a soldier. The rest of the time I was going about with gangsters.

# CHAPTER EIGHTEEN

I gave up the army at the beginning of 1991. While I was attempting to get full-time work on building sites as a mechanical digger driver, I was also running around with my brothers, trying not to worry Angie and the children. Diplomacy, I knew, was needed in my continued efforts to try to soothe the McGoverns into sitting out the fight, but Lobban seemed hell-bent on keeping the pot of hatred boiling. In leaving the army, I had given up killings and bombings on the streets of Belfast for a Glasgow riddled with the problems of drink and drugs. If you were on the happy drugs like cocaine, fine and well; if not, then the chances were you were out trying to kill somebody. As events just around the corner would prove, it was as dangerous a time as there had been in gangland Glasgow.

For people in that environment, it was really worrying. Not for those on the outside, but for the families of whoever was involved. I know Mum was worried sick all the time about us, but the foolish thing about Tam and me was that once we had a few drinks in us our inhibitions went. We just didn't care.

* * *

Those close to Alex wondered if there was an additional reason behind his choice of career change: his concern for his brothers. Had that helped fan the decision to quit the army? Certainly there were those who believed that his entry full-time into gangland with his skills and knowledge of weapons could tip the balance of power away from the McIntyre faction. Or did he sense there was someone on the loose who couldn't be trusted?

William Lobban had never been a shrinking violet. Most inmates fleeing prison lay low, hoping not to attract attention. Not so Gibby. His actions would leave a legacy of deceit, hatred and desire for revenge that remains in Glasgow to this day.

A few days after going on the run, like a substitute coming off the bench in a football final to score with his first touch, he immediately made his presence felt. In the knowledge that the feud between the Shannons and McIntyres was likely to turn into a full-scale war in which the strong McGovern faction might enter on the side of the latter, Lobban took a hand. It was not necessarily one that Alex appreciated. His army experience in Belfast had taught him about the morale-sapping effect of surprise attacks. In Glasgow, he found himself in a not dissimilar situation, being directly involved in a battle on the streets. His side could effectively be taking on the rest of Springburn gangland, a perilous and potentially deadly action. In Ireland, there had at least been the army to play piggy in the middle; there, the police only showed once there were bodies to pick up.

Hours after Tam and Pawny had fired shots during the run-in that followed the rumpus at the Talisman, a man strode into the Spring Inn on Springburn Road and, after looking around, spotted a close relative of Duncan McIntyre enjoying a harmless and peaceful drink with friends. In gangland circles, this relative would be regarded as a non-combatant, someone not involved in nefarious activity and therefore to be left alone. The visitor held no such respect for this unwritten code. He invited the drinker outside and as he reached Springburn Road whipped a pistol from his trousers, stuck it in the man's mouth and told him to take a message back to McIntyre that a reckoning would come soon for the attack in the Talisman. 'I'm giving you a break,' said the gunman. 'You have three seconds to get away from here before I shoot you.'

As he began his count, his hapless victim fled. When it reached three, true to his word he fired, but into the gantry of the bar. As the gunman left, startled drinkers noted how similar he was in appearance and demeanour to William Lobban. It was a nasty incident, but things were about to worsen.

# THE UNDERWORLD CAPTAIN

George Madden was a good friend of Duncan McIntyre and the McGoverns. His brother Charles, a friend of Pawny, had been only 27 when he was killed in a knife attack in Possilpark in 1985. George would later become a partner with the youngest of the McGovern brothers, Paul, in a legitimate and successful security firm, M and M Security. He was loyal and could be trusted, and the extent of that loyalty was about to be tested.

Knowing of his friendship with Duncan, Pawny, Tam and Lobban went up to George's house on Springburn Road. The madcap plan was simple. Lobban would go to the door dressed as a gas board worker with the others hiding at his shoulder and when the door was opened they would pile in and tie Madden up. He would then be forced to lure Duncan to the house, where they could shoot him. What they did not take into account was George's determination not to set anybody up at any cost, even though the potential was there for him to be seriously injured. Alex heard from his brothers what happened.

They got into the house, Lobban carrying a length of rope, but when they found Madden, they didn't have to tie him up. He told them there was no way he was going to telephone and set somebody up. He didn't want to be involved in whatever it was they had going. They could see where he was coming from and realised that there was no point in roping a guy in who had nothing to do with it. George saw at the time why they were doing it and as they left they told him they wouldn't take things any further – but they were determined to get their target one way or another.

The problem was actually getting to Duncan. If he was at home with his wife, then attacking him there would be a non-starter because of her presence. And usually if he was not in his house then he was in the heart of Springburn visiting the McGoverns. Timing was crucial. It was a case of waiting, no matter how long that took, and eventually someone would get their man.

Of course, business had to continue, even in the midst of a war. The incident on the Kingston Bridge had not deterred the successful operations of Pawny and Tam. Alex had by now moved to an area in Maryhill, Glasgow, known appropriately as the Barracks, and his family soon joined him there. Angie was glad to leave Lasswade, while he felt more comfortable now he was nearer to help out his brothers.

Not long before Lobban absconded, a bag had been left at Alex's new address. He knew the identity of the courier, but when he asked what was inside he was told, 'Nothing of concern.' When the visitor left, his curiosity won the day. Alex was shocked to see at least two loaded handguns, around fourteen kilos of heroin, approximately 20,000 temazepam tablets and £20,000 in cash. The contents were worth a small fortune – and a very lengthy prison sentence if the bag was discovered. What particularly worried him was that police were still sporadically visiting and searching the homes of known associates of Lobban, and sometimes these searches included the use of sniffer dogs.

He made a telephone call asking for the bag to be taken away but was told this could not be done for some time as those responsible for it feared they were under police surveillance. He was determined the bag and its contents would not remain in the house, a feeling made all the stronger when he told an enquiring Angie what was inside. She had threatened to leave him if anything like that happened again. One day two-year-old Danielle wandered into the living room carrying one of the loaded guns, causing her parents to instinctively dive for cover. Alex swore not just to move the bag right away, but to never again allow weapons or drugs in his home.

Remembering his army training, the patrols in Northern Ireland and the Winthrop Theory, which used features such as lamp posts and hedges to identify hiding places, that night he bought short sections of drainage pipe and, with Angie pushing Danielle in her pram, set off to the banks of the River Kelvin. While in Ulster, he had seen army colleagues dig up similar pipes from the ground and was told this was a favoured IRA method of safely storing weapons and ammunition. Now, while Angie kept watch, he dug holes and the following night went back, this time with the guns, drugs and money in the pram.

He firmly taped the ends of the pipes to ensure they were waterproof and buried them four feet down. Having used the Winthrop Theory to mark their position, he looked down and realised no one would spot where he had dug. His pipe hides were secure.

Alex knew his actions sounded selfish. He could have argued he was anxious to protect Angie and the children, but in reality he wanted the highly incriminating materials out of the family home, while at the same time wanted to make sure they were securely hidden. Loyal as ever, Angie had helped sneak guns out of the house to the hiding place. She felt she had to support her husband through her love for him and because of his love for his brothers Pawny and Tam. Had she believed any of this was to help Lobban, she would have had second thoughts. She didn't like Lobban, hated it when he visited their home, despised his links to crime and criminals and thought there was something odd about his behaviour. Angie was sure Alex had severed his connection to Lobban and was happy with that thought. But she was also angry at what she saw as Alex taking advantage of her wifely duties. And she felt guilty at using her daughter, by secreting weapons in the pram with the child, confident that should they be stopped by police no one would think of lifting the blankets to search.

Alex by his own admission was now running freely with gangsters. He knew things were beginning to get out of hand, a fact brought home to him by Pawny's close shave during a visit to a friend of the family who lived in Possil. As the two sat chatting, suddenly her front door was booted in and eight members of the Springburn crew piled in, among them two men still active in the Glasgow crime scene and a third, then a leading light in the underworld but now keeping his head down following a murder attempt some years ago. Pawny knew there was only one way out – through the living-room window. The fact it was closed made no difference. He ran, took a dive, staggered to his feet and fled to safety. It was only the sheer number of his attackers that made it difficult for them to get out into the street after him. Alex knew that had Pawny been caught, he would have been killed. In reprisal, the Shannons made another bid to murder Duncan McIntyre.

* * *

We were constantly trying to get to each other and on at least two occasions in Balgrayhill, Duncan was involved in a hit and run. Witnesses told the police they had seen the car drive into him, then reverse over his body as he lay on the ground. He survived.

One night after leaving the Tower Bar in Possil, Tam and I were crossing a footbridge over Galloway Street when we suddenly realised we were about to be cornered by all the main players in the Springburn Mob. Jamie Stevenson and Tony McGovern were among them. Some of them pulled out handguns. We ran in separate directions, hoping to split them up, and Tam got away, but for some reason I got the impression they had all followed me. I jumped into one of the drying areas and fortunately it was pitch black. Even so, Jamie stuck his head in, looked about and thankfully shouted back, 'There's nobody here.' To this day, I am convinced he must have seen me.

Anyway, it was a lucky escape for me. I would always be more careful from then on, but Tam was fearless. I would be with him when on the spur of the moment he would lead me straight to the Talisman to see who was there and who he could have it out with. There were never any takers. I believe that on the odd occasion this happened, the mob must have thought Pawny or a team backing us was waiting outside. In fact, it was just me and him, one knife between us.

# CHAPTER NINETEEN

I had become very friendly with George Redmond around this time. I had first met him when Pawny had taken me to a New Year party in 1990. He and George were in business together, moving drugs. People had gone from taking heroin to mainly Ecstasy, which could fetch up to £20 a tablet. The things were phenomenal, but, as youngsters like Leah Betts would later discover to their cost, could also be lethal. But that's where the money was and George was making a lot of it. He and Pawny dealt in batches of 20,000 to 40,000. They would collect the drugs when they were sent up from the London money men and have them either delivered to a list of given addresses or collected. Alongside this business, George was also running another, making money from all the pubs in town by selling drugs. He knew a lot of my pals, but until then I hadn't been introduced because I had been serving abroad with the army.

The amazing thing was that when I met him, George was on the run for murder. He had been accused of killing somebody at the Pinkston bar, yet there he was, living openly in Possil and walking about Glasgow as though he hadn't a care in the world. The police knew he was somewhere in the city; they were forever kicking in doors looking for him, but never the right doors. So, while they looked, he went on making money.

All the time his brother was inside doing a life sentence for a murder he had not committed.

George was a brilliant guy. On the night of my birthday in February 1991, I went to the Savoy with him. This was a time when you never had to pay for drugs. If you went to a party or out for the night, there always seemed to be plenty and they were free. We met up with Pawny, Tam, a pal of theirs from London and a crowd from Milton who were carrying guns.

Later that evening, Tam, the London guy and I were invited back to a party in Milton; however, it proceeded to go pear-shaped because Tam had taken an E and was spewing into a sink. It was one of those parties where everybody had their best gear on, was wearing suits. We saw a few teams we knew as bank robbers, but then they began laughing at Tam for being sick, telling him to get a grip. Well, unfortunately for them they didn't know who Tam was. When he cleaned himself up, he began asking who they thought they were talking to. Funnily enough, all of a sudden people were darting in and out of doors and coming back carrying bags. We knew there were guns inside and so Tam, me and the pal from London phoned Pawny to tell him to come down tooled up. He was outside waiting for us. Suddenly, it was stand-off time. It was crazy how these things happened.

There we were, tooled up, no fears, and them knowing we weren't bank robbers and therefore were more than likely to go ahead. So, that was it. As far as they were concerned, we were businessmen and they didn't want trouble. It was my first experience of the Milton crew. And the last. Next day Pawny had to intervene, make all the usual phone calls, get it all sorted and make sure there would be no comeback.

George was always there when we needed back-up and I knew we could rely on him. Similarly, if he needed help, we would do the same for him. I found George a really loyal and honest guy, always upfront, certainly never a liberty taker. For some reason, he took a shine to me, but there was often friction between his younger brother Sean and me, and George would often sort it out by grabbing him and telling him, 'Pack it in. Stop it!' Tam had a temper that went off like a grenade, whereas George never really showed that side of his personality, while I knew he was capable of that level of violence. There were lots of things happening at that time, but none of it really serious.

I remember going into Peggy Sue's, the club on West George Street in the town centre, one night with the pair of them. We had literally just walked in the door; I had asked George what he wanted to drink and had gone up to the bar but hadn't even been served when a guy came running out of the toilet, blood everywhere, with his jaw hanging off. I turned around and only then noticed George and Tam scuttling out of the door. The guy had a blade in his hand and was shouting and swearing at me: 'You fucker! You were with them. What was that all about?' And I was saying, 'What are you talking about, mate?' trying to calm him down and tell him I knew nothing about it. There was only one way in and one way out and he was blocking it. I managed to talk my way outside and left, but I never ever found out why they had taken his face off. Eventually, I met up with them again – I knew they would be at a big party in Hamilton Hill in Possil. There was loads of Red Stripe Jamaican beer and I was shouting, 'You arseholes! You left me,' but George was laughing and telling me not to worry. 'If anything happened to you,' he said, 'we were coming down to sort it all out.'

In those days, money was no object. We used to buy the dearest drinks, while the drugs were for everybody. And we never seemed to pay for it. It was a case of there you go, help yourself. I learned in that short period that in the drugs trade the higher up the chain you are, the less hands-on you need to be. The only time the men at the top use their hands is to make a phone call or two. Others do all the running around. George very rarely sold drugs himself. I'd be at his house and it would be a case of him making calls and telling someone to pick that up from there or take this there. But he never got the big money – that was for the men putting up the money. All he did was cream the profit. Still, any time I was in George's house there were people turning up with bags of Es and there would be lots of cocaine. 'Just dip your face in it,' you'd be told. He reminded me of Al Pacino as the cocaine baron in *Scarface* sitting behind a mountain of the stuff.

All the time the war with the McIntyres was ongoing. Now and then Pawny or Gibby would turn up. They had maybe become involved in an argument at the dancing and would want to know where the guns were. I'd take them over the fence, then I'd climb down by the canal, dig them up, hand them over and say, 'There you are, away you go.' When they came back, I'd bury them again. Anything, as long as they weren't in the house.

I knew Angie hated my lifestyle and I would have done anything to protect my relationship with her and my kids. Within weeks of leaving there had been talk as to whether I should go back into the army, but instead I tried to arrange my movements, especially my exploits with my brothers, as though it was a normal working day, leaving at breakfast and returning in time to play and chat with the children in the evening. I would not allow any of my family to come near my house after eight in the evening, unless it was an emergency.

I didn't enjoy this lifestyle and hadn't really wanted to get involved, but sadly I was weak and had allowed myself to be led into serious situations. I perhaps gave the appearance of not giving Angie and the kids a second thought, which wasn't the case. I always tried to keep Angie away from it all and would often be evasive or even lie to her, but this was only to protect her, as I knew she would constantly worry about me. I'm not proud of the way I acted in those years. Hindsight is a great gift, but I wish maybe I had done and said certain things differently.

* * *

While Angie suspected her husband was taking chances, she could not be sure. But still she worried. And just as she hated Lobban's unexpected arrivals, now she resented appearances at their door by Tam, who could be especially bad tempered. There was an incident when he turned up at the house covered in blood wanting a change of clothing. She told her husband to get him out of the house. After that, every time Tam came to the door it seemed it was because something was wrong.

Alex didn't work, but money was never short – his brothers saw to that – so it meant Angie could give the kids what they had been used to when Alex was getting army pay, which was one benefit. But often when he was out at night Angie would worry there would be trouble – and she was right to be concerned.

# THE UNDERWORLD CAPTAIN

Alex, who had spent his adult life upholding rules and obeying orders, was rapidly developing into an outlaw; he was becoming as much a part of gangland as the brothers who had so long admired him for staying on the opposite side of the divide. A classic example of how ruthless he could be was about to be demonstrated.

Alex knew of one family member who had sadly fallen into the drugs pit. Addicted to heroin and at the mercy of anyone willing to supply her next tiny bag, she had a big family and, like so many young women caught in the poverty trap, was seemingly forever pregnant and surrounded by screaming children. She had despaired and found smack to be a way of floating, if briefly, into a trance of pleasure in which she could forget her cares. The trouble with heroin is that one session is never enough. As she deteriorated, she complained of being beaten up by a male friend. After one especially nasty beating, when she was viciously punched and kicked in the groin, she had taken an overdose. Alex was furious.

In hindsight, Alex would wonder whether these attacks, however unjustified, were simply caused by the frustration of a man trying to cope with life amid demanding children and their near junkie mother, but at the time, in his rage, he turned judge and jury and decided to mete out his own sentence of punishment.

* * *

I look back and think to myself, 'God's sake, was I doing that?' I'm sure a lot of us feel that way, but one Sunday night at around ten o'clock I found myself at the back of the close where she stayed three floors up. Tam and Pawny were with me. We had parked our cars around the corner and I was now holding a machete. We weren't going to use a gun or anything like that – there would have been no point. Guns were used when someone was to be executed, or at least shot up; here, I had decided on a different form, a reduced level of punishment. These were the days when slashing somebody was a lesser punishment than shooting them.

As we stood at the foot of the stairs, I said to the others, 'Give me the machete. We'll go up there and if you just hold him down, I'll cut his two thumbs off.' The reason I had decided to cut off his thumbs was that if you are without a thumb you can't really do anything with the other four digits. It's like cutting your toes off. That's the way I had started thinking. There was no point in stabbing somebody when you could cut his Achilles tendon or take his toes off. Tam was normally the violent one, but along with Pawny even he was saying that was taking it too far. I was arguing that we'd just go up and cut his fingers off, but the others were still against this.

After about half an hour literally arguing at the back of this close, Tam says, 'I'll tell you what we'll do, we'll go up the stairs. If the pair of them are full of it, full of fight and rowing, then we'll do what you say. But if they are straight, cool and calm, we'll just walk away and leave them, and put what he did down to a bad experience.' We agreed on that and went upstairs. We walked through their door and found the place immaculate. They were sitting watching television, all lovey-dovey. I was still saying to myself, 'Wait a minute, here. I can't come all the way and not do anything,' so in the end I tried to start an argument with the pair of them. At that they asked if I was just there to cause trouble.

By now, my brothers were getting restless, telling me it was time to go, so we left. The guy didn't know how close he had come to losing his thumbs. If we had gone in there and the house had been a mess, or either of them had given us any excuse, then they were coming off.

This incident shows how I was already at a stage where I could totally put feelings to one side. Had I become callous? When I look back, I wonder how I ended up doing that. I believe it was a culmination of things building up over the previous two years, a deterioration in me from somebody who could differentiate between right and wrong, who had emotions and feelings. Why I had become so desensitised I neither knew nor cared. The fact is I was playing a new game with different rules. In other circumstances, it could have been me being threatened with having my thumbs chopped off. The margin between keeping and losing them could simply be a cuddle, as we had shown. Fortunately, the guy still had all his fingers. But it could have gone the other way.

While I had been in the army, I had done my best to stay in line and had avoided the temptation to experiment with drugs. Now in Civvy Street, I sampled Ecstasy and temazepams, and flirted briefly with cocaine, though I never ventured towards heroin. During leaves, I had been anxious to avoid trouble. Now, with the uniform and shackles off, I was being increasingly drawn into the gangland world of my brothers. My attitude towards violence was changing dramatically; the machete incident was just one example.

While I was anxious to build the family strength by cementing good relationships with, for instance, my old friends the McGoverns, sometimes my efforts seemed to take a backward step because of others. Lobban, a known affiliate of ours, was clouding our good name by becoming known as someone who could not be trusted and we needed to distance ourselves from him. Tam's bravery, and his penchant for violence, caused problems, too. Thankfully, it was his sheer reputation that often scared away potential retaliation.

Something would simply come into his head and he'd disappear. One night we were in the Tower Bar and I came back from the toilet to discover he had gone. I asked the barmaid where he was and she just pointed to the door and said, 'He's disappeared.'

I ran outside, saw a taxi and assumed it was him inside. I opened the door and leapt in as it was pulling away. Tam was there. 'Where are you going, Tam?' I asked. He said nothing and the taxi drove straight to the Talisman. It was a Friday night, full house. Tam opened the door and at the bar were about a dozen of the McIntyres and their crew. He walked right into the middle of them and said, 'I'm not here for any of you tonight. I'll leave you. But I'm here for him.' Everyone knew who he was referring to even before he pointed.

The individual, who I'll call 'Peter Coward', had instigated a dreadful attack some time earlier on my dad, by now a harmless and helpless alcoholic who sought and caused no trouble to anyone. As the old man was leaving the Talisman one night, he was set upon by a gang who were little more than animals and had given him a terrible beating. Now we could see that although Coward had cronies around to protect him, the expression on his face showed he was nevertheless afraid. Neither he nor his pack knew I was unarmed, or that Tam had only a single knife. I was asking myself how this was going to go down. The opposition probably had the same thought. It kicked off with a few punches being thrown, but that was as far as it went and we left with them cowering in a corner, Coward's mates protesting they didn't want trouble. The truth is that Coward and his crew were too scared to move, thinking that Pawny and a team of our friends were waiting outside for anyone venturing through the door. They also knew they had to be careful. The Talisman was one of our regular haunts; we were often in there and they could easily be picked off.

As the days passed, they became increasingly worried about us, wondering what we were planning. Adding to their paranoia was the fact that each day we would sit at the Springbank Cottage bar in Garscube Road with our friends Robert Taylor and Drew Elliott. Sometimes Frank McPhie, known as 'the Iceman', would appear. Maybe Coward and his pals had the idea we were watching for them.

Tam was determined he would have his revenge on Coward. One night he had sat for six hours in Springburn Park watching and waiting. When he had spotted his quarry, he had slashed him severely in retribution for the savage attack on Dad. Coward had to be taken to hospital. Others had also been eager to leave a mark of their own disgust on him and had set off to visit him only to find him guarded by police. It would not be the last chapter in that story.

\* \* \*

While I had been a serving soldier, I had little understanding of the extent of the violence facing my family. My brothers made little play of the risks they took or fights in which they became involved. Now, seeing the ongoing war against the other crews in Springburn brought home to me the level of hatred and viciousness.

# THE UNDERWORLD CAPTAIN

I became increasingly conscious of curiosity in my army background and knew my skill with guns was attracting interest. When you look back, you see things differently. I only realised much later that I had had an intimidating effect without actually doing anything. I was always just into having a drink and a good time, being nice to people who would say, 'He's a good guy,' but that would be in circles not involved in the bother. Once I was among those who were part of the trouble, there was a very different slant to my presence. 'Need to watch him. He's very deep, always thinking, always looking at things and analysing them.' That was more the impression I seemed to make. In fact, I wasn't conscious of doing any of that. I was simply out to enjoy myself.

* * *

Was his full-time presence creating too much interest in the brothers' activities? Pawny had been advocating for some time the need for a hideaway where the family would meet without fear of rivals knowing. He did not want to rent, so suggested the brothers buy a suitable house. Alex's commendable army record made him the logical choice to apply for a mortgage, with Pawny guaranteeing the deposit and monthly payments. It was left to Alex to choose and he settled on a house in North Carbrain, Cumbernauld, but it was a choice he would come to regret. The brothers had unwittingly moved into the Cumbernauld equivalent of Springburn or Posso, and it had more than its share of wild teenagers and hoods. Plus, the house ended up being a bolt hole out of the way for all sorts of people on the run from the police.

Buying the house would turn out to be a bad move, life threatening, and one the brothers came to regret.

# CHAPTER TWENTY

Lobban was known as 'Mr Benn' after the animated television series about a businessman who each day changes his outfit and becomes another character. Gibby had always been looked on as something of a mystery, his loyalties forever in doubt. Many thought of him as a cobra, capable of shooting poison into anyone around him regardless of whether they were friend or foe. For now, he wore the same colours as the Shannons, but for how long would that continue? As the months passed, it would be those who had been his friends who would be the victims of his treachery.

Meanwhile the skirmishes with the McIntyre team and their backers were an increasing irritant to the Shannons, who were by now fed up running about trying first to find their targets and then to shoot or stab them. One day, the snake Lobban came up with a solution. 'Let's go straight for the top. Cut the head of the viper off, two vipers, and then we'll be able to do our own thing.'

He convinced the Shannons it was the best way to go. He sounded almost like an army strategist as he expounded on his theory. 'There's no point in aiming for the foot soldiers because there will always be somebody willing to take their place. Just go straight for the top.' Alex agreed: take out the main man and it would be problem solved. It was time to rid themselves of the cause of this cancer that was eating at the family heart.

Two people were to be murdered in different parts of the ʹne was said to be a leader in the McIntyre camp who lived in the north end, the other a businessman who had offered support to this group. It would be a daring, audacious strike guaranteed to leave the whole of Glasgow gangland quaking. To take out two of the highest-profile figures in the underworld in a single swoop, much as the Corleone family did in *The Godfather*, would give undisputed control to those responsible. No one would offer a challenge, knowing it would leave them vulnerable to similar treatment. The assassins would be Alex and Lobban. Alex had reservations, though, about whether the man he was to kill was sufficiently high profile. His chosen target would have been someone else in the same crew.

The movements of the targets had been carefully watched, the plot to kill them worked out in detail. The hits would be made on a Sunday night when it was known both were in the habit of sitting in their respective homes watching television with their families. Neither had any cause to suspect they were going to be attacked and for that reason would almost certainly answer in person when someone knocked on their door. Alex would provide the handguns and Pawny act as driver. Everything was set, times and distances calculated to the last detail. The shootings would be simultaneous, leaving no chance for the families of one victim to telephone a warning to the other.

Alex had one major obstacle to overcome. Leaving the house late on a Sunday evening would leave naturally curious Angie to wonder where he was going. He could, of course, simply tell a lie by saying he was off for a few drinks with family or friends, but the relationship with his wife, by now into its sixth year, had been built on honesty. The couple believed in one another and in what they said. If something went wrong and Angie discovered the reason for his absence, how would she react? On the other hand, he could not tell her the truth. To have done so would have made her complicit in the heinous crimes he and Lobban were about to commit. So he devised a compromise.

He decided to tell her nothing. He would slip her a Mickey Finn, drug her, leave, murder, return and wait for her to wake up as though she had simply nodded off. She would have no reason to believe her husband had not been by her side throughout. And so, on the chosen night, the children had been put to bed and were asleep as he rested on the comfortable settee, his arm around Angie's shoulder. As the time to leave drew near, he offered to make tea and spiked the drink with around eight temazepams. Angie's head slowly drooped and she quietly went off to sleep.

Why did he choose such a course? Was it selfish, to make sure he had a cast-iron alibi by leading her to believe he had been with her all the time? Or was it because he didn't want her to be involved in any way? This way if she was ever questioned by the police it would be impossible for her to lie. All she would be able to say was she had been sleeping.

It was dark as he made his way to the banks of the Kelvin river. He used his knowledge of the Winthrop Theory to find, in the pitch black, where the pipe hides were located. The drugs and money had long gone to their intended destinations. He removed the pistols and replaced the pipes. That done, he walked to a phone box in Maryhill from which he telephoned Pawny to tell him everything was set. 'Right, hang on there. I'm on my way,' he was told.

It was around eight o'clock. Alex stood near the phone box and waited, and waited. Pawny should have been with him in only a few minutes. They had no mobile telephones then, so he rang Pawny's home only to be told he had left some time earlier.

Again, he waited, a bag under his arm holding the weapons. Curious police patrols passed by, scrutinising him but not stopping to question or search. At eleven, having stood in vain for three hours, he gave up, reburied the weapons and went home. Angie was still asleep on the settee. He sat down beside her, wondering what had happened to his brother, and within five minutes she woke up. He believed fate had warned him to give up waiting and get home when he did.

Next day, he telephoned Pawny. 'What happened?' Alex asked.

'Fucking car broke down. Couldn't get it going and no way of getting a message to you. No phone near.'

In a way, Alex was glad the murder plot had failed. He had

seen his target but hadn't spoken to him. He found it difficult to believe that he was going to knock at the man's door and, when he answered, put a bullet in his head. What he found most surprising was that he didn't have a care in the world about doing it. Once he'd carried out the murder, that would be the end of it. He had set out to kill a man who had never harmed him or his family for the sole reason that he happened to be in the opposing team.

There was a parallel in what he'd planned to do in the anonymous killings committed by the terrorists in Northern Ireland whom he'd not so long ago monitored. They too murdered men simply for being on the wrong side.

He debated with himself when to admit to Angie what he had done that night. Months later, when he was back in uniform, he told her the whole story. She listened and said nothing, but her anger was apparent. To this day, she has never forgiven him.

The plot to wipe out two of the leading lights behind the Springburn crew might have been aborted, but the desire of the Shannons and their friends to remove the opposition continued to escalate.

Meanwhile, Alex found himself in demand.

* * *

In this, the first half of 1991, the storm was leading to the hurricane. It was a time for taking sides and taking stock. Arthur Thompson, deprived of the services of Paul Ferris and Tam Bagan, was looking forward to the release from prison of Arty. The heir to the Thompson throne had been promised weekend leaves from open prison, but his threats and clumsy efforts at retribution on those he saw as enemies, mostly made on the back of his father's name, had left him more despised than he realised.

A short distance across the city Tam McGraw was building up strength in the Caravel pub, planning a coup that would make him and others millionaires. The idea was to smuggle huge amounts of Moroccan hashish from Spain in coaches by offering free holidays to young people and deprived Glasgow families. McGraw was already wealthy, and there were some who were envious of his riches and upset at being left out of the hash bonanza.

Paul Ferris, having split with the Godfather, had been briefly linked with McGraw, the Licensee. Now, since his departure from the Ponderosa, he discovered that he was increasingly a target for the police.

These three – Thompson, McGraw and Ferris – went about with £50,000 contracts on their heads. Was each trying to rub the other out? Were others further afield, in London and Merseyside, behind the bounties? Money by the bucketful was on offer, but only to the right man. Finding him was the problem.

At about this time word was quietly spreading that on the streets was an ex-soldier belonging to a tough north end family who was versed in gangland ways. Embroiled in a vicious gang war, he was highly skilled in weapons. Alex Shannon knew that he could become a rich man just by pulling a trigger. The offers were coming left, right and centre. He wasn't interested. But still they kept coming.

In fact, he was already mulling over a change in his career – but not to become a hit man. He was contemplating a return to the army. Angie had given him an ultimatum: soldier or separate. She was increasingly disturbed by the mystery surrounding so many of his actions and by his links to Lobban.

The Shannons had also suffered a blow in their fight against the McIntyre brigade, with the loss of their good friend Blink McDonald. Along with five other Glaswegians – Thomas Carrigan, Robert Harper, Michael Carroll and brothers Mick and James Healy – he had gone down to Devon to rob a bank in Torquay of £6 million. Mick Healy was on the run at the time from Shotts prison, where he had been serving ten years for robbery before fleeing in a butcher's van. The bank raid was wracked by bad luck and ultimately failed. Blink escaped back to Glasgow but was arrested when armed police burst into a Chinese restaurant where he and Sheila were dining. The angry restaurateur was left furiously waving his unpaid bill. Blink had a gun but was never able to use it. The men endured a wait of two years and a series of aborted trials to hear their long sentences.

During that time, there were many other developments in Glasgow and when the name Lobban was mentioned to Mick Healy, he had a frightening story to tell of betrayal.

Healy had been at home when he suddenly found himself looking into a pistol held by Ferris, who had been let into his home by Lobban. Ferris had been hearing tales that Healy had called him a grass, a hated police informer. Those tales came from Lobban. Ferris blasted a bullet into Healy's music player, then demanded to know whether the stories were true. Healy denied the accusation and Ferris left, but the incident had left both men angry and wondering about Lobban. Healy, in particular, would not forget Gibby's role.

Mr Benn had, of course, switched his allegiance from the Shannons to Ferris. That did not mean he was in an opposition camp, because Ferris knew the family from way back, especially Pawny. While they might not have been bosom buddies, there was at least a mutual respect. But the Shannons began wondering what Lobban might be saying about them. They already had to contend with one troublesome and dangerous gang from Springburn and did not want another in the form of Ferris coming at them from another of their flanks. Ferris had a lively and youthful team of men he trusted around him. Among them were Bobby Glover, who sometimes ran the Cottage bar in Shettleston, and Joe Hanlon, a one-time neighbour and friend of Tam McGraw and his wife, and a useful amateur boxer.

Lobban had evidently given Alex a glowing CV. One day in early summer Hanlon and Glover turned up, asking for a chat. They turned the conversation to a suggestion that he might want to enlist in the Ferris ranks. Perhaps it was his much admired and sought after army weapons background that had attracted their interest.

* * *

I think my army background was one of the reasons for Ferris's interest, but by that stage Lobban thought that I was capable of doing pretty much anything and that I could be trusted. He obviously spread the word and convinced others that I would be a good asset to the team. He showed up a couple of times with Bobby, probably for Bobby to check out for himself what Lobban said about me, but on each occasion I told them, no chance. It was nothing personal against Paul. My loyalties were to my brothers. However, I knew Paul would have liked me to link up with him.

Lobban was trying to make a name for himself. Joe Hanlon hated him because I believe people like Joe and Tam saw through the Mr Benn charade of having so many varied personalities. One hour he might compliment somebody to their face, the next put them at risk by spreading lies about them. I was always a couple of steps ahead of him.

One time he showed up at our home and demanded £1,000 from money I had been holding for Pawny. Bobby Glover had driven him. It was the same car in which the two and Joe would take a very tragic journey in the not too distant future. I sent Lobban packing but not before he tried yet again to persuade me to become part of Paul's firm. A condition would be my severing links to Pawny and Tam. That was unthinkable, and he was told where to go. But the decision came to bite us in the behind.

# CHAPTER TWENTY-ONE

The Saint Valentine's Day Massacre was one of the bloodiest episodes in American gangland history. On Thursday, 14 February 1929, seven men, most of them belonging to a gang headed by Adelard Cunin, better known as Bugs Moran, were lined up against the wall of a garage in Chicago, Illinois, by two bogus policemen and machine-gunned to death. The murders were on the orders of rival gang boss Al Capone, who was determined to wipe out Moran's crew, known as the North Side Irish gang. The incident has been featured in films and books, even songs. In mid-1991, Alex Shannon and his family decided to stage an audacious remake in Glasgow.

St Valentine's Day had passed, but then they reasoned the date hardly mattered if the attack was successful. Their targets were seven members of the Springburn Mob who had been causing aggravation for so long and seemed to be growing stronger each day. The plan was simple. The enemy base was the Spring Inn, but they also showed up at the Talisman from time to time. Where they were didn't matter. The Shannon gang would just walk in and start firing in the direction of the foes, spraying bullets everywhere. Years earlier when workmen were digging the foundations for the Spring Inn, they had discovered running water and this gave the pub its name. The Shannons promised themselves that it would now run with blood. Among themselves, they talked about the attack as a turkey shoot – the chance for a group to take advantage of a situation in which it was impossible to lose.

Blink McDonald would not be joining them. He did not even

know of the massacre plan because he was in prison in England and would not be released for more than a decade. But his friend Frank Ward, always ready for a fight and with a grudge to settle, had started to run with the Shannons. Frank's main argument was with the McGoverns. They would not be in the Spring Inn and by now the Shannon family had no issues with Tommy, Tony and the others. The Shannons would not embark upon a turkey shoot if there was a prospect of a McGovern being targeted. Frank knew this but told himself the targets were friends of his enemies, which justified his involvement. Tam McGraw was also a friend of the McGovern family, but McGraw had his own issues and there was money to be made. He would stay out of the dispute and the fallout from it.

What would be the Godfather's stance? Big Arthur was waiting to be joined by his eldest son. He might be tempted to side with the McIntyres, but in most fights the Godfather tended to wait and see which side was likely to get the upper hand or whether there was an opportunity to score against Paul Ferris. Until then, there was little likelihood of his involving himself in a bloody scandal that would have the effect of seeing police turning the east end upside down and smashing a whole series of lucrative rackets, which had been one effect of the Ice Cream Wars. What the Shannons had was not exactly a secret weapon, but an indirect foot in the Godfather's camp. One of his close relatives had for a time taken advantage of the house in North Carbrain by hiding out there for a while. The Shannons regarded that piece of help as small beer, but it had been appreciated and now they could rely on the man to keep them informed of any likely affiliations Arthur might have with their opponents and in which direction, if any, he was likely to move.

The Shannons and their cohorts kept in constant touch by telephone. Good soldier that he was, and conscious especially through his experiences in Northern Ireland of the importance of a good communications network, Alex insisted on ensuring everyone was up to speed with the plan. The advantage of the telephone was that one man could talk to another without prying eyes being able to discover they had been in touch. These conversations had included discussing the finer points of the massacre, like stealing enough cars to carry the gunmen and finding getaway drivers. But these were comparative irrelevancies. In the end, it was settled that the entire Shannon team would just walk in, guns blazing, and take out the entire McIntyre crew in one go.

Since his move to the Ferris organisation, Lobban had been seen less and less. In a sense, his self-imposed transfer was hardly a surprise. Following his escape from Dungavel, Lobban had needed somewhere to stay. Glover and Hanlon had briefly helped him out, and Paul, who had met Tootsie while both were in prison together, had given him the use of a flat in London to which he had access. He had then moved back to Glasgow, sharing not only a home with Bobby Glover and his wife but also their food and even money. They gave him their trust, made sure he was safe from recapture and wanted for nothing. All three benefactors would come to learn the cost of their kindness.

Alex trusted Lobban less and less. He was bouncing backwards and forwards, initially keeping both ends open, running up to Paul but coming back down to the Shannon brothers. And as the months went on and things were getting worse, they were seeing less of him.

The plan for the hit on the Spring Inn was complete but for one crucial factor, without which it could not go ahead. In total, the Shannon side needed six or seven guns, so each man could be tooled up. Their resources, however, were limited. Getting guns was not so easy as it was popularly believed to be. A few years back, even small-time gangsters with the means to pay could make a telephone call and within a couple of hours a delivery man would call and leave a grubby plastic bag with a deadly weapon wrapped inside. Arnold McCardle from Anniesland, Glasgow, for example, was a recognised expert in modifying and building guns for underworld clients, among them members of the Daniel family. Arnold, known as 'the Armourer', dealt with clients he knew. He urged discretion from his customers, but his days of freedom were running out. The troubles in Northern Ireland were also eating up an increasing number of guns from Scots with sympathies for the various factions.

# THE UNDERWORLD CAPTAIN

While there was no weapons famine in Glasgow, there was a shortage. The Shannon side had two or three but needed more. There was only one man they felt they could go to for help: Paul Ferris.

The brothers, accompanied by Angie's brother and a friend, went in search of Paul or Lobban, who they now looked on as a go-between as opposed to a reliable member of their team. They guessed that if Paul was about he would most likely be in either Bobby Glover's Cottage bar in Shettleston or Margaret McGraw's busy Caravel at Barlanark.

Arriving at the Cottage bar, Tam volunteered to pop in first to see whether there was any sign of Paul. He was only gone a few seconds when he returned to tell Alex and Pawny that there were only a few people in, but not Paul or any of his team, and that they'd better head to the Caravel. They knew Tam's brief appearance would have created a stir. This wasn't Shannon country and the grapevine would be buzzing with gossip.

No sooner had they clambered back into the motor than the telephone at the Caravel was buzzing.

'Tam Shannon just put his head in here.'

'What's he doing?'

'Dunno. He was asking if we'd seen Paul or Bobby.'

'Who's with him?'

'The brothers.'

'What do you reckon the Shannons want with Paul?'

'Dunno, Tam just said they were looking for him.'

At the Caravel, there was still no sign of Paul Ferris.

There was no need for the brothers to ask if he was likely to appear. They knew word of their enquiry would have reached the right ears. So they sat down by the pool table to have a drink, watch and wait. Most of the sidelong glances were at Alex. Tam's was a known face and Pawny had had friendly dealings with some of the Ferris crew in the past, but when Alex first left the army and took to the streets with his brothers, he had been a relatively unknown entity. Word then spread, and before he knew it he was becoming the main threat, the principal weapon in the Shannon armoury. For that reason, he suspected the strangers sitting a few feet from him would be asking one another what he was doing there and telling each other to keep an eye on him.

For a few minutes, nothing happened. Then Joe Hanlon walked in. Alex remembers that Joe, a young man with an occasionally odd sense of humour, was wearing an enormous coat, so bulky that it was obvious from the shape and size of the bulge beneath it that he was trying to hide a shotgun. It would have been expected because the Shannons had turned up in their territory. But it was the first sign something was not right.

As Joe was standing there, Bobby Glover put his head around the door and said, 'Paul's round the back and wants a quick word with you.' Tam, Pawny and Alex jumped up and went out the front door, leaving the others with their drinks. They made their way around to the back of the Caravel and suddenly there were people jumping out from everywhere. There were about ten of them waiting to meet the brothers and dressed, it appeared, not to thrill but to kill. Clearly, they thought they were trying to set up Paul to be shot. Guys were reaching into their pockets and under their coats, and at that Gibby jumped out in the middle of them all and started shouting, 'No, stop, stop. There's nothing going down here. Look, Tam, Ally, Paul's wanting to speak to Pawny. There's no offence meant. Tam, Ally, there's nothing against you, but he just wants a few words with Pawny. Leave it at that just now.' Alex was learning not to trust Lobban.

* * *

Now, Gibby knew Tam was a livewire. And he hated Tam with a passion. But the feeling was totally mutual. Had he said Paul wanted Tam on his own, we would have really thought something was going down, but when he asked for Pawny, me and Tam just said, 'Not a problem.' We went and sat in our car because we weren't keen on going back into the bar, especially with Joe standing there hanging onto his shotgun. We could see a wee red Ford Fiesta with Paul in it. Pawny climbed in beside him, the two men shook hands and Pawny told us afterwards that Paul was sitting with a handgun with a silencer on it on his knee. Paul was his usual polite self and said he was sorry to do all this, but these days you just don't know who you can trust. He had £50,000 on his head, so he really did have to watch what he was doing. He said, 'My people told me you were all up here asking about me and I thought, "Hang on a minute, what's going down here?" I apologise if anything has happened, Pawny. What can I do, how can I help you?' That made Pawny feel more comfortable, so he told Paul about us and the Springburn Mob, saying that it had gone on long enough. 'We've had a think and decided to go ahead with the whole lot,' he told Paul, 'but we need six or seven instant access guns. Can you help us out?'

He went on to describe what we had planned. 'We just want to walk into the Spring Inn when we know they're all there and wipe them out in one go.'

Paul must have thought it was a crazy idea, but he probably understood why we wanted to go down this road. When your back is to the wall, then the only thing to do is to come out fighting. Nevertheless, if it went ahead, it would see all of us locked up for the rest of our lives. Yet he didn't hesitate for a second.

'Aye, definitely, I'll see what I can do,' was his response. 'I'll help you out as much as I can.'

They shook hands once again and wished one another the best. When Pawny rejoined us, we collected the other two from inside the bar and drove off.

As the weeks went by, no weapons ever came our way, resulting in the entire plot going pear-shaped, even though Paul had said he would help us. We surmised that maybe he believed we had indeed lost the plot, but I also think Lobban played a part in Paul's final decision not to help. He was still making out to anybody who would listen that he was a member of our family, as good as a stepbrother to us. Despite all that sentimental talk, the fact remained he loathed Tam and would have been more than happy to have seen him killed. He probably thought that without guns from Paul to protect us and take out the Springburn crew there was a better chance of Tam being murdered or jailed. I think he drip-fed Paul all this bile about Tam, while making out to us he was doing his best to help us get what we needed. I don't think he was slagging me because as time passed he would turn up at our house with Bobby Glover and tell me he had spoken to Paul again about the guns. And while Bobby was there, he would again invite me to join Paul. 'Come up some time and I'll introduce you to everybody,' he kept promising, but I never had any intention of taking him up on the offer. By that stage, I had made up my mind to get away from this sort of scene and go back into the army.

I had a lot to think about at that time, one concern being the continuing worry that Lobban would try to kill Tam. Mind you, we would do our best to take him out as well.

But I had to think about Angie, too. She had told me she was pregnant again.

# CHAPTER TWENTY-TWO

From his plush palace in Baghdad, Saddam Hussein Abd al-Majid al-Tikriti, President of Iraq, dictator and mass murderer, ordered the invasion of the neighbouring state of Kuwait because of a dispute over an unpaid loan and the price of oil. Corporal Alex Shannon had avidly followed the build-up to the one-sided conflict from his base at Glencorse Barracks. The terms of his enlistment meant he was required to give one year's notice of his intention to resign. He had done so in January 1990 and was therefore due to leave the army at the beginning of 1991. In August 1990, Iraqi troops steamrollered their way into Kuwait, looting, pillaging, devastating towns and oilfields, bringing international condemnation and the certainty of retaliation. A coalition of more than 30 countries rallied to rout Hussein's armies. Britain and the United States would play the major roles. As his leaving date grew ever nearer, Alex was forced to sit back and watch as regimental colleagues and friends in Germany trained for desert fighting. He desperately wanted to share their excitement for the forthcoming battles. 'Send me back to Germany so I can go to Iraq and I'll sign back on,' he told his superiors. But the answer was no – corporals in the British Army do not dictate terms to officers. When he said that he was getting out, then, his response was met with silence.

In December, with only a few days to go until he was scheduled to quit, the Royal Scots deployed from Germany to Saudi Arabia as an armoured infantry battalion. From there, it prepared to push into Iraq. Desperate to join in, Alex tried again to be transferred back to Germany, but the response was the same. Helplessly, he listened as barracks gossip and ordinary conjecture implied units of the SAS had been dropped behind Iraqi lines to hunt down deadly mobile Scud missile launchers. He remembered his meetings with the SAS guys on the Brecon course and longed to be with them. He felt as though he was a schoolboy forced to remain at home while he watched his mates play a thrilling cup final in front of his window.

In January 1991, the coalition moves kicked off in earnest, just as Alex was taking off his uniform for the final time and heading for gangland. Operation Desert Storm began with an aerial bombardment of the interlopers and then the various allied forces, the Royal Scots among them, smashed their way towards Baghdad. It was a war fought in front of the media. Families could sit at home and almost have a seat on the fringes of the battlefields, with bullets, blood and shells whizzing around their living rooms. In between rounds, television teams chatted with and filmed the protagonists, many from Scotland.

For Alex, it was hard sitting watching soldiers who were his mates being interviewed in Saudi Arabia, then Iraq. He struggled to cope and began missing not only his friends but also the regiment itself. He wanted back in, but he'd made his choice. Instead, as each day passed he was drinking, taking drugs and trying to do his bit in the house to help Angie. The only thing he had in common with his mates now, even though they were going down different paths and doing different things, was that just about everything they both did was dangerous. In the early days of serving out his notice, he'd had no worries or concerns; now he did.

By then, of course, it was too late. He was a civilian living in another environment in which there were leaders and foot soldiers who were expendable. He tried making a fist of living a form of life that would be termed 'normal', but he had left the cocoon of the armed forces, where income was guaranteed every month to provide food, warmth, a roof over his head and sufficient to support his growing family. He had given up this security to seek work in a time of recession. Attempts at getting employment on building sites failed and he resorted to spending his days in the company of his brothers and being on the periphery of their various underworld dealings. All of this was against a background of squabbles between different factions. Everybody was fighting with each other and everyone was paranoid about everybody around them. People could sense this was a really dangerous time. Glasgow was dissected into territories and every one of those areas was having its own problems.

In their fight with the Springburn Mob, the Shannons had been joined by Angie's brother, Paddy, and his pal, Eddie Kennedy. Because of the relationship, Alex tried keeping a friendly watch over Paddy, but Eddie was a different kettle of fish. He was in the same mould as Lobban – he had no fear and was not someone to mess with. Unlike Lobban, however, Eddie was totally trustworthy and is still a very close friend.

Eddie once spent time in prison with the legendary Rab Carruthers. As a young man, Carruthers had left his native Glasgow and established a fearsome reputation for himself in Manchester, where he ran one of the biggest drugs smuggling enterprises in the United Kingdom – until he was caught and jailed for fifteen years. Rab took Eddie under his wing and gave him the education he needed. One well-known story is that Eddie, after years of being in trouble and being kept in solitary confinement, decided one morning that he had had enough of that existence and went to Rab's cell. Eddie explained that he wanted to be wiser and needed someone to guide him and give him sound advice on how individuals should work and act at the highest levels in the criminal fraternity.

Rab's advice was that he should first improve his education and learn two new words every day from the *Oxford English Dictionary*. Some people may find that a strange piece of advice, but to be educated, intelligent and capable of extreme violence is more of a threat than someone who can't think further than the next 24 hours and who wants everyone to know he is responsible for certain acts merely to gain notoriety.

Eddie mentioned his conversation with Rab to Alex one day. 'The mind can play havoc,' he agreed. 'If you let your enemy know it is you who has stabbed or shot him, then he knows who to seek payback with. However, if you attack an enemy with your face hidden, it's not the wound you have caused that creates a problem for him, but his state of mind. Because now the world becomes his enemy. He doesn't know who has done the deed or even why. So his mind begins running riot and depression and other mental problems begin to set in.'

The sight of his friends sunburned and evidently enjoying themselves in the desert had made Alex realise how big a part of his life he had removed by leaving the army. Now, he was sinking into a trough, swilling with the detritus of gangland Glasgow and in danger of drowning. He recalled the words of his former commanding officer in Germany, who had taken the trouble to watch a football match in which Alex was playing not long before his discharge and sought him out for a private word. 'Don't get out,' the colonel told him. 'You are going to go far in your career. I know you say you've made up your mind, but it takes a good man to realise when he's made a mistake. If you think you've made a mistake when you get out, be tall, stand tall and come back in because we need good soldiers.' An incident in April made up his mind for him.

\* \* \*

By now, I was really starting to wake up and look at my life, why and where it had all gone wrong. I began to think seriously about joining up again. Angie had announced she was again pregnant with our third child and given me an ultimatum that if I wanted a life with her and the kids I had to make a decision now before it was too late. 'You are going to end up in prison for murder, or you're going to get murdered yourself,' she said. I had to think hard and fast.

Next day, I went to the army careers office to speak about the possibility of re-enlisting. I came away with all the information I needed. Now, it was simply a case of making up my mind and signing all the necessary paperwork. It was the weekend and I decided to go out for a few drinks with an old friend from Posso. We settled on the Barracks bar in Maryhill, not far from his home. It had a bit of a history. A couple of years earlier,

Michael Greig had been murdered in the Barracks bar, his body wrapped in a carpet and buried in a shallow lochside grave. Graham Shields went on trial at the High Court in Glasgow charged with the murder. He denied being the killer and blamed another man. The jury found the case against Mr Shields Not Proven. Nobody else was ever charged with the crime.

We had no thoughts of trouble when we started drinking that night. I was chatting with my mate about possibly going back into uniform and the hours passed quickly. The evening was going great and, even better, at the end of the night I was asked if I wanted to stay for a lock-in and have a few drinks after the official closing time.

By now I was on my own, my friend having gone home. Something ought to have warned me that this wasn't right. I was being bought drink after drink and found myself standing alone at one end of the bar, while in a corner there were about ten other guys who I didn't recognise. They all kept looking at me. I thought maybe I'd met them before and didn't remember their faces, but then I became convinced they thought I was Tam. He and I were so alike we were regularly mistaken for one another, and so I told myself it was a case of mistaken identity and was nothing to worry about.

It was simply one of those nights when you're enjoying yourself and no matter how much you knock back don't seem to get drunk. When I needed to go to the toilet, I had to pass by them and they all moved to one side, which gave the impression they were being extremely polite, but still they continued to stare at me. It didn't bother me at the time and eventually, about five in the morning, I said to the guy behind the bar that it was time for me to go and asked if he would open the shutters to let me out. 'Aye, on you come,' he said, and I went home.

About four hours later the telephone rang. It was Pawny. He was going mental. He told me word had already spread that I was in the Barracks bar looking for somebody. I said, 'What are you talking about? I'm lying here with a hangover.' He told me I had been only minutes away from being murdered. The others in the bar thought I was Tam and it had all developed from there, as these things tend to do. Someone started it all off by saying to somebody else, 'I think that's Tam Shannon,' and by the time it got to the fifth person it had become 'It *is* Tam Shannon.' From there it grew from 'That's Tam Shannon and I think he's carrying something' to 'Tam Shannon is here with a gun and he's looking for somebody to shoot.' It was all lies, but it shows how easily an innocent situation can become distorted.

The effect of it all, though, was that the others were wondering how to stitch me up so I could be killed.

'You just don't realise how close you came to being murdered,' Pawny said. 'What the fuck were you doing?' I told him I was having a few drinks and a good time. He was convinced that what saved my life was the thought that I had been carrying a gun. I will never know what it was all about, but it was the final straw.

'That's it, Angie,' I said. 'I'm going back into the army.' As soon as Monday morning came around, I went back to the army careers office, filled in the paperwork and left being told I would be back in within two months. Now, all I had to do was stay out of trouble for a few weeks.

* * *

Angie was happy that Alex was returning to the army. When he finally decided to re-join, she felt relief because if he hadn't gone back they would have been finished. Re-enlistment meant losing one of his stripes and going back to the rank of lance corporal, and Alex lost a lot in pay, along with considerable seniority, which would have counted in the next promotional course, but he took it philosophically, believing that you would go up the ranks based on abilities. In reality this wasn't necessarily the case – it wasn't what you knew, but who you knew.

Alex had taken the break from the army to see what life was like on the outside; what he had walked into was trouble: murder, threats, drugs and all the rest of it. The day he signed the papers, he headed home telling himself: 'That's it. I'm doing this for life now.'

Tam Shannon had never been surprised by his brother's

decision to give up soldiering – and once he was out, he and Pawny wanted him to stay out. As far as Tam was concerned, Alex was really good at soldiering, so when he didn't advance as far as maybe he should have done, he wondered if he would leave. Tam had always been careful to protect Alex because of his career and there were times when his brothers had been careful to make sure he didn't walk into situations that could have led to trouble. For instance, the night Tam went to the Talisman, he left Alex because he didn't want him involved. When he realised Alex was with him, he knew he'd have to be careful. Had Alex not been there, the result could have been very different.

There was one urgent task Alex had to carry out before rejoining the Royal Scots. Late one night he returned to the banks of the River Kelvin, dug up the by now empty pipe hides, slung them into the water and smoothed over the spot where they had lain buried.

He re-enlisted on 18 June 1991, but was retained at Glencorse Barracks to wait for his regiment to return from Iraq and then from Germany before moving to Inverness. He would continue as a training lance corporal at Glencorse.

\* \* \*

I went back into the same job I had been doing before I left and was getting slagged off by the other guys about how I'd made a mistake. But I just had to get my head down and get on with it. It was all good-natured stuff. Nobody wanted to see you fall flat on your face. In a sense, I had to go back to Glencorse with my tail between my legs and admit to everyone that they were right and the outside world was not for me. But none of them had known what my life as a civilian had really been like and I thought they didn't need to know either. However, any time I came across a soldier who was going off the rails through drink and drugs, I would take him to one side and lecture him on what to do. When I had been out of the army, I had dabbled in recreational drugs, mainly because of peer pressure and the fact that I wanted to fit in and be like the rest of them. In hindsight, it made me a better person – I was now able to relate to recruits in a better way and could understand the pressures they were under.

I rejoined the regiment in Inverness, but it would be August before married quarters were ready and Angie and the children could join me. She was heavily pregnant by then, and I now felt I could look forward to a stable and decent future away from Glasgow. I was about to discover just how wrong I could be.

# CHAPTER TWENTY-THREE

Fort George, at Ardersier near Inverness, had been built as a base to keep the Highlands under control following the 1745 Jacobite Rising and the defeat at Culloden of Bonnie Prince Charlie a year later. It has been described as the greatest artillery fortification in Europe and after his move to the great fort Alex would frequently wish its mighty walls could also rebuff the consequences of fighting in the Glasgow underworld. About to unfold was a series of events to which he and his brothers had no direct link but into which they would be reluctantly drawn. Any supposition of their involvement was due to their relationship with one individual: William Lobban.

* * *

On the night of 28 July 1991, six weeks after Alex had re-enlisted, a slight man of medium height, wearing a blonde wig, gloves and glasses, walked into the Pipe Rack, a popular and busy bar on Crammond Place in Budhill, Glasgow. He had spent much of the day hanging about watching the comings and goings, and knew the takings would be reasonably good. Otherwise there would be little or no point in doing what he was about to do.

Much as others had done before him following prison escapes, he had made little attempt to go into hiding and went confidently about the Glasgow streets showing a disregard for the tracking abilities of the local police. Gibby was adept at dressing up. He had often disguised himself as a woman since his disappearance from Dungavel, allowing him freedom to wander around. For a time after his escape, he had been holed up in London in a Finsbury Park flat owned by Paul Ferris. Then he had headed back to Scotland to be looked after by the Glovers. While nothing had been said about his continued imposition in their home, others in his company had suggested that maybe it was time for him to move on. And that required money.

Earlier that day, he had told his host's wife, Eileen, that he was going to 'get a bit of money'. Now, strolling into the Pipe Rack, he was about to do just that. Lobban produced a gun, handed over a holdall and demanded it was filled with money. When the barman objected, he was bashed over the head with the gun barrel. Fearing more violence, frightened staff handed over £949 and Lobban fled. Where did he go? Back to the home of the Glovers, where, in front of Eileen, he counted out the cash haul.

In early August, a heavily pregnant Angie and the children moved to Inverness. The family started to enjoy life again, as Angie recalls. Friends were around them and they no longer needed to keep looking over their shoulders. Everything was beginning to look up. But if the clouds had seemed to disappear, an ill wind was about to blow them back.

In Glasgow, as the middle of the month approached, Lobban announced to the Glovers that he was moving out. They assumed the money he had made from the Pipe Rack robbery, a fairly mediocre sum though it had turned out to be, had enabled him to buy into some deal or another. They even wondered whether he might have gone to stay with his uncle, William Manson, a close friend of the Godfather, Arthur Thompson, in Provanmill. Where he was going, they really did not care: he was out of their home – that was all that mattered.

Meanwhile, sitting in the Ponderosa watching his favourite television shows, the Godfather too was thinking, just like Alex 200 miles to the north, that life was getting better. Arty's time for release on licence was drawing nearer; he had been moved to the open prison at Noranside in Angus and to acclimatise him to freedom he was about to be allowed his first weekend home. Arthur was fond of his son, as he was of all his family. He questioned whether his eldest was capable of taking over the various family enterprises, but he believed that with a little coaching, a few long talks and maybe teaming him up with one of the London gangs for a while he would learn sufficient discretion to inherit his business. Arthur knew that while in jail Arty had made enemies. He himself had had to step in on more than one occasion to provide his son with protection and had made a payment here and there to soothe offended pride. On the morning of Friday, 16 August, Arty, along with a dozen others given their weekend of freedom, stepped from a prison service bus taking them from Noranside to Glasgow's Buchanan Street bus station. The same vehicle would pick them up a couple of days later to return them and they had been firmly warned that to miss it meant a certain return to a closed prison.

Around the time Arty was stepping from the coach, a police inspector's car was being stolen by a well-known car thief from outside a railway station on the outskirts of Glasgow. The officer had taken a train in to work, so by the time he discovered the vehicle was gone and had reported it, the car was well hidden just outside the city centre.

The following night Arty went into the city for a meal with friends. Tam McGraw had also been dining that night in a well-known Chinese restaurant in Glasgow. His rival, the Godfather, was at home watching television. As Arty, on foot, having paid off a taxi a couple of minutes earlier, neared Provanmill, the stolen car emerged from the darkness. Its door opened and closed quietly. A young man walked towards Arty and shots rang out. Arty staggered into the arms of his younger brother, Billy, blood pouring from his head, body and backside. An ambulance was summoned, but 18 minutes after midnight on 18 August he was pronounced dead. Nobody, especially Arthur Thompson, called the police. That was left to the hospital where Arty had bled to death. The killer and his friends disappeared, maybe into the anonymity of London.

In gangland, Arthur began calling in favours. His many friends included influential and rich businessmen. Money was no object in return for good information. He was a hard, ruthless man who once had one of his debtors nailed to the floor. Those who offended the Godfather feared him more than they did the police.

A couple of weeks after Arty's murder, with detectives still chasing the killer, Pawny was at home when he heard a knock on his door in the early hours. He demanded to know who was there before opening the door. His shoulders slumped when he heard a low but familiar voice. Lobban looked dishevelled and agitated. His name had cropped up in idle conversation following the Arty shooting, when the brothers had been wondering what would happen next. The Shannons were not involved and, like so many others, were simply guessing at the outcome. Lobban hadn't been seen or heard since the tragedy, neither had he done anything to help the brothers in their quest to acquire enough handguns to massacre the McIntyre group.

When Pawny asked what Lobban wanted, he was told 'guns'. 'You've got some guns, I know you have. You told Paul you had a couple. Where are they?' he demanded. His excitement and nervousness were visibly increasing, and then he suddenly whipped out a pistol from his coat and put it to Pawny's head. 'Fucking get me the guns,' he shouted.

'You're getting no fucking guns,' Pawny told him. 'I'll tell you what, the person that has the guns is Tam. Go down to Tam and tell him you want them, but you know what he'll do if he sees you? He'll blow a fucking hole in your head.'

Lobban demanded that Pawny called Tam, then tried another manoeuvre, saying he'd go and see Tam and sort him. It was a threat made of desperation, and Pawny knew it. 'Gibby, you fucking go anywhere near Tam and he'll kill you,' he said. 'You know how he hates you and he can take you out.'

Lobban thought for a moment. Leaving Pawny to head for Tam's home would give Pawny time to telephone his brother, who would then be waiting for him. Lobban shuddered at the thought of appearing in the sight of a gun held by Tam Shannon.

Lobban never got any guns. When he eventually calmed down, he started to tell Pawny that things had gone wrong but decided not to expand on what he meant by this. As he was speaking, he realised that Pawny's wife or daughter might have already phoned Tam to tell him he was at their home. He was edgy, constantly looking around him, paranoid about Tam suddenly appearing out of the darkness. Lobban left as unexpectedly as he had arrived, leaving Pawny to guess at the reason for his desperation to have more guns.

In Inverness, Alex had more important worries than the murder of a Glasgow gangster on his mind. On 14 September, his third child, Nicole, was born. It was a naturally joyous occasion, but the immediate happiness of the delighted parents was short-lived. Doctors discovered the newly born baby had developed pneumonia and had an air bubble next to her heart which was affecting the organ's ability to pump blood around her tiny body. Alex and Angie were warned to expect the worst, but gradually their prayers were answered and Nicole crept slowly along the road to a full recovery.

Tam, meantime, had been told by Pawny of the early-morning visit from Lobban. Alex, too, had been given details of the conversation. He was still making occasional visits back to Glasgow to see his brothers and complete documentation in connection with the house in Maryhill. Tam had been enraged by Lobban's actions and had recruited Eddie Kennedy to help find Gibby. Although he did not openly say so, it was assumed that when Tam caught up with Lobban he would kill him.

Now, the brothers began wondering whether Lobban had been badmouthing them to Paul Ferris, Bobby Glover and Joe Hanlon, which would have accounted for the non-appearance of the promised weapons from Paul. 'Maybe Paul thinks we want nothing to do with Lobban,' suggested Alex, and he would soon come to hope that was indeed the case.

On 18 September, only days after he had tried to force Pawny into handing over guns, Lobban telephoned Glover and asked for a meeting. Glover's car had been impounded by the police because they suspected it could have been used in the shooting of Arty, so he rang Joe Hanlon to ask if he would take him to the rendezvous.

The following day was Arty's funeral. That morning a passerby in Shettleston noticed a car parked outside the Cottage bar, where Bobby had once worked. Two men were inside, apparently asleep, one slouched in the front well, the other on the floor under the back seats. The same man passed a while later and noticed neither car nor occupants had moved. When he looked closer, he saw blood. He tapped on the window, but the noise brought no sign of movement. The police were summoned and autopsies on both men revealed each had been shot in the head and chest with two different handguns.

Police hunting whoever was responsible later issued an appeal for anyone who knew the whereabouts of Lobban to get in touch. He was said to use disguises and a description was given of the tattoos on his right and left hands and left arm, whose removal he had used as the excuse to skip prison. Lobban was also named in a report by murder squad police to the Crown Office, but he was never charged.

The police, of course, did not know that shortly before the slayings he had called at the home of Pawny demanding guns. Nor that his uncle, William Manson, later boasted to another leading underworld gang boss that he, Manson, had been paid by the Godfather to execute the two men. The police might have been interested to know that Lobban had advocated the killing of two leading players in the gangland scene and had been a part of the Spring Inn massacre plot. But they were aware of none of this. And no one was talking.

Alex heard the news of the double executions in a call from one of his brothers. There was no need to talk in whispers; the murders had made the headlines. But Lobban's visit to Pawny had left Alex with a really bad feeling.

The visit occurred not long after Arty was killed and just before Joe and Bobby died, then Gibby had disappeared off the scene. As far as Arthur getting murdered was concerned, Alex had no interest. Arthur was an old man, finished. But Joe and Bobby? It was bad, especially the way it all happened. He started to think, 'There's more to this.' Everybody knew about the Shannon brothers and Lobban, but Alex had been getting offers to kill people. He'd been telling everybody he wasn't interested, but what if no one believed him?

# CHAPTER TWENTY-FOUR

The murders of Bobby Glover and Joe Hanlon were meant to level the account of the Thompson faction over the killing of Arty. That was the way of it with most gangland deaths. One was followed by another and then the book was closed, at least for a time. It was how underworlds everywhere conducted their business. But these were not business matters. All three were personal and therefore the aftermath was all the more bitter. The executioners, whoever they were, could not expect the customary protection of gangland silence.

Arty's murder had been only half the plan. Old Arthur was meant to follow his son to the graveyard, the thinking being that his death would almost certainly quash any likelihood of vengeance.

Arty's killer had fled to England, some thought maybe London. From there, he made a telephone call to Glasgow. The conversation was brief: 'I've done my bit, now you go and do old Arthur. It's your turn.' The individual at the other end of the line was no fool. He had been waiting for this call, but had long ago decided where his loyalties lay: to himself and his pocket. And he knew where there was profit to be made – but it wasn't by taking out the Godfather. While he was aware of the awesome reputation of the caller – was frightened, even, of the man – love of money conquered all.

'I'm no cunt's fire in. I'm murdering no cunt. I'll do what I want,' he spat back, then he hung up. It might seem like he was taking a chance with this show of defiance, but what, he wondered, if a quiet word naming the killer was dropped in the right ear and found its way to the police? The identities of Arty's enemies were widely known. What if the police were tipped off that one of them was the assassin? If they arrested the suspect and locked him up, it would mean he was safely out of the way, a situation the recipient of the call wanted for his own safety.

* * *

Paul Ferris was arrested and accused of being the Provanmill killer. While he was on remand, Bobby and Joe were shot. They were discovered in the same car in which they had driven off to meet Lobban. At the end of the road on which the grieving Thompson family lived was Hogganfield Loch, a local beauty spot favoured by courting couples. Shots fired there would be sure to be heard; however, some distance off, a motorway was being built. It was in this area that the car had been driven and when it came to a halt the terrible deed done.

By the time the men had been shot, it was late – their meeting with Lobban had eaten up time. The dead men had been taken from the motor, shot again and then their bodies carelessly thrown back inside. The man who had set up their murders then drove the car to the Cottage bar, where it was dumped. He was followed by an accomplice, who waited for him and then drove him to Glasgow Central station, where he was handed tickets that would take him to London. By the time he arrived there, word had already reached the capital. Arthur Thompson had many friends in London. When the traveller showed his ticket and stepped past the barrier, a man approached him, hugged him warmly, gave him a cuddle and whispered, 'That's from Arthur.' The two chatted amicably, their cockney and Glaswegian accents being no bar to disturbing the conversation, although the Scot was nervous. As they left, he looked to see what time the next train arrived from Scotland, then he was driven to a hideout near a notorious gay area to the west of the city centre and given money and a number to call in the event of his needing help.

Following the Hanlon and Glover deaths, William Lobban disappeared. When word leaked out about his telephone call luring both to the fatal meeting, he became a detested figure. Even some who had been close to him were appalled. Paul Ferris had been pals with Hanlon and Glover and he had taken Lobban in, looked after him when he was down on his luck. The Glovers had helped him out as well. People knew Lobban didn't like Joe, but they asked why Bobby? Why throw in his lot with a wasted old gangster? There were others who wondered why Lobban, who was seen as wild, dangerous like an animal, had been allowed to hook on to the Ferris team.

At Fort George, news of the double killing was telephoned to Alex before the newspapers began screaming out the blood-curdling details. In Glasgow, police were looking for Lobban and now they set out to trace his associates. Alex knew precisely where Gibby was holed up, as did many in the underworld, but nobody was passing that on to the police.

\* \* \*

I was in the army now, but I had been in the same circles as these people. If something happened in the street, I knew about it straight away. The police went to our ma's house, trying to find Tam and Pawny. I'd had such a low profile that they weren't aware there was another brother who was in the army. Of course, Tam and Pawny had nothing to do with the murders, but the police wanted to find out if they knew where Lobban was and they were hardly going to tell them that.

Four weeks after Joe and Bobby died, I was still being told that Lobban was staying in a hotel in London, constantly telephoning all sorts of people connected to us, wanting to know what was happening. Everybody was still sceptical about all the rumours dropping names as to who had done it and nobody knew where Lobban fitted in to all of this. Then the police found out exactly who I was, what I did, where I was and they became very interested in me. My attitude at this time was that the whole thing was none of my concern. I was concentrating on getting my career back on track by going on a Platoon Sergeant's Battle Course. It was really important and I was determined to do well.

Then one morning a telephone call came through to the

training wing for me. At the other end of the line was the sergeant major, who left orders to 'tell Shannon I want him down in my office straight away'. It was about a mile and a half to where he sat and so I set off running at top speed, a host of things, most of them stupid, going through my mind as to why I was wanted in such a hurry. I started wondering if maybe I hadn't paid my mess bill and whether that might affect my chances on the course, had I failed to do this or that? I was still in that frame of mind when I arrived.

The sergeant major at the time was a guy called Tam Butler from the south side of Glasgow. When I reached his office, I could see he was on the telephone, so I halted at the door but could hear him talking, saying, 'I've got Shannon here.' Then he put his hand over the mouthpiece, looked up at me and said, 'I've got London Road murder squad from Glasgow on the line wanting to speak to you reference the killings of Hanlon and Glover. They want to come up and interview you.'

The old me returned and I said, 'Well, sir, you can tell them I don't want to speak to them. Nobody's interviewing me about anything. Tell them I have nothing to say to them.'

Butler started speaking into the telephone again. 'You'll not believe this cheeky cunt. He's telling me to say he's got fuck all to say to you, so you'll be wasting your time coming up from Glasgow.'

There was more discussion on the line and eventually a compromise was reached. If I wasn't going to talk, they would turn up next morning and lift me from my home. But if I was willing to be interviewed, they would do so in my house and leave it there. I wasn't caring. I knew at the end of the day it wasn't me they were after.

Next morning, four detectives turned up. Angie and I sat and answered their questions, but everything related to Lobban, who seemed to have so many different names by now. The newspapers were calling him 'Tootsie' and 'Gary'. The police tried to lay it on that they were looking for Lobban because they thought he had been murdered. 'We really need to get hold of him,' they kept saying, but everybody knows the way the police operate. It was the usual approach – try to panic you, make you think you have somebody else's life in your hands, but I know the streets anyway. It was a case of hear no evil, see no evil, speak no evil until you knew exactly what it was all about. Of course I knew where Gibby was, but this wasn't my affair and I didn't want to be dragged into it. I knew he hadn't been murdered; so did the police. After a time, Angie got up to leave. They tried to prevent her going, but she just said, 'Look, I have no dealings with Lobban. He was not allowed in our house because I disliked him.' Then off she went.

For the next two and a half to three hours, I was given a severe grilling. They threatened me and even in my own house tried to push me about a bit. They began threatening me that Paul Ferris and his crew knew about me and if I was ever to go near Glasgow I would more than likely be killed. They said they had already found out I was a marked man and was going to get murdered. But I paid no attention to that because I didn't really believe it. They tried scaring me with a description of the murder scene, the number of rounds that had been fired by the killer and how, in their words, 'the only thing the bastard didn't do was to nail them to the front door of the Cottage bar.' I must admit that that had me shaken a bit, but by then I had worked out they would say and do anything to get the response they wanted from me, the information they were after.

I wasn't really interested in what they said because I knew it would not affect my way of life or my movement between Glasgow and Inverness. At the end of the day, even though I was back in the army I was still wearing my civilian head. No matter what they said or what threats they used, I wouldn't have said anything. When it came to the crunch, although I had a career in the army, I knew where I was in Civvy Street, what I had to do and where my priorities lay. I was street wide and wise.

They eventually left, muttering all kinds of threats. They telephoned me a couple of times after that to see whether I had anything to say, but I hadn't. They were still trying to persuade me to go to London Road police station for a talk. But I wouldn't entertain them. It was just that you didn't deal with the police and that was it. Even if it had been one of my brothers who had been done in, I would probably have had the same attitude. That's just the way it is. As a result of where I am from and the circles in which I have moved, I am a party to many pieces of information, including what some might term gangland secrets. Frankly, I don't like knowing what I do. It is said that too much knowledge can be a dangerous thing, and that is true. While I totally disagree with the violence and crime that went on at that time, I don't like talking about it. Knowing as much as I do sometimes makes me feel I was actually implicated in matters in which I was not involved. But while I wasn't there, the fact is that when I look back and piece everything together, I tell myself, 'Now, I know.' And I do.

But that wasn't the end of the matter. Obviously, before speaking to the sergeant major the police had talked to the officer commanding and told him he had a soldier in his company who was involved in this and that. They wanted to know my history and what he knew about me. Although the army should not have done so, they told the police about me – where I had been, what I had done and what I was capable of, and as a result I became of interest to the police. That's when they began thinking that maybe I was involved.

After they had gone, nothing was said to my face, but I knew, through conversations with mates who used to tell me what was going on and what was being said, that a senior officer had tagged me as a 'gangster', a 'hit man', a 'gun runner' and a lot of other things. I tried to just ignore them and carry on training.

I was still conscious of talk when it reached Christmas and the company party. That's when I met the officer who had been slagging me off. I told him the life I had led in Glasgow was now behind me, that he could trust me not to bring embarrassment on the company.

'What went before is finished with,' I said. 'Forget it. Let's move on. Give me the benefit of the doubt.'

He promised he accepted my word and would back me 100 per cent. Soon after, I was arrested and accused of three attempted murders.

# CHAPTER TWENTY-FIVE

Private Tam Gow of the Royal Scots (The Royal Regiment) was a hero. Earlier in the year he had been out in the Gulf War, courageously crawling through an enemy minefield, ignoring heavy fire to clear two bunkers using grenades. He then rounded up three Iraqi officers and four soldiers. Tam, originally from Glasgow but who went on to settle in Inverness, was rightly awarded the Military Medal for his exploits and the Citation detailing the honour said he was a brave man who showed 'initiative, aggression and determination'. He was also a good pal. I had known Tam before joining the army, one of his family had grown up in the same children's homes as me.

The day after I'd pledged to the officer that I'd be on my best behaviour the company travelled to Edinburgh to do Castle Duty, which involved formally guarding the city's imposing structure over Christmas and New Year. It meant that, while most of the rest of the country were enjoying themselves and having fun, we had to stay sober, smart and alert.

Tam knew how much I would have loved to have been with my brothers on 31 December and he showed just how good a friend he was by offering to do a couple of my duties. It would allow me to go to Glasgow for the New Year. His offer was a last-minute thing, so I accepted, but did not tell Angie what I was going to do. She did not like me going through to Glasgow and Cumbernauld to drink with all the guys. I understood her point of view. She was worried and just didn't want anything to happen to me. I knew if I told her what I was planning, she would be upset, so I said nothing and simply headed off to

Cumbernauld to meet up with Pawny, Tam, Eddie Kennedy, Andy Thompson, who was a distant member of the Godfather's family, and Angie's brother, Paddy.

To say it turned out to be a disaster is one of the great understatements of all time. The whole night was actually boring, so I drank a half-bottle of brandy and some cans of beer before the bells. For hour after hour, I just sat there getting sozzled. I wanted to get drunk early on, having decided I would have an early night with a view to getting up sharp next morning and returning to Edinburgh.

Pawny and Andy left the rest of us to move on somewhere else and I went off to bed in the house we had bought in North Carbrain. I remembered Paddy coming into the room to wake me and say they were going a few doors down the road to another party. He asked if I wanted to join them, but I told him just to let me sleep.

I don't recall how long it was after Paddy's visit, but next thing I heard Tam's voice below the window of the room where I was sleeping. He was shouting and swearing. I got out of bed, went downstairs to the front door and found Tam and Eddie standing there. There was blood everywhere.

They were surrounded by a screaming crowd of about 20 teenagers, all drunk and cursing, seemingly intent on tearing them apart. Tam had his hand in the inside of his jacket, while Eddie was waving a black machete or sword about. It appeared he was trying to hit as many of these yobs over the head as he could reach.

They looked to be aged from 16 to 20, but were out of their heads on drink or drugs. I must have had about four hours' sleep and that, combined with the sight and noise, sobered me up. Blood was spattered on the walls and floor of the house. Some of it was so thick it had congealed, which told me someone had been badly hurt. I knew the victims were neither Eddie nor Tam because the mob was by now screaming and trying to run away.

'God,' I thought, 'this is bad. I need to get away from here now because if I don't Angie is going to kill me and the army will wash its hands of me.'

I managed to drag Tam and Eddie indoors. Neither seemed to have a care in the world. They had no idea of Paddy's whereabouts or if he was OK. My instinct was to get out of there fast before the trouble got worse, so I raced back to the bedroom, bundled my stuff together into a bag, went to the veranda and jumped off onto the pavement. My plan was to make my way to Pawny's house in Kirkintilloch. It was ten miles off, and it was raining heavily, so I put up my hood and made ready to set off.

Immediately, I walked straight into about ten of the youths who had been outside the house yelling. I didn't recognise them, but as soon as they saw me they began shouting and swearing, 'It's you, ya bastard. You stabbed our mates!' There was no way I was going to argue with them, so instead I turned and headed back to the house. It was only about 30 metres away, but I had to go in by the front door. That was a bad move. Police were everywhere.

There was worse to come. The house nearby where the party had been held had now emptied. Everyone had piled into the street and all of them seemed to have noticed me at the same time. They surged forward, trying to get to me, but four or five policemen surrounded me and wedged me against the wall beside my front door. It was as if a screaming horde faced them. Then I saw paramedics taking casualties away on trolleys. It was obvious there had been severe stab wounds; blood was running from the bodies. Blue lights were flashing and the looks on the faces of the medics showed real concern. Other youths, the walking wounded, were also being led away.

As I watched, I noticed a young guy with a cut on his head walking towards the police and myself. He was carrying a half-bottle of vodka. As if in slow motion, as he walked past he smacked it onto the bridge of my nose. I fell, stunned. The police grabbed him and hauled him away. It was a bizarre scene. There I was at the door, having been smashed in the face by a bottle, while inside I could see Tam and Eddie still drinking away as though nothing was wrong.

The police eventually put me into a car for my own safety, but it became a magnet for the entire mob of youths, who tried smashing the windows and overturning it, so determined were they to get to me. It was scary. I couldn't believe what was happening. The car was being rocked backwards and forwards, and the police seemed to have disappeared. Eventually, they realised the safest strategy was to get me to the police station as quickly as possible before the riot got out of hand.

At the station, I had expected to be put in a cell but instead was asked to wait in an office. I found this strange and wondered what was happening. Every now and again the police would come in and check on me, give me a cigarette and tell me they would not keep me long. I wasn't used to this sort of treatment from the police and wondered if the fact I was in the army was making them more sympathetic to me. They obviously knew the mob that had been attacking me consisted of pond life, all the wee troublemakers from that area. Clearly, though, the police did not know that here they had a member of a family from Glasgow that had a pretty bad reputation. They had promised I wouldn't be detained and, true to their word, about half five in the morning someone took a brief statement, asked me to sign it and let me go, telling me I was being released on police bail.

I wandered back to the house in North Carbrain and found the forensic team still there, examining the scene. They said it was OK to go inside. I had to step over congealed blood. It was like having a mad dream. I found my bag, which someone must have taken from me and thrown inside, and left. I headed through to Glasgow to find Tam and Eddie, knowing this whole business was serious, and managed to track them down in a house in Maryhill completely off their heads on cocaine and Ecstasy. Yet again, they didn't seem to have a care in the world. I told them what had happened to me, described the people carried away on stretchers and pointed out I hadn't even been there during the fighting. Both promised that if I was arrested, they would hand themselves in and explain the truth of it all, that it was nothing to do with me.

'Stop worrying,' they told me. 'Look, as soon as we hear the police are on their way to lift you, we'll hand ourselves in.'

The words and sentiment were fine, but they came from guys

who had been in prison. I remembered the case of a friend of George Redmond who was still serving a life sentence after being convicted of a murder he didn't do. Innocent people did end up in prison.

So, I went back to the army. But in the back of my mind I was thinking to myself that this was going to go horribly wrong. I couldn't get out of my thoughts the sight of the guys being wheeled out on trolleys, drips stuck into their arms, masks over their faces and covered in blood. I remembered trying to get away and hearing the yells, them blaming me for the injuries. Obviously, it had been the others – probably Tam. My stomach was turning. I had been through all this before. When you are guilty of something, when you've done something wrong, then there's no fear, you accept it – you remember the old saying, 'If you want to do the crime, do the time'. But when you weren't involved, that's when you start to feel the emotions. I couldn't think, couldn't eat and was drinking. I kept asking myself what was going to happen, but deep down I knew it was inevitable: I'd be arrested.

As soon as I had time off, a couple of days, I went back to Inverness to see Angie, fully intending to tell her everything, but when we met up I found I just couldn't bring myself to do that. Instead, I went for a pint with a mate to discuss how best to tell her the whole story. While we were in the pub, the barmaid, who knew me, said I had a telephone call. When I picked up the receiver, I found it was one of my best friends ringing to tip me off that the civilian and military police were on their way to my home to arrest me. It meant I had 20 minutes to get there and explain everything before they showed up.

As soon as I got in the door, I told Angie I had something to tell her but had only five minutes in which to do it. As I raced through the story, she collapsed onto her knees and burst out crying. Dreadful though it was, I had to just leave her there on the floor and get out of the house. I knew I needed to hand myself in at the police station in Cumbernauld before midnight. By doing so, I could be in court the next morning and released on bail. If I waited for the police to arrest me, it would be hours before I would be taken south and because the next day was a

Friday I would in all probability be remanded over the weekend before a court appearance on the Monday.

So, I set off to drive to Cumbernauld. I stopped on the way to ask my lawyer to meet me at the police station. As I did this, the police were arriving to find me gone. They explained the whole story to Angie and at least stayed with her, realising she was in a state of total shock.

In Cumbernauld, following a brief chat with my lawyer, I handed myself in. The police were understanding and treated me well, but when the desk sergeant read out the first charge I felt my stomach churning. It was alleged that I, Alexander Shannon, did assault and attempt to murder so and so with a machete or similar instrument and did strike him to the extent of leaving him severely disfigured. It was repeated twice more.

By now, the reality of it all was sinking in. After my fingerprints were taken, I was led to the cells. On the floor outside the cell next to mine, I noticed a pair of training shoes and immediately recognised them as belonging to Tam. True to his word, as soon as he found out from the police and my friends in Inverness what was going on, he had handed himself in. So I sat, miserable and cold, with a blanket wrapped around me, wondering how I had got myself into this mess and how, now, my life, career and possibly marriage were over. How would I cope without Angie? I was sure I could handle a prison sentence, but not life without her.

As the night wore on, I heard Tam shouting. He had noticed my shoes and was upset that they had arrested me, even after he had handed himself in. When he calmed down, we started talking, but he insisted on singing over and over to 'always look on the bright side of life'. Well, I didn't see there was anything to be cheerful about. After hearing the charges, I fully expected my army career to be over. I'd be remanded in custody and spend three months in prison waiting for a trial. It wouldn't matter if I was found not guilty. I would be a civilian in prison clothing by then.

We were allowed out of the cells that morning to wash and shave before showing up in court. Tam pulled out a packet of cigarettes and gave me some, along with a few matches and a couple of temazepams to calm me down. 'Don't worry, I'll make sure you are 100 per cent sorted,' he assured me.

Within twenty minutes, I was ready for anything, even a seven-day remand to Barlinnie prison. By now Eddie too had given himself up but because of the seriousness of the charges we were given an escort to the court in Airdrie, where we were placed in a cell for high-risk prisoners. Happily, when we eventually appeared at court later in the day we were granted bail on condition we attended an identification parade and a judicial review hearing.

At the identification parade, thirty-four witnesses turned up and eight of them picked me out as the machete attacker. I knew they had got it wrong, mistaking me for Tam, but us looking so alike had been a constant thorn in my side. A couple of years previously, I'd found myself in a cell after allegedly being caught in possession of a big machete in the centre of Glasgow. I'd never seen it, but the police had come and arrested me.

Next day, when I'd been released on bail, I'd said to Tam, 'Fucking knife's got nothing to do with me.' It turned out to belong to Tam's mate. He'd always carried a knife, but because I was in the army I could not afford to do things like that – although I didn't mind fighting and, if it came to it, would use whatever was on hand and then get rid of it. By luck, I had insisted on having the machete fingerprinted and, of course, the police ended up dropping the case. Again Tam had promised, 'If it comes to it, we'll say it belongs to us.' Thankfully, it had not come to that, but I always had the feeling the issue of mistaken identity would come back to haunt me. And now it had.

\* \* \*

While Alex went through the agonies of waiting for his trial and the uncertainty of the outcome, he learned of the arrest in London of William Lobban. Police had picked him up in January in Earls Court and he was taken under escort back to Glasgow, where he was questioned about the murders of Arty, Bobby and Joe. In the end, no action was taken. But Eileen Glover, for one, was not going to forget his treachery. Nor were the Shannons.

* * *

As the trial neared, I was going through a gamut of emotions, including denial and fear. I was having nightmares, too. Worst of all, sometimes I had no fear of anything or anyone, life or death, I just accepted the fact, as my lawyer had warned me, that I could expect a prison sentence of between eight and ten years.

None of this mattered, though, compared to my concern for Angie. While she stood by me, and believed me, then mentally I would be strong enough to cope with anything. I owed her so much and loved her more than life itself, but what if she wasn't there?

The attitude of the army remained as it had always been – I was a gangster and guilty until I could prove my innocence. My brothers continued to reassure me they would make sure my army career was safe.

One thing that worried me was that each time we had to turn up for a court hearing our lawyer told Tam and me: 'You two are too alike. Who will a court believe? One of you did it.' Tam insisted he would plead not guilty, but he assured me if they insisted on continuing with the charges against me and we ended up in the dock, he would plea bargain and change his plea.

The case dragged on for a year. During that time, George Redmond promised he would do all he could to help and he would show just how good a friend he could be.

* * *

Now that he was back under lock and key, William Lobban had been accused of the Pipe Rack hold-up and was awaiting trial. More worrying to him than the prospect of a further prison sentence was being sent to Perth prison. It was there that he would be joined by Paul Ferris's brother, Billy, nearing the end of a life sentence for a murder in England. Billy had been friends with Bobby and Joe; indeed, they had visited him not long before their deaths. Lobban needed to be wary and he knew it. He had a small coterie of friends to act as minders, but paranoia that he was on the verge of being killed had set in.

First, someone tried to poison his food. Then, in July, he needed 17 stitches to a head wound after another inmate had battered him with a last in the cobbler's shop. Inexplicably, the prison authorities locked the attacker in the next cell to his victim, with the result that Lobban determined on revenge. Desperate to get at the other inmate, Lobban took prison officer Terry O'Neill hostage using a pen as a makeshift weapon. He then set about trying to smash his way into the neighbouring cell. As he ripped and tore and almost succeeded in smashing off the door to the cell where the other man cowered, staff, realising that if he succeeded then in all probability they would have a murder on their hands, set about negotiating an end to the drama. After 14 hours, they persuaded Lobban to give up. O'Neill was released unharmed.

\* \* \*

You can only imagine what must have been going through that guy's head in that cell. I've no doubt that if Lobban had got in to him, he would have killed him with his bare hands. Shortly afterwards he was shipped to Peterhead in Aberdeenshire, where me, Pawny and Tam went to visit him. This was the first time we had seen him since the murders. We wanted to know where we stood and to find out if he'd had anything to do with them. Of course, he was never going to admit to anything like that, so we assumed that he may or may not have been involved. That was more a concern for Paul Ferris, rather than us.

Clearly, the Peterhead staff were keeping a very close eye on Gibby. When I was growing up, I had heard all about Peterhead. Nowadays, it holds mainly rapists and paedophiles, offenders thought to be in need of protection from the mainstream prison population, but at one time it guarded the most dangerous men in Scotland – rough, tough characters who feared nothing. Conditions had been appalling and brutal, beatings of inmates frequent.

On the day we went, we sat among all the other visitors and then officers came in and told us to follow them. We naturally went along with everybody else and ended up in a big room. Everyone was sitting at tables and we started looking around for Gibby. There was no sign of him, then a whole pack of screws came rushing in, surrounded us and told us we shouldn't have been there. We protested, but they hurried us out. We discovered later that they'd stuck us in a room with the sex offenders. The screws must have thought, 'Fuck, we've stuck three gangsters in among them, there's going to be a riot.'

Gibby was in Peterhead having been recategorised as a prisoner who could not be trusted to conform to the mainstream system. He was both a danger to and at risk from other inmates. This followed the incidents at Perth and the whispers about his possible involvement in the Joe and Bobby murders. It was deemed too risky to let him loose in the general system, not knowing how many friends Paul Ferris had there. As a result of his status, we were taken to a tiny separate area of the jail. Guys with riot shields were guarding it. They had to move aside to let us in and sit down to wait for Gibby.

He was too wary to say anything important. He was always conscious of cameras and people lip-reading as he spoke, so we left none the wiser. On the way home, I wondered why nobody else had made a move on him in Perth. I came to the conclusion it was because everybody knew he was a highly dangerous person.

# CHAPTER TWENTY-SIX

Alex had enjoyed his first tour in Northern Ireland, despite the dramas and dangers he had experienced. Now, he was looking forward to another. He received word he would be going to the province as a multiple commander in charge of 12 other soldiers. The tour would begin in the autumn, but instead of returning to West Belfast he would find himself in Crossmaglen, South Armagh. It was a nervous, worrying time for him and Angie. The risks all soldiers took in Northern Ireland didn't bother him; he was well trained and, he knew, would be well prepared. Mentally, he was well up to the tasks that awaited him there. It was the waiting at home that made him edgy.

His frame of mind was not helped by continuing friction with the Springburn Mob, in particular the McIntyres, Duncan and his brother Joe, commonly referred to as 'Fat Boy'. Alex had cemented his peace with the McGoverns, but they could not be expected to begin an all-out war with the McIntyres, a fight that would effectively be on behalf of a rival family.

Elsewhere, Alex hoped the jailing in the summer for 14 years of his co-accused, Eddie Kennedy, for a series of bank and building society raids was not an omen for his own forthcoming ordeal over the Cumbernauld fighting. There was nothing he could do except work hard and wait.

Alex was due to go to Northern Ireland in November, but in October the Procurator Fiscal refused him permission to leave the mainland until after the attempted murders trial, which had been set for January 1993. All sorts of assurances were given by the army that Alex would be back in Scotland well before the court hearing, but it made no difference. To Alex, it seemed that as far as everyone was concerned, his lawyer included, he was going down. It certainly wasn't looking too good for him.

Angie did her best to reassure her husband. She had never doubted his innocence, knowing that when he was drunk he just fell asleep. She had asked him to tell her the truth and when he did she had believed him.

On the day of the trial, the Procurator Fiscal seemed to have had a change of heart where Alex was concerned. A deal was made with Eddie under which he pleaded guilty to a lesser offence and was given five years to run concurrently with the fourteen he was already serving, which resulted in the charges against Alex being dropped. After much more bargaining, Tam's charges were dropped as well. Why the change of heart by the Fiscal? Well, none of the 30-plus witnesses turned up for the court hearing, so he didn't have many options left open to him.

And why hadn't they shown up? Perhaps because it turned out that George Redmond knew most of the guys who had been at the party that night. Alex could never be completely sure whether this had anything to do with it, but by two o'clock the following afternoon he was patrolling through Crossmaglen. Only twenty-six hours earlier he had been looking at eight years in prison. It was just the IRA he had to worry about now.

* * *

Crossmaglen had earned notoriety 200 years earlier as the site of a thriving but illegal shebeen whose owner gave his name to the village. Now, it had a reputation as a real hotbed of Republicanism. During the troubles, nearly 60 police officers and 124 soldiers were murdered in and around Crossmaglen. This horrific toll included at least a dozen troops killed by a squad known as the South Armagh Sniper Team of whom Alex would come to have first-hand knowledge. To suggest the area was highly dangerous came nowhere near the reality of the situation. Indeed, nobody or nowhere was safe. Booby trap bombs were a frequent cause of slaughter, one of their victims being Edmund Woolsey, an IRA sympathiser who, after being told that the car he had reported stolen was abandoned near Crossmaglen, went to retrieve it and was blown up. This was the setting into which Alex and his colleagues were introduced. Because of the Official Secrets Act Alex cannot talk in detail about specific operations or individuals on whom he was tasked to gather information.

*  *  *

Days into the tour, I knew things were not going well, as the guys in Borucki Sangar were constantly being shot at. A sangar is a small, temporary fortified post and this one was named after Private James Borucki, from the 3rd Battalion, The Parachute Regiment, who was killed by a bomb hidden in the basket of a bicycle at Crossmaglen. He was just 19. The sangar was constructed on the spot where he died. The commander of the sangar team was an old friend of mine from Posso. I'll call him 'Mac'. I knew him and his family very well. He was older and had that particular job because of an old injury that prevented him from patrolling. Now, his job was to sit in the sangar, monitor movements and report everything that went into and out of Crossmaglen. To us soldiers, the sangar was just a big target used for shooting practice by the terrorists, especially snipers wanting to test out their weapons or bombers testing different types of explosives.

Some guys spent their entire six-month tour on sangar duty and sometimes found the length of this duty difficult. Mac was among them.

Our attitude at that time was the quicker you went back into the place where you had just been blown up, the sharper your mind was in being able to deal with any resulting issues. Easier said than done, of course.

I remember one of the young soldiers refusing to go back in after the South Armagh Sniper Team took out the supposedly bulletproof windows with 7.62 mm and .50 calibre ammunition. His face looked like the top of a pepper pot, pitted with cuts from flying glass fragments. However, after the company sergeant major had had a chat with him, the young soldier was back in, cracking on with the job and awaiting the next attack. That took considerable bottle.

South Armagh was known as Bandit Country and we were having a particularly bad time. All the other companies were being hit in one way or another, but we in Crossmaglen were under constant threat. It had a reputation as the worst place in the province to serve as a soldier and multiple commander, and I soon learned why. I was responsible for the main radio communications back to base and would receive daily threat updates. These would generally be intelligence linked. When a message came over warning, 'High threat, sniper shoot in the Crossmaglen area,' we all knew it had to be taken seriously, but most of the time I would not tell the rest of the guys about the level of these threats. To pass on information of this nature to soldiers is to risk changing the way they work, which might result in them making mistakes or putting their lives or those of others in danger.

Don't get me wrong, I would change my patrol techniques, move in and out of cover quickly and always be very vigilant, but it is impossible to cater for every eventuality. One important factor to remember is no matter what happens, you must, in these circumstances, keep moving. I've seen the biggest men crumble under the pressure of working in this environment. Once, we were about four miles outside Crossmaglen when one of my team commanders broke down and refused to go any further. This was a guy around six foot five and weighing 17 stone. Yet there he sat, in a ditch crying, with a tiny graze on his hand. I have to admit that in the weeks leading up to that incident I'd noticed something was going wrong with him. On occasions, I would sit down with him, talk to him, encourage him to lead by example and not to show his soldiers signs of weakness. If he showed he was cracking up, I would tell him that letting others see this would destroy his name and career. But the day he sat in the ditch I realised talking had not worked. There was only one thing to do. I grabbed him by the throat, gave his weapon to another soldier and dragged him, despite his crying and apologising for his breakdown, all the way back to base. It was a worrying situation. The guy was a mate. If I called in a helicopter to evacuate him, gossip would soon have spread all over. He wouldn't have been able to continue in those dangerous surroundings any longer. His career would have been as good as over. Cruel though what I did might sound, I was more or less carrying out a damage limitation exercise, and it worked. He recovered his composure and his dignity, though he was replaced in the multiple team and was not allowed out of base until we returned to Inverness at the end of the tour.

The strategy in South Armagh was to always patrol with two multiples on the ground mutually supporting each other. My supporting multiple commander was an old friend. We were good pals and related well to one another, and professionally were very alike. One day as we were on Quick Reaction Force duty, specially trained to deal with situations requiring rapid response, an RUC officer told us that a group of IRA Volunteers suspected of blowing up one of our guys a couple of weeks earlier was in a bar in Crossmaglen Square. His information revealed that when they had finished their drinking session, they would head by car down Culloville Road, which ran past our base. 'If you're quick, when they leave you can head onto the road further down and set up a vehicle checkpoint,' he suggested. We were up for this. Stopping them would give us an excuse to search their motor and question the group. It all sounded great in theory, but things did not quite go according to the textbook.

Things started off well. When word came over the intercom that the party was leaving the bar, we made our way to the predetermined spot and set up the checkpoint. As their car approached, it was signalled to stop. We went through the usual routine, asking for names and addresses and searching the vehicle, but things very quickly got out of hand. There were four in the car and two of them got out and started fighting with the team commander and me. The other two Volunteers remained in the car, watching as we grappled and punched. I was wearing full kit, so I was having difficulty moving freely and my opponent was getting the upper hand. So I broke all the rules. I took off my kit, gave it to one of my colleagues and went at it again. This time it was a different story.

The RUC had been informed we were setting up a roadblock and came along to see how it was going. By now, all four of us were cut and bruised, and it took the police several minutes to pull us apart. Eventually, everything settled down and the Volunteers climbed back into their car and began driving off. However, after only travelling a few metres, they stopped; one of the rear windows was wound down and my opponent stuck his head out and shouted to me to come over.

'What the fuck do you want?' I spat at him.

'The next time I'll see you is when I have the crosshairs of a weapon sight bang on your fucking face,' he told me, ever so calmly. 'One in the head, ya Brit scum.'

'Fuck off, ya wee prick. You want another fight?'

He looked back up and said, 'Arsehole! Don't you realise for the last 30 minutes I've been studying your face. You forgot to smear your camouflage cream on when you left the base.'

They drove away and I could almost hear them laughing in the car. The exchange left me chalk white and feeling sick, not because of the threat about the weapon sight but because camouflage cream gives soldiers a false face to hide behind, so they cannot be recognised. When I discovered who my fight had been with, my worry increased. I realised I should have been really worried over his weapon sight remark.

'That's "Patrick Pitt". He's a member of the South Armagh Sniper Team,' I was told. On hearing that, I knew, for the rest of this tour and any other I did in Northern Ireland, I would never go on patrol without first coating myself with cam cream.

The South Armagh Sniper Team was the name given to members of the Provos South Armagh Brigade. Terrorist snipers, dedicated to the expression 'one shot, one kill', murdered around 180 soldiers, police and prison officers during the troubles. A senior police officer said they were 'undoubtedly one of the most vicious, callous teams to be run by the IRA'. Pitt was one of their number.

Shortly afterwards my team commander friend and I were briefed on a patrol we had been ordered to carry out. We were kitted and ready, but with about ten minutes to go the officer commanding announced there had been a change to the plan. Instead of two, just one multiple would go on the patrol. It was an easy enough patrol. The unit would be carried by helicopter from Crossmaglen and then work back to base, carrying out checks at the homes of suspected troublemakers along the return route. It was a total distance of about five miles and would take around two hours. I thought about this and asked if it was safe, not having a supporting multiple, but was assured I would be fine. The officer commanding assured me all the observation towers were watching me and had been issued with my route plans and timings. So, I thought, 'OK, let's get on with it.' And off we set. I completed the patrol and returned, wondering if it had all been a complete waste of time.

I was due to head out on a double multiple patrol with my friend's outfit the following day, 25 February 1993, when it was cancelled with a couple of hours to go and this time we stayed behind. He took his guys out, but as they were around 500 metres from base, heading back towards Crossmaglen, a loud bang rang out. I was in the cookhouse having lunch with another mate, who was wearing all his gear and had his radio switched on. Within seconds, the radio blasted out, 'Contact shooting, one casualty.' I recognised the voice of the other multiple commander and was sure someone had been killed.

Sadly, I was correct. Constable Jonathan Reid, aged 30, of the RUC, had been shot in the chest by the South Armagh Sniper Team as he patrolled Castleblaney Road, Crossmaglen. The killer had fired a single bullet and fled before soldiers with the police officer could return fire. Constable Reid was flown to hospital in Newry but died despite efforts to save him. The patrol took the customary follow-up steps, searching, asking questions and so on, but the killer had gone. As soldiers, you just move on and accept it, as though it is just another blip in the day. That may sound callous and lacking in remorse, but it's part of the strategy soldiers use for coping. We just carry on. To be brutally honest, we tend to deal with death by using black humour. To someone outside the military community, this may sound disrespectful, but it is our way of getting by.

I was later sent to take charge of another multiple whose

commander, a young lieutenant, had lost the ability to lead. I was welcomed by a legendary character known as 'Big John'. The name was appropriate. He was a giant of a man, about seven feet square, and despite being only a corporal took no nonsense from anyone regardless of rank or size.

My first encounter with my new team was to be a move by helicopter to patrol a sector close to the border. They had been gradually congregating by a shed next to the helicopter landing pad and I was the last to arrive. As I walked in, they all burst out laughing. One of the soldiers asked why I was wearing cam cream. 'We leave here in two minutes,' I said. 'Those who don't have cam cream on are staying behind.' I had remembered my earlier encounter with Pitt and his promise to recognise me.

There was silence, and everybody looked towards Big John.

'Sorry, Del,' he said, then asked, 'Does anyone have a cam stick?'

In a matter of seconds, they had coated their faces with cream and were ready to go. In the weeks that followed, I had a few other exchanges with Big John, but the unit knew I was in charge for a reason. I refused to cut corners or take risks. It was my job to be 100 per cent professional and I knew that if they followed my work ethic and ethos they might just make it through the tour alive. I was determined to see them all safely back home.

As we neared the end of the tour, my multiple had been dispersed as soldiers started heading back to Scotland. I was sent to one especially troublesome sector as stand-in commander while we prepared for the handover to the regiment that was to take over from us. It was 17 March, St Patrick's Day, and I was alone in an observation tower around midday when I noticed the volume of radio traffic was increasing. Suddenly, my radios went silent. I tried the usual trusted method of punching and kicking them to see if they would come back to life. At first, there was nothing. Then, out of the blue, the telephone rang. I recognised the voice of the families officer back in Inverness. He was looking for me.

# CHAPTER TWENTY-SEVEN

Armed and masked raiders had pounced on the post office at Kirkintilloch to the north of Glasgow, not far from Pawny's home, and had made off with a sizeable cash haul, as much as £110,000, some said. As soon as the police arrived to begin investigating, Pawny was placed near the top of the list of those whose movements at the time of the robbery would be checked. When the knock on his door came, however, it remained unanswered.

Alex spoke to Tam on the night of 16 March and was told he was heading to Spain with Pawny and the family for a two-week holiday, as they had recently made some money. He told Alex they would catch up when he returned from South Armagh.

As St Patrick's Day dawned, Alex thought about his brothers and guessed they would be lying in the sun, drinking beers and enjoying themselves. In South Armagh, the coming hours would bring little cheer. Lance Corporal Lawrence Dickson, aged 26, from Inverness, was married with an 18-month-old daughter. His career had closely mirrored Alex's, signing up as a boy soldier in 1983, training at the Bridge of Don and then joining the ranks of the 1st Battalion the Royal Scots. He had seen service in Northern Ireland and Iraq. That day, as he routinely patrolled near the Irish border at Forkhill, a single fatal shot from a high-powered rifle held by a member of the South Armagh Sniper Team struck him in the chest.

\* \* \*

As messages about Lance Corporal Dickson's murder were

passing through the army communications network, I was taking the call from the families officer in Inverness. I asked how I could help, and he said, 'I have some bad news for you. Your brother is in a coma in Spain. He fell from a motorcycle and it's likely he won't live for more than 48 hours. We can get you back to Inverness as soon as possible, but will you organise your flight to Spain?' All I could think of to say was 'I'll phone you back.'

I knew something was wrong at my location and, as soon as I replaced the receiver, the three main radios all switched back on at the same time. I knew straight away there had been a killing and within minutes a clear picture had emerged. Lawrence Dickson was the brother of one of the men in my company and a team commander. Dickie was a really well-liked guy and his death had a huge impact on our morale, as, until then, while some of our men had suffered serious injuries, nobody had died. He was the first Royal Scot to be killed and what was even more tragic was that his death came so close to the end of our tour.

I was still thinking of him that night as a helicopter picked me up to take me to base at Crossmaglen, where I was to collect my kit. Lawrence's brother George climbed in beside me. There we were, two soldiers, one expecting to lose a brother, the other already having lost one just a few hours earlier. George hugged me and said, 'Don't worry, at least you should get to see your brother before he dies.'

We were transferred via the army's casualty evacuation system all the way back to Inverness and then went our separate ways. When I had last spoken to Tam, I'd told him to make sure he enjoyed himself and that we'd have a few pints together when he was back. Now, I too was heading for Spain, wondering if we would ever stand at the same bar again. I wasn't looking forward to what lay ahead.

* * *

It had been a bad crash. Paramedics had performed a roadside tracheotomy so he could breathe and their skill had helped save his life. At hospital, he underwent an emergency operation but his heart stopped twice on the operating table. He was in and out of a coma for months and once a Roman Catholic priest was brought in to give him the last rites.

There were many who believed it was the presence of his brothers and their love for him that helped him survive. Brotherly love can be a powerful force – the blood bond overwhelms other ties built on affection.

There is a little known story concerning two brothers belonging to a Glasgow underworld family. As one lay ill, his wife was bedded by his sibling. When the wronged brother recovered and discovered what had transpired, his animosity was aimed not at the other man but at his wife, who was blamed for taking advantage of her lover's weakness. She was thrown out and divorced.

Alex got to spend a fair bit of time with his brother, and as the days went on he was getting stronger, not to the extent that he was OK, but just enough to survive. To what extent he would recover, nobody could tell. When he was sure Tam was going to pull through, he returned home and to the army. After a few weeks, Tam followed. He would continue his treatment at the Southern General Hospital in Glasgow

While Tam lay recovering, it became apparent that the police were looking for both him and Pawny in connection with the post office robbery that had taken place a week before the brothers flew to Spain. Realising Tam was vulnerable, it was decided to spirit him out of hospital to a safe house where he could remain until he felt fit enough to face the police and a possible court trial. The safe houses turned out to be a series of caravans in sites dotted all over Scotland.

Before long he was caught when someone close to him told the police of his whereabouts. It was done solely out of greed for money. So he and Pawny had to face the music. They were charged with holding up the post office, but Pawny's case was dropped due to a lack of evidence and the case against Tam was judged Not Proven. However, Tam still had years of healing ahead of him. And there were apparently a lot of people from Springburn happy at his situation.

Tam himself had heard about the premature celebrations.

# THE UNDERWORLD CAPTAIN

When he was in a really bad way, people were dancing on the tables. The McIntyres and their cronies were especially happy to hear he was in a coma and wasn't expected to pull through. They certainly weren't laughing when they discovered Tam was going to survive because they knew he and his friends would be looking for them.

Just days prior to Tam's accident, Arthur Thompson had died in his bed from a heart attack. He was only 61. On the day of his funeral, someone planted a device in the cemetery at Riddrie, a few metres from his home, where he was to be buried, and telephoned the police. Bomb squad officers, called in to carry out a controlled explosion, discovered it was a crude hoax. The mourners included police officers, representatives from the legal profession and a host of shady underworld characters, some of whom were part of a delegation from London. His death, following that of Arty, brought an end to the empire. His surviving son, Billy, lacked the clout or reputation to stave off fighting over the Godfather's territories and would ultimately suffer permanent brain damage as the result of a cowardly attack near his home.

It was inevitable that at the wake following Arthur's funeral there would be talk of the killing of Arty and the murders of Bobby and Joe. And, of course, the name William Lobban kept coming up.

Following the arrest of the Glaswegians after the Torquay bank fiasco, the trials in Devon were aborted when word leaked out that one of the men had a pistol and would use it in court to effect an escape for the gang. As a result, it was decided to move the case to the Old Bailey in London, where security was tighter. Lobban was cited as a defence witness. He was already in custody, having been arrested in London and charged with escaping from prison, and then accused over the hold-up at the Pipe Rack bar in 1991. He agreed to give evidence, provided he was not named. But word was that some of the defendants had an extra motive for wanting to be near to Lobban. Michael Healy, for one, had not forgotten that it was Lobban who had allowed Paul Ferris into his home, carrying a gun. Nor who it was who had said Healy had been badmouthing Ferris. Blink McDonald, too, had similarly been put into the Ferris bad books as a result of rumours spread by Lobban.

Rumour reached the Shannons that Lobban had been set up, cited not so much for the reason of any usefulness he might have as a witness but simply in order that he could be murdered in prison. And there were plenty of takers.

Lobban would have known the risks when he went to London. Later on he told friends how in prison one morning he had gone for his water to make tea and was on his way back to his cell, carrying two pots filled with boiling hot water. He was conscious of people staring at him; guys had been looking daggers at him for days because obviously word had spread about the rumour that he might have been involved in Joe and Bobby's murders. Then he had been called down to give evidence even though he had nothing to do with the bank robbery. People were trying to get him from Scotland to London so he could get nipped there. As he stood holding the pots, Gibby shouted, 'Come near me and you're getting boiling water over your faces!' The incident was seen by warders and, although the other inmates left Gibby alone, he was moved into another wing and as soon as he had given evidence he was shipped back to Scotland.

The appearance of the not-so-mysterious 'Mr A' in the witness box was bizarre. Everyone in court knew his identity as William Lobban and that night word of what happened was the subject of bar gossip and laughter all over Glasgow. Blink McDonald, sitting in the dock, remembers Lobban arriving in the witness box clutching a Holy Bible and at one stage rebuking the jury for not giving him sufficient attention. Newspapers reported that 'Mr A' alleged Ferris had been responsible for the deaths of Arty, Bobby and Joe. In the end, Lobban was of no help.

All the robbers were destined to spend many years in prison. The following month, September, Lobban was sent down for six years for the Pipe Rack robbery. Eileen Glover, the pain over the loss of her husband still visible on a face wracked by grief, had determined to make him suffer; in her evidence, she had said that Lobban had told her the money counted out in her home came from the Pipe Rack hold-up. When she said she believed he had been involved in murdering Joe and Bobby, even if he was not the actual killer, he had shouted from the dock, 'Eileen, Eileen, it wasn't me.' But it was not her he needed to convince. It was hundreds of others in the prison system with allegiances to the dead men and their friend, Paul Ferris.

The Shannons, too, had their issues with Lobban. Tam, still recovering from the Spanish nightmare, continued to rage over the gun threat against Pawny. And they had felt aggrieved by his moving his loyalty away from them towards Ferris, even though they had no grudges against Paul. In their opinion, though, it was better to keep their enemy close and so they continued to visit Lobban in prison.

Lobban entered Alex's thoughts very rarely, though; his concerns were with his career and, even more so, Angie. As most couples do at some time or another, they found their marriage going through a difficult time. She was still not convinced he had severed his links with gangland, a belief that was correct; however, he was determined to show her he had the desire and ability to build his career.

\* \* \*

After the trials and tribulations of the previous two and a half years, I told myself things can only get better. I used to sing the words along with D:Ream, who had a huge hit with the song. I just couldn't get the lyrics out of my head. They kept running around and around until I was sure someone was sending me a message. Perhaps things were on the up. I hoped so.

But it wasn't to be. I was selected to go on my Platoon Sergeants Course, starting in January 1994, but after seven weeks of hard graft and then nearly being kicked off for fighting with another soldier, the selection board failed me for having a bad attitude. I was told it was not the way I was expected to carry myself as a future Senior NCO. It was a real blow and set me back a couple of years mentally. In hindsight, they were correct: my mind was still not settled. While I loved soldiering,

I had a mouth and a temper to match, and in the army you need to learn quickly that there is a time and place to be seen and heard. I'm afraid I was a slow learner in this department and tended to challenge authority on behalf of everyone else; I could never just shut up and play the game like the rest of my close friends. I suppose I can say, 'Look at me now.' Although I was ostracised and criticised at times over the years, I still made it, and I'm proud of the way I did it.

During the summer that year, along with the rest of my company, I went to Cyprus for six weeks on a training course. It was an amazing experience and then, training over, we were allowed five days of freedom to go to Ayia Napa, one of the main seaside resorts on the island, for a spell of rest and recuperation.

When we arrived, we all hired mopeds and rode round like a gang of Hell's Angels. One night, I was in one of the main nightclubs when I overheard a group of girls talking and could tell right away from their accents that they were from Glasgow. After a while, one of the girls came over and politely asked if I was one of the Shannons from Springburn. When I told her I was, she asked my name. 'Oh, then you're the one in the army,' she said. 'My brothers talk about you all the time. They think the world of you.' My curiosity was really aroused, so I asked who the brothers were. 'The McGoverns from Springburn,' she said. I told her I had always felt the same way about Steven, Tommy and Tony.

We spent the next hour talking about what had gone wrong and who was behind all the mixing that led to the troubles of a few years earlier. Before we parted, she said that as soon as she was back in Glasgow she would tell her brothers about our talk. 'They didn't know the whole story,' she said. 'They were only getting one side, which was coming from Duncan and Joe McIntyre.'

She was true to her word. A month after returning from Cyprus, I received a message through a third party to the effect that Tony was asking for me, that all was well and he wondered if in the future we could meet up for the drink he had first suggested a few years earlier. Sadly, things happened that prevented me from accepting Tony's invitation. I'd love to have spent an evening in his company, but by now I was totally focused on my career and adamant that after all the troubles of the past I was going to get myself in order and make a life for me, Angie and the kids with the army.

# CHAPTER TWENTY-EIGHT

Each summer the royal family traditionally heads north to Balmoral Castle, a beautiful estate home near the town of Ballater in Aberdeenshire. The castle looks as though it's been dropped in from a fairy tale, with its ivy-covered granite walls and spectacular turrets. Nearby lie fields packed with shaggy, long-horned Highland cattle and through which runs the River Dee, where the Duke of Edinburgh at one time loved to fish. In the distance, snow-covered hills and mountains look down on the scene. Balmoral is the personal property of the Queen. Frequently, she will invite guests to share this wonderful house with her. These may be members of other royal households and heads of state. On warm August days, royal parties will head off in search of game or a quiet hillside on which to picnic. Every year, she and her family work hard for these pleasures, but the annual holiday represents a security nightmare. Local police are augmented by members of the Metropolitan Royal Protection unit, which comes under the control of Protection Command, and at times of medium to high alert, members of the SAS will secretly hide out in the hills and woods surrounding Balmoral, but the task of showing high-profile security is left with the army. Each year, a regiment will be tasked with guarding Balmoral. It is a prestigious operation, giving ordinary soldiers unprecedented access to the royals. Hardly the setting for a man with a Glasgow gangland background; one accused of attempted murder and knife crime, no less, and with a criminal record. Yet in the summer of 1994 Alex found himself dancing with the Queen and enjoying a boozing session with the Queen Mother.

\* \* \*

Guard duty at Balmoral? Totally fantastic. Something a soldier probably only gets to do once in a lifetime. We were in Inverness when the order came through that we would spend three months based at the Victoria Barracks in Ballater as the Royal Guard. We were divided into three platoons. One is Pony Platoon, going up into the hills to stalk deer with the royal party; the other platoons mainly do guard duty at the various entrances to Balmoral and within the area around the castle. Until you are tasked with duty at Balmoral, you cannot understand just how amazing a duty this is, not least because of the access you have to the royal family. Guys who are used to guard duty at Buckingham Palace just don't understand how close Balmoral duty takes you to the most exclusive family in the world.

One of the highlights is the Ghillies' Ball. Soldiers and some members of the police get invited and it gives you a chance to let your hair down and have a drink with the royals. Ghillies go out on fishing or stalking expeditions and ensure all goes well, offering advice and help when it is needed. They are glorified gamekeepers, really, but they are highly regarded and often chosen for their discretion and good manners. The ball is one of the highlights of the summer holiday at Balmoral.

I looked forward to the big night and made sure my uniform was immaculate, buttons and medals gleaming. When I arrived at the castle, I was told I was being given a very special task. I was to stand at the head of the staircase in the private accommodation area and wait for the Queen Mother. I was then to escort her all the way through the castle and down the staircase to the room where the ball was taking place. As I waited upstairs, I watched footmen calmly and professionally going about their business and I must have been there for up to an hour. As the time passed, I would now and then be offered a drink. Well, the night wore on and the drinks became more frequent. In fairness, I was tanning them. I'd had a couple before I started just to calm my nerves and was pretty close to being half cut when I spotted the Queen Mother making her way towards me. I tottered down the staircase with this wonderful and gracious lady on my arm and on reaching the bottom she asked if I would get her a gin and tonic. I did, and was about to leave when she told me just to stand there with her. And so I ended up standing with the Queen Mother for about an hour and a half, as the officers at attention behind us tried to find excuses to get me away. All the time, the Queen Mother was chatting to me. It was crazy. But she was brilliant.

Eventually, I went off to join in the ball. And here, to put it mildly, I made a bit of a mistake. For one of the dances, the females take the inside, with males outside, and you go in opposite directions. When the music stops, you dance with whoever is standing opposite you until the music stops again and then the whole thing begins over. I had joined in and was enjoying this when the music stopped and I discovered I was standing in front of the Queen. She put out her hands and told me, 'It's your lucky day'. She stood waiting for me to take her hands and commence dancing. At my side was this old guy who must have been in his 70s. He was shaking with excitement. I felt sorry for him and said, 'Ma'am, I hope you don't mind, but I think he needs this more than me. It's his lucky day this time. I'd like to step to one side.' Then I just switched places with him.

I'm sure the Queen looked stunned, but later on that night my chance did come again and this time I took it, dancing the Eightsome Reel with the Queen and Princess Anne. It was a truly unforgettable experience. Ask any soldier and they will tell you they love Balmoral guard duty. You get to experience the royal family at a very personal level and see how much they enjoy their holiday at Balmoral.

# CHAPTER TWENTY-NINE

A few hundred yards from where I lay, I heard the sound of firing and knew what it was coming from. A farmer was blasting a shotgun into bushes. This wasn't an idle waste of pellets; he was doing it just in case there were any soldiers lying in hiding. It didn't matter that he couldn't see anything or anybody. He had probably heard whispers that an undercover army team was somewhere in the area hiding up, watching the home of a leading terrorist, reporting back on his movements, photographing and snooping. I hoped he wouldn't come any closer. If he did, I would have to decide whether to give my little group away by taking evasive action, thus ruining a very well planned and vital operation. It was my operation and I wanted it to succeed, but this was South Armagh, danger country, where dozens of policemen and soldiers had been murdered simply because they wore a uniform. You never knew what to expect next.

And there we were, huddled in the middle of a gorse bush, tired, unwashed, stinking, cold, hungry, wet and cut off. We had been there for ten days. There were four still to go. I'd waited for eight before having a crap, and now that was in a bag inside my pack. 'Leave nothing, not a trace,' I had been told. I longed to feel a bog seat under my backside, taste a warm drink, eat hot food, lie in a bath, live like a human again instead of an animal.

It didn't pay to move too much. I had sited us in the middle of gorse bushes. At night, rats and furry things ran over us. Things crawled inside our stinking clothes. I was hungry. My wife was leaving me. Maybe she had already gone, I had no way of knowing. But this was the life I had chosen, the one I had picked. I wondered whether Tam and Pawny had caught up with the McIntyres, if Lobban had done another runner, if there was a chance of holding onto Angie.

It had been my job to pick the spot where we lay because I was now a specialist member of a Close Observation Platoon. Others might have called it a hiding hole. To me, it was a Greenfield Observation Post. Just how it sounded. Normally, it was a spot somewhere in the middle of an anonymous green field from where we could watch somebody else. Only in our case it was a set of giant gorse bushes on the side of a railway line. We were keeping watch on a suspected terrorist who lived a few hundred metres off. It was a difficult and dangerous task that could only be done by men dedicated to their army calling. But I had so nearly not been there.

For a long time after the disappointment of not making it on to the Platoon Sergeants Course, I had thought over whether the army was for me after all. My confidence had taken a major knock and now I was doubting my ability as a soldier. I considered calling it a day, moving back to Glasgow and picking up where I had left off. Yet, once again, it was Angie who shook me to my senses, pointing out the reality that I was good at my job, there was a career for me and I should simply get stuck back into work. She put me back on the road to recovering my self-belief, but I sensed all was not well with us.

The regiment was due to go on another tour of Northern Ireland, to South Armagh, later in the year. Now, I decided I wanted to do something different, so I put my name forward to be a team commander in the Close Observation Platoon. Getting in wasn't simple nor was it straightforward. The best six sergeants and corporals were chosen after a contest involving the top soldiers in the regiment. That stage lasted six weeks. Competition for places was really keen and anyone getting a slot thought of himself as extremely lucky. Going through the selection fight was pure hell. It involved sleep deprivation, constant fitness work and just sheer hard work. The intention was to prepare you for what lay ahead.

## THE UNDERWORLD CAPTAIN

I knew it was going to be a dogfight to win a place, but at the end of it I was absolutely thrilled to be told I was one of the lucky half-dozen who had been selected. It wasn't all good news, though. We would have the weekend off, then we'd set off on the actual training course itself, which would last another seven weeks. Nothing ever seemed to run smoothly for me, however.

The night before I left to join the other soldiers on the course, I was out drinking with Angie. We needed time together because we had been going through our worst spell since we had married ten years earlier. Now, things had reached the stage where we were on the verge of splitting up. I blamed myself for taking Angie for granted and always putting myself, my brothers and the army before her. I loved Angie to bits but had taken my eye off the need to convince her that loving me was the right thing to do and was, for me, so all-important. Without Angie, I was nothing. But our talk just didn't seem to take us anywhere. It was as if we were drifting down a river, each of us heading into streams running ever further apart.

Our relationship had reached rock bottom and the dread of what would happen to us next was whirling around in my mind at five o'clock the next morning as I sat on my bags with a hangover, pondering over the future. At that point, one of the guys approached. I'd always looked on him as a friend, but when he began mouthing off some silly remarks I got up to speak to him. Unfortunately, that was as far as it got. Without warning, I felt blow after blow to the face. It took only seconds for me to come to my senses and begin chasing him all round the camp.

I was furious, intent on killing this guy, but he was saved by the intervention of the sergeant major, who reached him first. Already, I was having trouble seeing out of my right eye, where his fist had caught me.

There was no way I was going to let him get away with punching me for no reason. The crazy, sad thing was that on the very verge of leaving for a really significant challenge in my career, had he offered to fight I would have taken him up on it. However, having thrown punches and run away, he wasn't up for facing me.

One thing life, and living among people who survive the

dangers of gangland, had taught me was that you bide your time. Everything comes to those who wait, goes the old saying, advocating patience, and I had plenty of that. I'd bide my time and strike when the opportunity arose, I told myself, but that morning as I set off to take part in the course, I was nursing a cracking black eye with the prospect of my wife leaving me and an uncertain future.

From the first moment I arrived at Hythe and Lydd Army Camp in Kent, however, I completely focused on the job ahead. The ultimate intention of the course was to teach us how to watch something but ensure that nobody knew we were doing so. I loved this and within a short time was noticed by a sergeant major who asked whether I had considered going for selection to the SAS, telling me this was an option open to me.

But before going anywhere else, or even thinking of transferring, I had to get through this course successfully. It was probably the hardest, but also the most enjoyable I've ever done at any time in the army. I was also looking forward to putting into practice what we were learning when I reached South Armagh, the worst, most dangerous place in the province.

We returned home to Inverness, but then it was off again, this time to bandit country. It might sound stupid, but my mind was taken up with what we had been sent there to do. Thoughts of Angie took a back seat. While it was true that there you needed all your powers of concentration, sometimes just to give yourself a chance of survival, pushing Angie back in the order of importance was foolish. At the end of the day, no matter what happened with the army, it was her I'd fall back on. She was my rock, whose actions would determine whether I had an existence worth living or one that was empty and hopeless. It's always easy to be wise after the event, but the way I treated Angie at that time was wrong.

Within a short time of arriving in Northern Ireland, I was busy gathering as much information as possible using covert means. This was sent back to experts who analysed and used it to plan further operations.

\* \* \*

A good example of how this worked was the operation at Loughgall, County Armagh, in May 1987. The IRA had previously used a stolen JCB digger to ram and bomb. Now, another digger had been stolen and an intelligence gathering unit of the RUC discovered it hidden at a farm. Security forces got wind it was to be used in an attack by the Provisional IRA East Tyrone Brigade on the unmanned police station at Loughgall. Units of 22 SAS are predominantly used in covert actions and now they were brought in to perform just such an operation. Soldiers were hidden in the police station and in the fields and woods around it. When the terrorists attacked, the soldiers opened fire, killing eight of them.

In October 1990, two other members of the Provisionals, Desmond 'Dessie' Grew and Martin McCaughey were killed by undercover soldiers as they retrieved three AK47 rifles from a derelict farmhouse near Loughgall. The location of the weapons had been established by 14 Intelligence Company, and the information was passed on to 22 SAS, who lay in wait. It was another example of how the various arms of the services combined.

* * *

I had only been in the province a matter of weeks when I was tasked by Tactical Command Group (South) to recce a Greenfield Observation Post near Forkhill, where Lawrence Dickson had been murdered, and the Kilnasaggart Railway Bridge with a view to gathering intelligence on a suspected member of the IRA who lived in the area.

It meant finding a place in which six of us could lie up for two weeks, totally cut off, and live, watch, photograph, report back and survive.

The first job was to find a suitable spot in which to hide and this had to be done without drawing attention. So, I went about looking for a location. Since my regiment was already in the area, I was able to retain my normal headdress. Had I been with another unit, then it would be odds-on some local would spot the difference, pass word back that a member of another outfit was in the area and probably set alarm bells ringing as to what I was doing there. The terrorists would quickly realise something was going on in their patch and begin asking questions and investigating. So I simply joined in with other patrols, watching and looking, though the others I was with didn't know why I was there. The fewer who knew what I was up to, the better – and the safer.

To start with, I'd done a helicopter recce, flying around the area and selecting potential hiding places, then I examined these more closely in daylight while on patrol. The best observation posts are gorse bushes, the thickest gorse bushes you can find, simply because nobody likes going near them. Wander in and you get jagged with the sharp and painful gorse needles. But for my type of work they were brilliant. During the various daylight reconnaissances, I had chosen three likely spots. Then, at night, when it was dark and most people were in their beds, I went back to them all, going inside the bushes knowing nobody would be watching what I was up to. I couldn't risk taking even a torch but needed to see how suitable each spot would be. What were the entry and exit points? Could we get out quickly in an emergency? How thick was the cover? And could I see the target's home? Most importantly, would anybody see us once we were inside? After repeatedly checking out all three, I decided which one I would use.

It took three nights for me to build the den because I had to work alone. It wasn't like the streets of Springburn, where everything was done during the day and you go out scouring the local area for bits and pieces to make it the best den ever. This was carried out in the early hours and in silence. I took in chicken wire to act as walls and flooring. At the end of the day, the post had to be sustainable but unrecognisable, and any work I did in it should not interfere with surrounding features. Once we were in, nobody was to know we were there. The post I had chosen happened to be on steep banking close to the side of a railway line. It needed to be banked to stop us sliding down, which meant building platforms. Luckily, about two miles further along the line, I came across some disused railway sleepers and humped these back to help build the areas on which we would sleep and work. Had I taken sleepers from around the bushes, locals might well have noticed they had disappeared. When it was completed, I congratulated myself that it was the best gang hut or hole in the ground I had ever made in my life. And it was, as time would prove.

On the third night, we went in with all our kit, including weapons and enough rations to last two weeks, though we almost didn't make it. As we quietly headed for the hideout, we came across a couple having a quiet kiss and fondle. They obviously didn't want anybody to know what they were up to and, for that reason, were hidden in shadows and silent. Fortunately, we heard a groan, probably of pleasure, and stiffened against a wall until they finally had finished their lovemaking and moved away. But it could have been awkward. Had they spotted us, the likelihood was that gossip about our presence would have been heard in the local bar, from where it would be passed to a local IRA player and then on to active service units. Before we knew it, everybody would have been searching for us. This time luck seemed on our side.

Once inside the post, we sealed ourselves behind a curtain of gorse and settled down to watch the home of our target, looking to see who he visited, where he went and who called on him. It was our little box, and nobody else knew where our box was. Not even our own troops, who were pulled out of the area in case they accidentally came across us and gave the game away. We were effectively on our own.

That first night was exciting, as we got used to our surroundings. We knew it would be cold. Winter was approaching. We had taken with us three sniper suits, worn by men whose job it was to lie for hours, maybe days, in a single spot. They left your hands and feet exposed, but everything else was zipped up under cover. They were waterproof, but having them on was the equivalent of wearing a sleeping bag.

It was my job, despite the conditions – the cold, the wet, the constant worry of being discovered – to make sure the other guys were permanently on their toes, even though we couldn't stand up. We took steps to leave no trace of our existence. We urinated in bottles and defecated into cling film in front of one another. After a few days, the smell of urine was appalling. As I said, I waited until day eight before doing the toilet – one of the others managed to hold on until day ten! The bottles and cling film went into bags in our Bergen packs. Our rations were eaten cold because a fire was out of the question.

Some of the guys tried making humour out of our situation, but I found nothing funny about it. Day after day, night after night, one guy would be operating the cameras, while another manned the radios, ready to send off signals informing base of any movements or developments; a third covered the exit point, while the others were resting. In the early days, we learned to listen for every noise, lay back and looked up through the gorse bushes at the stars in the cold, night sky, thinking. Later on it drizzled, rained and snowed.

I thought about my whole life during that time. I went back through everything I had done, anything I had ever said. Because Angie and I had just about fallen out before I left, my thoughts constantly went back to her. I wanted to be able to tell her I loved her and was sorry, but I couldn't, and there was no point in moping about that fact. We were apart and that was it.

After about three days, we settled into a routine, working out how to do everything in silence. If it was essential to speak, then it was done in whispers and generally late at night when nobody was about. Movement was terribly limited. If you were lucky, you managed to find enough space in which to kneel. Rest periods became the worst part of being in there. I wanted to lie down, to fall asleep, but mostly I just lay with my eyes closed, trying to nod off but not succeeding. Sometimes I would wonder about the guy next to me, pondering if he felt the same, then realising he must be because it was exactly the same for all of us.

I also wondered and worried about Tam and Pawny. The latter had been building a fearsome reputation as a dangerous villain. He had been in the dock of the High Court three times, facing charges with the potential to bring him a sentence in double figures. One allegation involved no fewer than 14 charges of armed robberies on banks and building societies; another of robbery from a security van. On each occasion,

Pawny walked free, but he knew police were itching for an excuse to arrest him again.

As the days dragged on, we became more conscious of noises around us. I heard all sorts of rodents and other tiny creatures running about, over our bodies and even scuttling across our helmets and kit. Even though I knew where I was and who was with me, it could still be frightening. The hairs on the back of my neck would rise as I wondered just what the creature was.

We were in a bubble, a cocoon, all of us with different thoughts and fears, but determined to act professionally and not to show weakness. The longer we remained in the observation post, the slower time seemed to pass. Minutes seemed like hours.

After a while I began thinking I was seeing people or even cars in the middle of the fields around us. When daylight came, I realised they were cows.

By now, it was day ten and I needed to keep things going. I began playing mind games with the other guys to keep them alert. I would tell one guy, 'He thinks you're an arsehole.' It was kidology, but it set off two of the guys bickering, one trying to punch the other. I realised just how quickly things could go from being quiet to exploding and compromising the entire post!

Some of the guys, through lack of discipline, ran out of rations and I ended up selling them some of mine, using the money to buy everyone drinks when we finally emerged.

We continually ran the risk of being found. The terrorists knew that when patrols were pulled back from any area, then something must be happening within that zone. They were aware of the existence of army methods and observation posts because their ranks included former soldiers. Rather than use the time-consuming and risky strategy of peering into every likely hiding place, terrorists and their sympathisers, including farmers, would go out into rural areas and simply bang away at bushes and trees, knowing that if anyone was hiding inside they would in all probability be hit. Throughout our time in the post we knew this was a possibility and on about the tenth day I heard the sound of firing from a few hundred metres away. Someone was shot-gunning bushes. I tensed, but then worked out from the diminishing noise that the gunman was moving away from us.

Fourteen days was the maximum we would be allowed by the army to stay in the post because any longer than that and the mind starts to wander and play tricks. On the night we were to be extracted, my mate came down to take care of us before the changeover and we managed to clamber onto the railway line. I was standing there, shouting his name, calling, 'Where the fuck are you?' Due to the length of time I had been in this type of environment, I now felt secure in it; he wasn't yet and had dug himself into some bushes about 200 metres away. When I found him, I told him, 'Get up! You're the team commander. Guys are looking at you for orders.' I could sense the rest of his squad looking at him and saying to themselves, 'He's shitting himself.' Eventually, I got him out of his hole and showed him the post where we had been for the last fortnight. We did a sort of formal handover, even though it was only a bush. I was the last to leave and had checked all was in order; we had put it back exactly as it was before we went in. Nobody could have known that there was, or had been, a post there. We passed over all the kit and moved away.

We had about two miles to walk. Remember, I hadn't stood up for 14 days and must have looked like an old man, bent over and finding it difficult to move my legs freely. The further we went, the more the blood began to flow and the stiffness eased. After we'd gone about a mile and a half, I saw the Puma helicopter coming to pick us up. I needed to shine a Firefly light to guide it to us. The light is so bright you would blind a pilot by shining it upwards and so you point it towards the ground. The helicopter pilot saw it and moved to us. It was about half past midnight, pitch dark. He opened the rear doors and we jumped in and I heard an 'ugh'. I thought, 'That's not because of us, is it?' But then I remembered we hadn't washed for 14 days – and realised what we were carrying in our Bergens.

# CHAPTER THIRTY

Had our two-week task hiding in the bush been worth it? I thought so. At the end of the day, it was an achievement for everybody because it was the first time for a very long period that there had been a covert observation post in that particular area. Everything we had worked and trained for had made it successful. Our targets had been an individual and a location – I am not allowed to say who or where. We knew we had provided good information and gave ourselves a pat on the back for that. Even nowadays the guys remember it and when we meet up it dominates our conversation. Some now admit they found it mentally hard but didn't want to say so at the time for fear of losing face.

In a tiny observation post like that, the only privacy you have is in your own mind. My mind has always been my buffer against the outside world. I've always been interested in psychology, and so I have nurtured the ability to have an internal me, in the mind. It meant I was able to deal with whatever situations I came up against in that unusual environment by myself without anyone else being involved and I was able to cope with all the mental problems that resulted from our situation. I know some of the others were struggling with issues in their own lives, but we all came out of it in one piece.

I knew we had left a post that could have been sustainable for a year or even two. I am sometimes asked, 'Why live like that for so long in those conditions?' and one of my replies is that by doing so we were gathering information that was saving the lives of others. I know we managed to get intelligence on vehicles, makes and models that were intended to be used later by a terrorist group in a bombing in that area.

The team that followed us into our gorse bush stayed there only five days before they were withdrawn. Meanwhile, after returning to Bessbrook Mill, our base and the centre for counter terrorism operations in South Armagh, we were debriefed and cleaned up. It was two in the morning, but a lot of pals had waited up to speak with us. One of my mates had bought a case of lager so we could enjoy a decent drink and next day I was told to take my team away to Belfast to relax. We took him at his word, went to Banbridge, an old coaching stop on the route from Dublin to Belfast, and drank until we were legless. On the return journey, two of the guys began fighting, one of them biting another in the face, with the inevitable result that he was quietly kicked out of the platoon and replaced.

Back on active duty, we had numerous dealings with men we knew to be players. They got to know our faces and in some cases even our first names.

One of the people I often spoke with at this time was a local farmer, Seán Gearóid Ó hAodha, well known as a member of the IRA Army Council. He and I would try winding one another up. For instance, I'd tell him the word on the street was that the Loyalist fanatic Billy 'King Rat' Wright had been talking about him. Wright was the leader of the Loyalist Volunteer Force and was killed in a prison van as he moved about the Maze jail in 1997. 'Billy's been making threats and you'd better watch what you're doing,' I'd joke. His reply would often be, 'You sure you'll make it back to base for your tea?' I'd pretend I didn't know what he was talking about, and he would say, 'Look at the signs on the poles.'

As the reputation of the South Armagh Sniper Team grew, notices planted by Republicans would go up on road signs and telephone poles warning they were in the area. These were meant to scare soldiers but had little, if any, effect.

Sometimes I would stop Seán as he was accompanying a member of his family to the ferry for the crossing to Scotland in order to watch Glasgow Celtic playing and that would take my mind back home. But I would always let them go on their way. After a time, I felt I had watched the main players in the area for so long that I knew them better than their own partners. All the same, I knew not to take chances. There were things you learned from others who had sometimes paid a heavy price in order that we could benefit from their experiences.

For instance, you never used normal entrances to fields, as these were favourite hiding places for remotely detonated bombs, nor beaten tracks for the same reasons. We avoided halting at road junctions, became accustomed to climbing fences rather than opening gates. Safety first was drummed into everyone.

My work included providing protection for other members of the security services, who occasionally visited us while carrying out very sensitive intelligence work. There were many rumours flying around at this time about how the homes of well-known terrorists had been bugged as part of the fight against those who indiscriminately killed innocent non-combatants by bomb and gun.

My experience with the gorse bush observation post was put to other uses when I was asked to set up another post to watch the home of a suspected terrorist bomb-making specialist. He lived in a village in South Armagh and intelligence branches wanted a post established about 150 metres from his front door. It was a difficult and dangerous task. There were some major natural obstacles between his home and where the post was intended to be set up, including a river and wooded area. I examined about five potential sites before selecting one. When I checked it out, I was confident that while it might have seemed too close for comfort, there was no way he could see us, while we in turn would be able to watch him. I was asked to attend a meeting with some highly placed individuals from the security services at Aldergrove airport and showed them plans, maps and aerial photographs of the proposed site. There was a considerable amount of discussion before I was asked to leave. When I was recalled after a quarter of an hour, it was to be told the operation was being shelved until further notice. I never heard anything further about it, but much later I did read about the individual I had been going to watch. It was following the terrible Omagh bombing in August 1998, when 29 people were blown apart by a car bomb. It was said to have been planted by members of the Real IRA, yet another splinter group of the Republican Army.

Throughout my South Armagh tour, a ceasefire had been in operation, but the thought of peace was not to the liking of some terrorist groups. In February 1996, the ceasefire was broken when the Provisional IRA planted a huge bomb weighing half a ton in the Docklands area of London. It caused damage estimated at £85 million and, more importantly, and tragically, the deaths of two men who had been working in a newsagent's shop opposite where the bomb had been left in a lorry. At the time of the explosion, I was working on an intelligence operation in East Tyrone and was immediately recalled to Bessbrook Mill. Everyone was placed on standby for immediate deployment.

Our accommodation was in a secure location within the Mill itself and no one was allowed in without permission from the highest authority. There was considerable activity involving strangers who arrived from London wearing suits; all of us assumed they were part of the security services intelligence-gathering set-up. We were not to know it at the time, but it is widely known now that the vehicle used to carry the bomb had been monitored and filmed heading off towards what would be an appalling incident. In 1998, farm worker James McArdle from Crossmaglen was convicted of conspiracy to cause explosions and sentenced to 25 years in prison. But just a couple of years later he was released under the terms of the Good Friday Agreement. At the time of the bombing, it was said that there would only be peace in the province if South Armagh members of the Provisional IRA agreed to it and here was evidence to support that view.

As the tour neared its end, it felt as though I hadn't seen Angie and the kids for an eternity. In fact, it had been virtually ten months, taking into account the tour itself and the two courses preceding it. As those months had passed, I had been hearing less and less from her and was beginning to accept that our marriage was doomed. I didn't want to convince myself we had reached the end of the road, but the damage was done as far as she was concerned and there might be no regaining the bond that had held us through so many difficult times. If I was to have a chance of saving the marriage, I needed to get back to her – and soon.

When it was announced that an officer wished to see us, I thought, 'He is coming down to thank us and say well done for all our hard work.' But what he had to say shocked and angered me. In future, he said, tours would no longer be of six months' duration. To allow a proper handover and training to the incoming Close Observation Platoon, which was to be based at Ballykinler in neighbouring County Down, we would need to stay on in South Armagh for up to another month. Well, that hardly went down a treat. I stood up, said, 'Fuck you,' kicked over my chair and walked out.

Of course, I stayed on, and have ever since regretted this show of temper, but it was simply a case of a soldier trying to get home to do his bit and, if possible, patch up a breaking marriage. So, it was a further month before I could head back to the beautiful sights of Inverness and my gorgeous wife and children. Sadly, what awaited me was not what I wanted.

As for the guy who had punched me many months earlier, by the time we returned from the tour to South Armagh he thought we were the best of mates. I had accepted his apology, but there was no way I had forgotten what he'd done. One night, one of my relatives had called to see me and we had plotted revenge. The idea was that the relation would wait until the guy took his dog for a walk, then attack him, but when dog-walking time came, the target emerged with his daughter. I knew we couldn't do anything while the youngster was there – that would have been wholly out of order – so hostilities were suspended, but had there been another chance to get him during the next few days then the opportunity would certainly have been taken. Everyone would have known I was behind the attack, of course, but then there were always rumours linking me to this and that and other un-pleasantries. Then, as time passed, I asked myself what the purpose was to all of it. 'Leave it and move on,' I told myself. And I did, but to this day what happened all those years ago is still a sore point. It was the first and only time that I would ever use my family to settle a score with someone who upset me in the army.

# CHAPTER THIRTY-ONE

In South Armagh, I had experienced the death of a brother soldier, the fears of friends and threats from terrorists. My own brother had come back from the dead. But nothing compared with the pain of losing Angie.

Within a day of returning to Inverness, I realised it was all over between us. Nothing I could say or do – no apologies, tears, pleadings for reconciliation – could change her mind. Maybe our love had grown stale with time.

Angie had met someone else and wanted a fresh start. The worst part of all of this was knowing I was to blame. She had stood by me through gangland wars, army fights, attempted murder charges; I had drugged her and terrified her, and now I'd lost her. I knew I had to get on with my life. It was no use moping and feeling sorry for myself, even though a voice somewhere was telling me that now there was no future and I may as well kill myself. I had met someone else, too, but we were just friends; I still longed for and craved Angie and that was the truth of it.

Angie and I staggered along for two miserable months and then I transferred to the great army garrison at Colchester in Essex where I met up with some old mates, including Tam Gow. There I had time to think, space in which to move about and discover that absence really did make the heart grow fonder. I sensed that in Inverness Angie too was coming to the same conclusion.

Every couple of months, when the chance came, I'd head back north to see her and the children. She made sure her new partner was nowhere near when I was around and from her reactions during my visits a tiny shoot of hope that there might be a reconciliation began to emerge. Maybe, I thought, our marriage was a casualty of the battles I had fought both in and out of uniform and, given time, it would recover. Deep down, I was sure we would end up back together because we were the ultimate soulmates who had just lost our way.

While we remained apart, my career began to take a nosedive. It staggered through a haze of drink, late nights and parties until my lifestyle became a talking point. There were those around me who doubted my ability to emerge with my sanity. Some officers were becoming concerned that I was on the verge of becoming a welfare case, a basket case, as we call it, and would openly voice their opinions and concerns about my and Angie's marital situation.

I was saved by my friends: Frankie, Stevie, Tam Gow and Colin all stuck by me, even when I contemplated suicide. They were friends then and remain so to this day. The odds on my new relationship becoming serious were long to begin with, and lengthened with each slip of the tongue when I found myself calling her Angie. During one of my trips to Inverness, I told Angie I was thinking of leaving the army once again and starting a new life in Glasgow. She knew that meant a return to gangland, and probably prison, and talked me out of what was a reckless idea.

'Alex, there's nothing for you in Glasgow but trouble,' she warned. 'Why sacrifice a career into which you've invested so much of your life. You have lots to offer the army. Stick with it.'

I reached the nadir of despair around Christmas 1997 when I rejoined my family in Inverness. One of my friends had gone with me because he was worried about my state of mind and was the type of guy who was always there for me if I needed someone to rely on. After a few days, Angie asked me to leave, saying she was finding my presence too difficult to handle because the children continually asked me to stay while the pressure of the break-up was depressing her. I spent New Year with my mum in Glasgow. She could see I was in a mess. When you reach those depths of hopelessness, nothing anyone says or does succeeds in giving you the lift you need. Only you, yourself, can provide that.

Just as all seemed lost, I realised those seeds of hope had continued to grow. Danielle's birthday falls on Valentine's Day, 14 February, and two days later is my birthday and our wedding anniversary. I planned to surprise Danielle by turning up for her birthday. Only Angie was in on this. Catching the sleeper train from London to Inverness, I arrived early on Saturday morning. I couldn't know it, but this day was to be a turning point for the family.

By now, I had accepted that it was all over between us, and I believe Angie could see that too in the way I acted around her. Later in the day, we set off for a meal and a few drinks. It was then that Angie began crying.

'Alex, I've made a mistake,' she sobbed. 'Shouldn't we think about starting again?'

Her words brought me to tears. I began blurting out that I had made so many mistakes.

The kids began crying, too. Within five minutes, Angie and I had our problems resolved. We agreed to tell our current partners that we were getting back together and she would move to Colchester to be with me. We talked over how we would deal with all the idle chit-chat and gossip when we got there. It was a wonderful moment for us, but I cannot forget that two very good people were also hurt because of Angie and me.

I wasn't going to kid myself. Angie wanted a reconciliation for the sake of the children – but I was sure that as time passed she would fall in love with me again. I knew I would never again let her go.

Within two weeks, we were together in married quarters in Essex and I can honestly say that this was the point in my life where once and for all I completely changed for the better and refocused as a husband, soldier and father. Of course, there would be hurdles ahead, but we would deal with those together as they came along. What mattered was that I trusted Angie and she trusted me.

Maybe splitting up for a time did both of us good. We had been with each other since we were young, too young perhaps, and had begun taking one another for granted. Being apart taught us a lot about ourselves. It was like testing the temperature of the water before going into the sea. Once we had been there and tried it, we realised it would never happen again. We have never looked back.

Within a month of the reunion, I was off once again to Northern Ireland, this time to Fermanagh. The county, in the west of the province, had suffered its share of heartache and tragedy during the troubles. Men from all sides of the disputes – soldiers, policemen, Provos, Loyalists and civilians – had died, the worst atrocity being the Remembrance Day bombing at Enniskillen. By now, things had calmed and, remembering the dramas of South Armagh, I almost wondered what the point was of us being in Fermanagh. My frustration wasn't helped by knowing I needed more time with Angie to cement our relationship.

I was confident we had resolved our problems, but then the man she had dated travelled twice to Colchester in an effort to persuade her to change her mind and return to Inverness to be with him. Angie told me about these visits as they happened. The news left me feeling unhappy, sad and lost, but I was thankful for her honesty and her promises to stick with me. There are, and always will be, problems in every marriage, but we showed that with hard work these can be overcome. We have never hidden what happened and still speak openly about it to family and friends. We learned to be open and honest with one another, never to take each other for granted. I knew then, and I know now, that I truly want to be with Angie for the rest of my life. But still I feel guilty for all the crap I put her and the kids through.

About three months into the Fermanagh tour, a major who had always had a soft spot for me decided I should transfer to his company and at the earliest opportunity return to Brecon to complete the Platoon Sergeants Battle Course, one phase of which I had earlier failed. The officer ordered me to spend the next three months preparing so I was ready to join it in January

1998. Knowing its importance, I threw myself into this and managed to reach a stage where I was physically and mentally the fittest that I had ever been in my time in the forces. This lifted my confidence sky high. I just knew I was on the up and nothing would stop me advancing my career.

I passed easily enough, but not without the inevitable scare. I don't know what my problem is, but every time I'm at Brecon I seem to end up fighting with other students and this time it was no different, except that I was caught red-handed by the company sergeant major and the officer commanding, Major Ken Hames. Ken is now a very well-known and familiar face on television. After 25 years in the army, serving in the Falklands, as one of the last guards of Rudolf Hess in Germany and then in the SAS, he became in civilian life an expedition leader, presenter of travel programmes and he even helped design one of the camps for the bizarre television series *I'm a Celebrity . . . Get Me Out of Here!*. When I came across him at Brecon, the circumstances were not so light-hearted.

As part of the course, I was involved in an exercise in which we were carrying out a night attack on a building. I was role-playing the section commander and trying to tell the guy taking the part of platoon sergeant that the 'enemy' were just outside the window. However, we ended up arguing and he said to me he'd sort it out with me after the attack. As far as I was concerned, he had just told me he was going to have a fight with me later on.

Now my temper came into play. 'It's now or never,' I thought and gave him a traditional Glasgow kiss, a head butt, and as he hit the ground, I finished him off with a few punches and kicks. Something brought me to my senses and I carried on with the exercise; however, when it was over Ken Hames and the CSM came over, tapped me on my helmet and asked who I was. They wanted to know what had happened inside the building. Both the guy I'd knocked down and myself gave the same version of events: that we ran into each other in the dark and fell down. There had been no scuffle or fight, we assured them. Unfortunately, both had been wearing passive night goggles and had seen everything as clearly as if it had happened in daylight. Since the other guy, who is now a commissioned officer, stuck to his story, however, they could take the matter no further. I owe him a massive favour, as both wanted to return me to my unit with an instruction that I was never to be allowed back.

Word of that got round. Before the course ended, I was having a conversation with an NCO when he asked me for a fight. 'Come on, nobody is going to know. I'll knock you down to size. Fancy yourself as a hard man, don't you?' I listened but ignored him, well aware it was a wind-up. He wanted to provoke me into a punch-up, but I was not falling for that one.

Shortly after passing the course, I was promoted to sergeant and sent from Charlie Company to 1 Platoon Alpha Company. Frankly, it was the worst platoon in the regiment, packed with men who had drink and drug problems. In other words, my kind of people. Not long after I took over, two of the guys found themselves under investigation for allegedly breaking into the office of the commanding officer and one of them for defecating on his desk. Military police ordered a DNA test on the offending pile, which proved it had not been left by my man. I got on with the platoon like a house on fire and, within a very short time, it was accepted as the best in the battalion, a fact we proved in many inter-company competitions. I stood up for my soldiers at every opportunity, always putting them first, and in return was given 100 per cent respect. I still keep in touch with a lot of these soldiers and my reputation in the battalion remains.

Once, I took the platoon on a visit to the Houses of Parliament then on to 10 Downing Street, followed by a tour of Buckingham Palace. At the time, the CSM and officer commanding warned me that in the event of trouble I would be severely reprimanded or even reduced in the ranks, as some senior officers just would not accept that my men had changed and could be trusted. On the journey back, two of my best men wanted to fight each other, so we pulled our minibus off the motorway and let them crack at it. After ten minutes, I opened the window and asked, 'You finished yet?' There was a shout of, 'Yes.' They got back into the motor, I made them shake hands and apologise to each other and they each opened a can of lager and said, 'Cheers, now let's forget this ever happened.' I had a very strong relationship with the whole platoon. Some of the members are now sergeant majors or officers and take pride in telling me that they have modelled their management skills on my methods, truly a great compliment of which I feel very proud.

# CHAPTER THIRTY-TWO

William Lobban just would not go away. He had been transferred, at his own request, to the English prison system. Social workers had managed to trace his father to England and Lobban felt meeting him could represent the opportunity for a new start. But his reputation followed him south of the border and there were fears for his own safety and that of his fellow prisoners. However, he neither cared for nor feared others and was left within the mainstream system. So he completed his sentence in England and now he was back out of jail. I knew that meant trouble.

After being attacked in Perth, then taking an officer hostage, he had gone on the English circuit. At one stage, he was in Hull nick during a major riot. Trouble seemed to follow him around.

Tam had wanted to kill him for sticking a gun to Pawny's head. Then there had been an incident where Tam was sent to murder Lobban near the Forth and Clyde Canal that runs through part of Glasgow. It was my fault Lobban even got wind of that. I had foolishly opened my mouth to someone Angie knew and who used to go out with Lobban. We'd been having a chat one night over a drink and Gibby's name cropped up. I was saying that he was an animal and was lucky to still be around, and when I was asked what I meant by that I said Tam had been going to kill him at the canal. It was a comment made among people who we thought of as family and I did not expect it to go any further. I forgot about it at the time, but a couple of years later a woman who had been present during the chat mentioned it to Gibby.

He tried a few times to trap Tam, once ringing him up and inviting him to a meeting at Glasgow airport. 'Come by yourself, there's no need to bring anybody else,' he'd told Tam, who knew what he was up to and so didn't show up.

Now he was back on the scene and I could do nothing about it because I had been posted back to South Armagh, to Forkhill, where there had been so much tragedy. It was all very different now, the talk almost exclusively of preserving peace, but the last thing I needed to hear was Angie telling me Gibby had turned up at our married quarters in Colchester. He had arrived with a Spanish girlfriend and camped himself in our home, pleading with Angie that he had nowhere else to stay. He was not welcome. He had even tried to persuade Angie that it was OK for her to hand over to him my bank books and cards, saying I would be OK with that because we had always helped him out when he was broke. I knew that was just a ploy to allow him to clean out my accounts. Angie was not having it. She didn't like Lobban. She was aware he had a reputation as a dangerous person, but she wasn't scared of him.

Eventually, I telephoned him one night and we had a blazing row. There was no way I was going to be intimidated by him. There were strong words and threats, but I ordered him to get out and he left. Angie and the kids were glad to see the back of him, but his presence had put a lot of pressure on them, especially as they continued to worry about me being in bandit country. Lobban made his way back to Glasgow.

Before going to South Armagh, I had dropped a clanger career-wise. A former platoon commander of mine had asked if I wanted to join the Royal Military Academy at Sandhurst in Surrey, the very prestigious training centre for all British Army officers, as an instructor. I decided against the move, as I had my own career plan worked out to move up the ranks, but in retrospect it was a mistake on my part because by going to Sandhurst I would have been guaranteed further promotion. However, I believed my own strategy was the right one.

As a result of my vast experience in South Armagh, I was given the position of company operations Senior NCO. It meant that basically I would plan all operations that the company and platoons would have to do on a daily basis. In addition, I was to act as liaison with the local community, news reporters, elders, gatekeepers and councillors, mainly members of the Social Democratic and Labour Party, as Sinn Fein refused to deal with us. SDLP representatives would come to me with local concerns and complaints, such as helicopter movement after ten at night. It was my job to try to sort out these problems and appease local people.

We had all grasped the fact that the way to get the community onside was not through bombs and bullets, but by winning over their hearts and minds. I was very good at assessing individuals and situations and was seen as someone the people of Forkhill could talk to without compromising the lives and security of our soldiers.

It was a much changed area from when I had been there before. On patrols we used to see signs on poles showing drawings of big guns with long barrels and warnings such as Sniper Team in Action, or Sniper. Beware! In fact, the snipers had had their day. They were no longer the worry they had once been. It was to be an event at home at the beginning of July 1999 that would cause me the most grief.

One of my closest mates, Robert Simpson, originally from Hamilton and a member of the First Battalion of the Royal Scots, had just risen to the rank of captain, but was having marital problems. Angie and I were extremely close to him. Every day while I was in Northern Ireland he would telephone and we would talk through his difficulties. Now, he was saying he seriously wanted to commit suicide. I had so far managed to talk him out of this, but the difficulty was affecting him not just mentally but physically. From being over six feet tall and weighing fifteen stone, and being extremely fit and recognised throughout the infantry as a top-notch soldier, he told me how he had lost three stone in a matter of weeks and was looking grey and gaunt. Even when he persisted with his threats to kill himself I still didn't believe him. Then one day came a terse announcement that he had hanged himself.

I couldn't believe it. He had a brilliant record, having done four tours in South Armagh and being among the first ground troops to liberate Kuwait in the first Gulf War. His promotion had come only three months earlier, yet he had evidently been involved in a scuffle in the mess and the next day was found dead. Only that night Rab had telephoned me to say he and his second wife, Lorna, were going to a function.

'Don't get stupid and screw things up. You've just been promoted. Watch what you're doing,' I had told him.

'Aye, it'll be sorted,' he had replied.

At the function, he and Lorna had talked to Angie.

The next day Angie, who had found work in the NAAFI, was returning from a day out with the family and Rab's stepdaughter. The military police were waiting. Somebody shouted that they were looking for Angie, that there had been trouble. She said her heart sank because she immediately thought it was me, that I must have been killed. The police told her they were there because Rab and Lorna were our friends and he had committed suicide. It was almost a relief to her that it wasn't me, but she was so sad for Lorna.

Rab had gone home, where he got the dog's chain. But the strange part about it was that he opened one of the big old creaking garage doors, pulled it half down after him and then put the dog's chain around his neck and basically fell asleep and choked himself standing up.

At an inquest in August, the coroner recorded an open verdict, but those who knew Rab thought he hadn't wanted to kill himself – his action had been a plea for help. I flew back from Ireland to be one of the pall-bearers at his funeral, but for years his death left bad blood between some of his other mates and Angie and me. They assumed we'd known more than we had about the reasons for the tragedy. Feeling was strong and sometimes we felt like lepers. The truth was we had only tried to be a good friend to someone who needed us. There wasn't a lot I could do from where I was in South Armagh, as Rab did not want me to speak to anyone else about his problems. He and I knew that for others to think he had mental problems – or, even worse, for him to show signs – could have become a career-stopper.

One night after I had eventually completed my tour in South

Armagh and had returned to Colchester, Angie and I were in the mess enjoying ourselves. I'd had quite a bit to drink and we were kissing and cuddling in a corner for half a minute or so. Next day one of the officers had me in his office to tell me about his displeasure over what we'd been doing. He did not realise that after Rab's death I really didn't care much about people like him. I remember standing in front of him as he sat at his desk and looking over the top of him and out of his window. This irritated him and he was shouting, 'Look at me,' so I would look down at him for a few moments until I found what he was saying irritating and then just look over his head again, setting him off once more. In his rage, he was turning beetroot red. I was asking him, 'What are you going to do? All I've done is kiss my wife.' Finally, he came out from behind his desk and stood right beside me. He was about six foot two, thin, and he put his nose on my cheek. I just burst out laughing. In my mind, I was saying to myself, 'Make a move,' because he had shut the door and there were guys waiting outside. 'Make a move because I'll fucking kick you up and down this office.' I knew it would have been my word against his. When he put his nose on my left cheek again, I burst out laughing once more. At that he told me to get out of his office.

I think word of that incident spread because my career, which had been flying, went on to hit a brick wall. In fact, I know of one guy who put down an entry in the Mess Wagers Book to the effect that I would never rise higher than colour sergeant. I had been glad when that tour ended, as by then I had realised that the higher up the ranks you went, or the more experienced you became, the further back from the front line you moved. That was destroying me. I was a soldier and needed to be out patrolling rather than tied up in the planning side. Probably this lack of excitement was the cause of my short temper and my need to be constantly challenging authority. Almost every day I was openly, within hearing of other soldiers, challenging a man whose rank was higher than mine to fight.

Early in January 2000, I deployed to Alberta, Canada, for an eight-week-long Winter Warfare Instructors Course and when we returned, the family and I went off to Ballykelly in County

Londonderry on an eighteen-month tour. The village had seen one of the worst atrocities of all those during the troubles.

On 6 December 1982, the Irish National Liberation Army planted a bomb in a disco at the Droppin Well inn, a bar frequented by off-duty soldiers. Eleven troops and six civilian patrons died. Among them were three teenage girls just out for a night's dancing.

Now, the area was peaceful. I was promoted to colour sergeant and took over as signal company quartermaster sergeant, another step up the career ladder, but I still felt the fallout from Rab's death and believed some individuals wanted to ensure my path up the ranks would be as rough as possible.

\* \* \*

Things might have been quiet in Northern Ireland, but not in Glasgow. Jamie Stevenson and Tony McGovern, once the best of friends, had fallen out and in September, outside a family-run bar in Springburn, Tony had been gunned down. He had been wearing a bullet-proof vest supplied by Tam McGraw. The killer had known and shots to the head and body ended the life of the man who had been looking forward to a drink with Alex.

Jamie Stevenson would ultimately be charged with Tony's murder but after spending time in prison on remand he would be released and the charge dropped. But more shootings would follow.

The following year, also in Springburn, someone tried to shoot Duncan McIntyre in the head. He survived, but there would be at least one further attempt on his life. Tommy McGovern, too, found himself a target after being lured to the car park of Blink McDonald's old pub, the Talisman. A hit man tried pumping three bullets into Tommy, who fired back. Neither man was hit.

\* \* \*

We were enjoying being together in Ballykelly, but then Angie's mum Margaret was diagnosed with cancer and we knew she was dying. Angie, not unnaturally, was taking it badly. She had a special bond with her mother and at every opportunity travelled to Glasgow to be with her. There were days when Angie found it difficult to cope, but she managed to see herself through; however, when the inevitable came, what made it all the more difficult was that her mum and Nicole, our youngest daughter, shared the same birthday and so each year a day of celebration was also one that reminded them of great sadness.

It was during this period that I learned not to trust anyone. Not even so-called friends with whom I had joined the army and grown up. Some had learned to play the game better than others, climbing the ranks faster by brown nosing or, as it is termed in the army, 'pole sucking'. Sometimes their desperation to get ahead of one another, even at the expense of close friends, was too evident and even ridiculous. Normal people ask, 'Where are you from?' In the army, it is 'What school did you go to?' Where you begin in the ranking chain depends on your answer. And even once you are on the ladder, until you can show that you know how to think, speak, act, dress and which knife and fork to use at dinner, then you'll remain standing in the corner with no mates. I look back and see how class can make or ruin a career. It's sad when snobbery kicks in. At least I can say that throughout my time I have never brown nosed; I have achieved what I have through ability.

The regiment was posted back to Dreghorn Barracks, Edinburgh, in April 2002. It would turn out to be the most important stage of my life. I believed I had only five years left in the forces before I would concentrate on my family and future. I was promoted to warrant officer class 2 and sent to the training wing as regimental training officer. This suited me to a tee, because if I wasn't on actual operations then I was thrilled to be able to pass on my knowledge and experience to the up-and-coming stars of the regiment.

In August 2002, we were posted to Bosnia for a six-month tour. As brigade training officer, I was based near the infamous complex outside Banja Luka, which had been used as a prisoner of war camp during the Balkan War. It meant I was responsible for the personal development, assessment and selection of all soldiers attending regimental career courses and would provide general support, advice and direction on all regimental training issues. I loved this job, but the posting would almost finish my career.

I had no difficulty picking up the language and when Angie came over for a short visit she was astonished at how well I was able to converse. Her visit had been marred by a dreadful assault on her sister, Babs, who was in a coma for some time. There was some doubt at one time as to whether she would pull through. After a very long time she did, but she has never fully recovered.

As the end of the tour drew near, I ran a massive multinational live-firing exercise, involving troops from Britain, Canada, America and Holland. The planning and preparation tested my ability to its extremes and as an added pressure I learned it was to be watched by at least 50 VIPs, among them the grand-sounding High Representative for Bosnia and Herzegovina, the former Royal Marine and politician Paddy Ashdown. Two weeks before the exercise was due to take place, we did a practice run. It was at this stage that an officer who had helped me in Fermanagh appeared on the scene and was about to destroy me.

My job had been to act as host to and brief the VIPs, but at a meeting of all those involved this officer told me he did not think me the type of person who should be doing this. The task was, therefore, given to someone else. I was delegated to make tea and coffee. Was it my background? I personally think it was a form of snobbery – he did not want a Glaswegian with a strong accent being the focal point for the guests. But imagine how I felt. I was ridiculed and made to feel worthless in front of everyone.

I put aside my personal feelings because I wanted the exercise to be a success. One of the jobs involved erecting an enormous marquee from which the VIPs could watch the proceedings in comfort. Next morning I went to check it and discovered it had vanished overnight. Locals must have stolen it, creeping past thousands of soldiers in darkness, dismantling it and loading it onto a horse-drawn cart. Then they disappeared. I found this hilarious, but the fact was the officer delegated to take my place should have placed an overnight guard on the marquee. Not surprisingly, I found the blame being laid at my door. And before I knew it I was informed that on return to the UK I would be leaving the regiment and be posted to Warminster in Wiltshire. I protested, and even offered to go back down the ranks, but was told by the officer concerned, 'This is my train set and I don't want you as part of it.' In the end, instead of England I was posted to the TA in Edinburgh, where I spent three of the happiest years of my life.

Babs was eventually released from hospital and went to live in a flat for those with mental health issues. She had to be taught how to live all over again – how to walk, talk, cook, do every conceivable chore. At weekends, she would come to stay with us and we did our best to try to help her regain at least some of her self-confidence, but she could not force herself to look in a mirror. And still cannot. Now, she lives in sheltered accommodation next to her own children and ex-husband, who has done a wonderful job of helping her.

Devoting so much time to helping Babs caused difficulties with Danielle. Lots of young people go through a phase of wanting to be totally independent, but Angie and I at times felt guilty for not giving her more of our time and attention. Thomas and Nicole were, thankfully, doing fine.

Angie had put up with so much since we had married and I was determined to show the strength of my love for her. I always wanted to renew our wedding vows as a form of saying sorry for our problems, my mistakes and for putting up with me for the past 19 years. We renewed our vows on 14 September 2004 in Saint Margaret's Chapel in Edinburgh Castle. It was a memorable day, made even more special by being that of Angie's, Nicole's and, had she been alive, Margaret's birthdays. We did it in style, arriving in a stretch limo. My three nephews, who were by now in my regiment, wore their No. 2 dress, me my No. 1 Dress Ceremonial, while Angie looked stunning in white. As we entered the chapel, hundreds of tourists looked on, probably believing we were royalty. Afterwards, we held a private function in the Sergeants' Mess at Dreghorn Barracks for our guests, a mixture of civilians, family and very close mates. I made a short speech: 'I know there's a lot of you here from Glasgow. The silver on the walls is hundreds of years old. It's priceless. Can we keep it in the hall and not steal it because I'll get charged for it.' My mum and dad were there too, and one of the best things to come out of that day was Mum seeing me in all my glory with all my medals and looking so proud of her son.

On occasions I would see Pawny's car in Posso and I'd call in for a chat with him and Birdman O'Hara. We would chew the fat about life in general and how the army was a good way out for everyone. They would tell me that had it not been for the path they chose, they would have loved to have joined up. We never discussed drugs, guns or ongoing feuds, as there were others present. We all knew the rules: don't speak in front of anyone unless you can trust them with your life. In these circles, loose tongues can cost lives. Sadly, the following year, Birdman was jailed for 20 years after being found guilty of a murder.

By now, I was thinking about and planning for the likelihood of my engagement ending. I needed to find a job and began shopping around. But I was about to discover it wasn't going to be easy.

# CHAPTER THIRTY-THREE

'Forget it. Leave it. Get on with your life,' the senior policeman told Alex. 'You're wasting your time.' The soldier, worried about impending job cuts, had applied for a job with Strathclyde Police. He had enclosed his criminal record with the application forms. Both had been returned, marked with a note saying thanks but not interested. The reason? He had been admonished for a minor offence more than 20 years earlier. Strathclyde police force said it did not want men or women who had broken the law. It made no difference that since that offence Alex had served his country, wearing khaki with distinction, winning promotions and praise.

'We wouldn't touch you in a million years,' he was told, when he telephoned to appeal the decision.

'What about the Rehabilitation of Offenders Act?' he asked. 'Are you saying that whatever I may have done as a teenager I can never put behind me? In the army, I can get a Long Service and Good Conduct Medal, work with the secret services, the police in Northern Ireland, but because of something minor two decades ago I am not wanted?'

'Yes, that's it,' came the reply.

His convictions, however old, had blighted the entire remainder of his life. But did Strathclyde Police refuse to allow convicted persons in their ranks? Shortly after that conversation Alex was astonished to read newspaper reports revealing that statistics the police had been forced to provide under Freedom of Information rules showed 80 Strathclyde officers had criminal records for road traffic offences, assault and breach of the peace. Throughout Scotland the police were employing 200 officers who were criminals.

In one confidential appraisal, a senior army officer had written Alex was 'a bright star who has been missed by all'. Another glowing testimony warned, 'He would be a massive loss to the army were he not retained.' In yet another, 'He certainly has the presence, intellect and ability to attract further promotion.'

\* \* \*

What I was accused of doing all those years ago had, unknown to me, been a Bergen I had carried on my back. I wondered why it was that with my record of service to my country I was being rejected, while all those others retained their jobs. At the time, I was a warrant officer, based at Barrow-in-Furness, having been accepted on to the army's Long Service List and working as a senior recruiter in the army careers office. There was considerable uncertainty about the future and I had been looking around at alternative careers, including the police. Then I was told an army job might be in the offing in Aberdeen as a permanent staff administration officer. I was appointed to the post and found myself back at Gordon Barracks, Aberdeen, where my career had started all those years ago with my belongings in a carrier bag.

\* \* \*

In the meantime, his good friend George Redmond had been murdered, shot along with a friend as he stood outside the Waldorf bar in Cambridge Street, Glasgow, in October 2008. The friend survived, but the drive-by killing went unsolved. Alex had known so many who had died or wasted so much of their lives in prison cells. Once, when he had taken Angie, Nicole and Danielle to visit Lobban in the Special Unit of Shotts jail in Lanarkshire, he had spotted Andy Walker, the payroll killer. He had urged Gibby not to mention to him who he was. He had last seen Walker when he offered the killer a cigarette minutes before his arrest.

Lobban thankfully seemed to have departed the Glasgow

gangland scene, living in the north of Scotland and having lost part of a leg due to cancer. He and the dead had chosen their route through life, Alex his. It was June 2009.

Weeks later he found himself at Sandhurst joining a Late Entry Officers Course. It meant being commissioned from the world-renowned academy whose past students have included Winston Churchill, James Bond creator Ian Fleming, the actor David Niven, *Dad's Army* writer David Croft and King Hussein of Jordan.

\* \* \*

When I was at Sandhurst, there were around a dozen of us in the Sergeants' Mess. One guy whom I hadn't set eyes on for years came up and said, 'The last time I saw you, you were up for three attempted murders.' It was some conversation stopper. I looked around to see others staring at me and saying to themselves, 'He's an officer, highly thought of.'

'Aye, thanks,' I told my companion.

\* \* \*

As Captain Alexander Shannon stood on the steps at the entrance to the academy for the course group photograph, the famous pillars in the background, he paused and thought how far life had brought him. And rightly he felt proud. But problems and sadness lay around the corner.

Just when he hoped his career had once again settled, he discovered cutbacks would lead to his being unemployed. He learned of an identical position becoming available in Glasgow, applied and was appointed. Then his dad, having battled against drink addiction for decades, finally succumbed. He died in December 2009 but not through alcohol. Lung cancer killed him, and he had never smoked a cigarette in his life. A doctor told Alex his father's lungs were like those of someone who had smoked 40 cigarettes a day. Passive smoking did kill.

Alex took up his present post in April 2010. By then, his family had settled in North Lanarkshire. Working among men from every walk of life, from every background, of every character, the good and the bad, the weak and the strong, helped develop in him a passionate interest in psychology. He has already successfully completed a Level A psychometrics/ psychology course and is working on the next level. Once these are completed, he plans to work with young professional footballers and has the blessing of the army to do so. One of Scotland's major soccer clubs has already agreed to allow him to work with players and pass on his findings to members of the coaching staff. Other clubs have expressed an interest. That, though, is for the future. His life now revolves around the British Army and his family. He is close to them and they to him.

\* \* \*

Angie's love shines more brightly than ever. She says: 'Since joining the army a second time, Alex has been a very different man. He is wiser, but I think more ambitious since our separation, more determined to make the army a real career. He always tried his best, but I believe that for a lot of the time he has been held back by some individuals and had it not been for that he would have reached his present rank much more quickly. Has his background been responsible for that? Yes, but at the same time he is proud that the army gives those with his upbringing a chance to go far.

'He and I have always been close. I tell my children I still love it when the door opens and he walks in. I love it when I talk to him on the telephone. I'd rather go for a night out with Alex than with a friend. I have no regrets about his army life because it has taken us away from the childhood we had. My mum and dad were alcoholics and food was scarce, but my kids have never known hunger. True, there have been times when my heart has missed a beat. For instance, on the day in 1987 when the corporals died, I knew Alex would be in an unmarked car heading into Belfast. When it came over on the news bulletin that they had been attacked and killed, I was instantly worried. There was nothing I could do and it was a huge relief when he called me that night to tell me he had arrived at his base safely. But despite incidents such as these, I have loved the army life.

Nowadays I miss the socialising, the Messes we had. But we wouldn't change even the bad things because learning from them has made us what we are.'

Tam Shannon, proud father of an army sergeant son, is also unashamedly proud of his brother. 'I think there was always a desire in Alex to stand up for what he felt was right. Once, when we were younger, I spent money on a pair of training shoes at a time when I had a wife and young child. He came to see me and bollocked me, saying I should have spent the money on them. So I jumped up and attacked him. Next day he came to apologise, and I attacked him again. If I was writing a testimonial to Alex, it would read, "His most remarkable achievement is emerging from all he has gone through as a decent citizen."'

John 'Pawny' Shannon, like Tam, does not attempt to hide his past and is glowing in his praise of his officer brother, the captain who emerged from gangland. Pawny admits he first broke into a shop at the age of four and has been a major player in drugs rackets. He has been arrested and questioned over murders he did not know had been committed, but his worst moment came as a teenager when Alex announced he was joining the army.

'We were really close and I felt as though I was losing my best friend. Now, I don't know if I could put into words just how proud I am of what he has achieved. At one time I thought of joining the Merchant Navy, but an outstanding criminal charge meant that it was only a pipe dream. So often I thought of joining the army, of doing something else with my life, but my convictions put an end to any hopes there, too. When Alex left the army in 1991, we were aware of people sizing up his capabilities. It was a time when the Shannons were at war and I don't know whether he felt that was a factor influencing his decision to join us. It was a dangerous time, and we were all targets, but we were respected not only by our friends but by our enemies, too. I often thought to myself, though, "Maybe he would be better off back in the army." He had his family to consider and I was glad when he rejoined.'

As for Captain Shannon, what does the army mean to him? 'I cannot thank the army enough because it gave me a stability and direction in life. Even when I fell off the edge from time to time, it pulled me back and gave me core values of honesty, loyalty and courage, although these assets were instilled in me as a consequence of my upbringing on dangerous streets and among dangerous people. I say to those who have become my friends, "If you have a problem or a question, ask me direct and I will give you an honest answer. You can trust me." But if I come across someone who reveals they are neither loyal nor trustworthy, then I don't give them a second chance. The army has built that into me. If it were not for the army, I would definitely be in jail, or murdered. And so I love to think that out there are other young people, perhaps feeling hopeless, despairing, who will read my story and realise that with the army there is a future.'